AMERICAN GOVERNMENT:
MINORITY RIGHTS
VERSUS
MAJORITY RULE

AMERICAN GOVERNMENT: MINORITY RIGHTS VERSUS MAJORITY RULE

HARLAN HAHN
University of Southern California

R. WILLIAM HOLLAND
University of California at Riverside

JOHN WILEY & SONS, INC.
New York   London   Sydney   Toronto

Library of Congress Cataloging in Publication Data
Hahn, Harlan, 1939-
American government : minority rights versus majority rule.

Includes bibliographical references and index.
1. United States—Politics and government—Handbooks, manuals, etc. 2. Minorities—United States. 3. United States—Race question. I. Holland, Rolland William 1943- joint author. II. Title.
JK274.H145   320.4'73   75-15925
ISBN 0-471-33921-0
Printed in the United States of America

10 9 8 7 6 5 4 3 2 1

To our fathers
Robert Holland, Sr. (1912–1974)
Harold E. Hahn (1900–1974)

AUTHORS' FOREWORD

This book has evolved from many years of discussion and friendship. In the course of this undertaking, we have learned much from one another. We hope our readers will discover a similar experience.

We believe, however, that it would be intellectually and morally dishonest to conceal our true identities. In a certain sense this book was written by a member of a dominant white majority and a member of the black minority. However, another dimension needs to be added. In reality we are both members of minorities, one racial and the other is a member of a minority consisting of people who are physically different from the remainder of the population. This minority, and perhaps many others, has not yet been recognized or understood. It is in the belief that there are many similar segments of the population remaining to be identified that this book has been written. If this book can prod its readers to an increased appreciation of the problems and aspirations of all segments of the society—including people who have obtained the status of an identifiable minority as well as those who have not yet earned that prominence—we will consider it a success.

Harlan Hahn
R. William Holland

PREFACE

This book is about the American governmental process. It explains that process by examining the many obstacles confronted by minority groups in their quest to obtain major political goals. Unlike other texts, which have been infused with the values and aspirations of the dominant white majority, this volume investigates and appraises the operation of American politics from the perspective of racial and ethnic minorities. It has two important objectives. First, it reflects our firm conviction that all phases of the American political process can be effectively understood by studying the manner in which governments have dealt with the issues raised by minority needs and demands. Although political institutions in America may not have been established purposely to frustrate the will of minority groups, these institutions encompass many barriers and obstructions that have prevented minorities from realizing their ambitions and that require careful analysis. Second, this book explains American politics in such a way that we understand the manner in which minority demands are frustrated by the political system. If large segments of the population understand what is wrong with the system, they can change the present political structure intelligently. After decades of intense and bitter controversy, it is clear that minorities, including blacks, Chicanos, Orientals, Puerto Ricans, and native Americans will continue to struggle to improve their socioeconomic position, and, in this struggle, politics will almost certainly determine the outcome.

As more and more minority students enter college and university classrooms, as more high school students begin to understand and pay closer attention to minority politics, and as instructors recognize the importance of acquainting other students with the perspective of minorities, a need arises for a textbook that illustrates and illuminates the American system of government by assessing the role of minorities in that system. We hope that this book will fill the need.

American Government: Minority Rights versus Majority Rule, therefore, is not intended to describe and analyze the socioeconomic condition of racial and ethnic minorities; that subject is described extensively in other volumes, and such an approach would focus on the minority groups rather than on why the American political process has not devised a complete remedy for those problems. Instead, this book focuses on the institutional features of American politics, that have hampered minority efforts to achieve their goals, rather than on public attitudes concerning racial and ethnic minorities. Although important data are given on the behavior of persons within political institutions, this traditional approach avoids the common pitfall of assuming that the blame for the lack of progress on minority rights can be ascribed to personal inadequacies rather than to structural constraints. The study explores how several major values, which were enshrined in the Constitution as a critical means of fulfilling political interest—including compromise, accomodation, coalition-formation, and satisfaction with incremental gains—have had a crucial impact on the political goals of minorities. Those values have been translated into institutional characteristics that have impeded minority aspirations. As a result, the efforts by minorities to pursue their objectives through political parties, interest groups, legislative assemblies, administrative agencies, and the judicial system have not produced total satisfaction of their demands.

This emphasis on the structural characteristics of American politics also has important implications for the analysis of policies affecting racial and ethnic minorities. Instead of concentrating exclusively on a single issue or a series of issues, such as welfare or economic programs, we discuss the institutions that are responsible for the adoption and execution of those programs. In Section 5, we review Supreme Court decisions in several important areas, such as education, housing, public accommodations, and the right to a fair trial. Because of the impact that the police exert on everyday conduct and the special problems that they have encountered in relations with minority communities, a section also has been included on law enforcement to provide an in-depth analysis of the implementation of laws. Generally, however, the focus is on the fundamental features of the American political system rather than on the details of specific social and economic controversies. This emphasis offers special advantages to the student and to the general reader. With a broad understanding of American politics, the citizen can promote his political values, regardless of the nature of the particular issue in which he is interested.

At the end of each section we have provided a dialogue that focuses on major issues about which we, as coauthors, were unable to agree. These dialogues give additional insight into the workings of the political system. Preceding each dialogue, we have included "Points to Remember." These two features provide a focus for further inquiry and various points of departure for further discussion.

We also examine "the politics of moderation," a phrase that best describes the American political process. We explain that minorities have achieved changes in American politics, but they have been accomplished primarily through minor gains and gradual advancements rather than through decisive triumphs.

Section 1 examines the historical foundations of American government, the manner in which the Founding Fathers dealt with racial issues, and the political values that have permeated our political institutions.

Section 2 investigates voting, political parties, and interest groups—the traditional means available to citizens for the satisfaction of their political demands. Even though relatively powerless groups frequently are advised to use these alternatives for political advancement, the experience of minorities in the American party system has shown the limitations of relying on this approach for the attainment of important goals. Much can be accomplished by mobilizing parties and interest groups in behalf of political interests, but racial and ethnic minorities have encountered special problems in seeking to utilize this form of political persuasion.

Section 3 explores the relationship between voters and their elected representatives in legislative assemblies, and it probes the institutional obstacles that prevent minorities from securing legislation that would fulfill their political ambitions. The nature of those barriers to political change and the specific means by which they have frustrated the desires of racial and ethnic minorities constitute an important chapter in American politics.

Similarly, minorities often have looked to the President and other executive officials as a focal point for the adoption of their demands. But even the most powerful leaders of the governmental process have failed to provide a solution to racial conflict in America. Special attention is given to the position of the President as head of the federal bureaucracy and to the public trust and confidence that is bestowed on him as the nation's highest elected official. However, the resignation of Richard Nixon demonstrated that the exercise of presidential power is limited and that trust and confidence can be withdrawn as quickly as they were granted. The relationship between minorities and administrative leaders and the dependence of the leaders on public opinion are the major themes of Section 4.

Perhaps the greatest gains for racial and ethnic minorities have resulted from successful litigation in the courts. The crucial role of the judiciary in imposing social and legal regulations on human behavior is the subject of Section 5. In this connection we examine critical law enforcement agencies. Although the system of justice in America has been responsible for major progress, it also has imposed sharp limitations on the pursuit of crucial political objectives.

Sections 7 and 8 describe the efforts of minorities to exert influence on governmental decision through protests and violence. Both the incentives for the participants in these manifestations of political discontent and the effects that they produce are essential elements of a comprehensive understanding of American politics.

Finally, in Section 9, we debate the major issues posed by this examination of America's most persistent and vexatious political conflict. In 1787 some of the nation's best minds met in Philadelphia because they recognized that the Articles of Confederation failed to adequately serve the needs of the American people. Perhaps, the time has come to call for another Constitutional Convention.

H.H.
R.W.H.

CONTENTS

1 CONFLICT, COMPROMISE, AND THE CONSTITUTION: AN INTRODUCTION TO AMERICAN POLITICS

In the broad spectrum of issues that political leaders are forced to confront, none has been more crucial or more difficult than the role of minority groups in American society. For members of the dominant white majority, America has seemed to fulfill the promise of the Declaration of Independence. For many minority groups, including blacks, Asians, Chicanos, Puerto Ricans and native Americans, however, phrases such as "life, liberty, and the pursuit of happiness" seem to have a hollow ring. The controversy over the status of minorities in America has been a persistent source of conflict, resulting in the country's only experience with a civil war; and the struggle to gain equality and freedom has been a major chronicle in American history.

Perhaps most important, however, efforts to cope with this issue have confronted political institutions and leaders with their most severe test. An investigation of the methods by which governments have attempted to grapple with the issues raised by minority groups, reveals both the weaknesses and the strengths of the political system. The purpose of this book, therefore, is to illuminate major facets of the American political process by examining the means by which that process has sought to resolve the issue of minority rights.

Coalitions and Majorities

In a society founded upon the principle of majority rule, racial and ethnic minorities encounter seemingly insurmountable obstacles to the fulfillment of their political objectives. Since the will of the majority requires the support of more than half of the citizenry, any segment of the population that comprises a smaller fraction may be doomed to political neglect. Many of the men who were responsible for writing the American Constitution felt that this problem could be avoided by encouraging minorities to transform themselves into majorities. Interests that represented less than half of the people could compete effectively for political rewards either by expanding their ranks or by joining with similar groups to form an alliance for their mutual benefit. The spirit as well as the nature of American politics is designed to provide a climate of compromise and accommodation in which this transformation can take place. As a result, numerous elements of the public such as farmers, laborers, and business interests eventually have succeeded in achieving at least a minimal satisfaction of their political ambitions by gaining the support of the majority.

Persistent Minorities

Racial and ethnic minorities, however, seem to present another problem. Since membership in those groups is determined biologically rather than by interest or voluntary affiliation, they have little likelihood of increasing their numbers. In addition, both the effects of prejudice or discrimination and the lack of incentives for other groups to align themselves with a minority have reduced the probabilities of gaining the status of a majority. Centuries of struggle have indicated that the political demands of minority groups may not be fully satisfied, but it is also unlikely that those demands will disappear. As a result, black Americans and other ethnic groups have been compelled to assume the posture of a *visible and persistent minority*[1] in American politics.

Single-Cleavage Issues

The size of the black population in America adds another dimension to the relationship between minorities and the white majority. A major confrontation along racial lines might threaten the stability of the body politic. As Lewis Coser has argued:

> "Stability within a loosely structured society often inadequately identified with the absence of conflict can be viewed as partly a product of the continuous incidence of various conflicts crisscrossing it. The stability, for instance, of bureaucratic structures may be accounted for, in part, by the fact that a multiplicity of conflicts prevents the formation of a united front. If, on the other hand, one conflict cuts through a group, dividing the members into two hostile camps, the SINGLE CLEAVAGE will probably put into question the basic consensual agreement then endangering the continued existence of the group."[2]

Overlapping group memberships are partly responsible for the general stability of the political system. For example, a parent who is a Catholic and who has children in the public school system belongs to groups that cut across

---

[1] Our concept of minority group status thus is based upon two major characteristics. First they are visible or easily distinguishable from the remainder of the population. Thus blacks, Asians, Chicanos, Puerto Ricans, and native Americans can be differentiated from European ethnic groups by their skin color, customs, and cultural norms, which prevent them from merging imperceptibly with the dominant white majority. The second element that we regard as a criterion for a racial or ethnic minority revolves around their perpetuation; that is, they will, in all likelihood, never become extinct and they will never obtain the status of a majority. Most racial and ethnic minorities are, of course, genealogically determined.

[2] Lewis Coser, *The Functions of Social Conflict* (Glencoe, The Free Press, 1956), p. 77.

religious lines, which tends to prevent him from advocating one position at the expense of all other interests. In contrast, race in America tends to be a "single-cleavage" issue.[3] In a heterogeneous society, the existence of racial identity that coincides with a geographical territory could mean that loyalty to the racial group might rival loyalty to the nation itself. Black Americans have found it difficult to be blacks for some purposes and Americans for others. The low economic status and geographic segregation of blacks in urban centers of America has produced a situation in which many public policy questions such as education, criminal justice, poverty, welfare, and housing are perceived primarily as racial issues. If the implications of a controversy are perceived to be "problack," hostile whites are angered. If the issue is regarded as an "anti-black" one, blacks are angered. Either perception tends to heighten racial hostilities and increase group solidarity. Sharp divisions along racial lines have produced a social polarization in which America may be evolving into "two societies: one white; one black; separate and unequal."[4]

The salience of conflict between black and white Americans in almost all decades of history can be traced to the failure of the framers of the Constitution to resolve racial issues in the early days of the republic. The men who met in Philadelphia to draft the Amercian Constitution produced a document that reflected a fundamental ambivalence toward the rights of non-Europeans that has remained as an integral part of American politics. In many respects, they seem to have designed a political system that has proven to be incapable of resolving political issues with strong racial overtones.

CONSTITUTIONAL AMBIVALENCE

The Founding Period

In 1787, representatives of the 13 states met in Philadelphia to write a national constitution to replace the Articles of Confederation that failed to provide adequate authority for a central government.[5] Blacks and native Americans ("Indians") were not represented among the delegates, but they were not conspicuous by their absence. Few whites suggested that either native Ameri-

---

[3]Since many issues are defined by their impact on minority groups, both the members of those groups and the dominant majority often feel compelled to take positions on these issues according to their racial or ethnic characteristics regardless of other interest. Conceivably, a white parent in a low income neighborhood may find the busing of children to another school advantageous to the child's education; but he may feel constrained about expressing his support for busing because of the overriding racial nature of the controversy.

[4]National Advisory Commission on Civil Disorders, *Report of the National Advisory Commission on Civil Disorders* (New York, Bantam, 1968).

[5]Accounts of the Constitutional Convention taken from Max Farrand, *The Records of the Federal Convention* (New Haven: Yale University Press, 1911), Vols. I, II, and III.

The Constitution is formally adopted by the delegates on the closing day of the historic convention at Philadelphia. (Painting by Junius Brutus Stearns, from the Clarence Dillon Collection)

cans or blacks would be able to participate in an undertaking as important as the formulation of a constitution. The atmosphere of the country was generally hostile to racial minorities. "As early as 1669 Virginia law virtually washed its hands of protecting the Negro held as slave. It allowed punishment of refractory slaves up to and including accidental death, relieving the master explicitly of any fear of prosecution on the assumption that no man would destroy his own estate."[6]

Although the Constitutional Convention was an earnest attempt to institutionalize the rights to "life, liberty and the pursuit of happiness," the Convention assumed that such rights belonged only to persons of European descent. During the discussion of admitting new states to the union, concern was expressed solely about the claims of European powers; no questions were raised about land occupied "only by Indians." The delegates were reluctant to incorporate blatantly prejudicial statements in the Constitution, but their thinking was dominated by implicitly racist assumptions.

[6]Robert C. Twombley and Albert H. Moore, "Black Puritan: The Negro in Seventeenth-Century Massachusetts," in *The Making of Black America,* Meir and Rudwick (eds.) (New York: Atheneum, 1969), pp. 103–110.

Slavery

Three major issues forced the delegates to consider the question of slavery and the inconsistency between this institution and the principle of freedom. The subject of slavery arose when the Constitutional Convention considered the manner in which the House of Representatives would be apportioned, the importation of slaves, and the taxation of imports.[7]

Of the three issues, the delegates devoted the greatest attention to apportionment.[8] There was no thought of extending suffrage to nonwhites, and no one proposed the representation of blacks in Congress. The Convention was preoccupied by the question of whether the House of Representatives should be apportioned on the basis of land, population, wealth, or a combination of these factors. Pinckney, of South Carolina, argued that the number of inhabitants was the only just and practicable rule of representation.[9] This formula implied that blacks would be counted equally with whites. Equality simply meant that one black man was the *numerical* equivalent of one white man, not his legal or political equal. This proposal favored Southern slaveholding states. Ironically, delegates from the largest slave state, Virginia, rejected the plan because they did not regard blacks as equal to free men. Butler and Pinckney, of South Carolina, continued to "insist that Blacks be included in the rule of representation equally with Whites."[10] The South Carolina motion to consider blacks equal to whites solely for purposes of apportionment was supported by three of the 13 states: Delaware, South Carolina, and Georgia.[11]

The defeat of this motion demonstrated that most convention delegates, though for differing reasons, were opposed to even the slightest suggestion of equal representation for blacks. Northern states objected because voting for full equality would give the South an advantage in the House of Representatives and would continue to protect the institution of slavery. Morris of Pennsylvania was of this opinion.

"[He was] compelled to declare himself reduced to the dilemma of doing an injustice to the Southern states or to human nature and he must therefore do it to the former. For he could never agree to give encouragement to the slave trade as would be given by allowing them representation for their Negroes, and he did not believe those states would even confederate on terms that would deprive them of that trade.[12]

[7]Farrand, *op. cit.*, Vol. I, p. 580.
[8]By apportionment we simply mean the number of legislative representatives allocated to a geographic area.
[9]Farrand, *op. cit.*, Vol. I, p. 580.
[10]*Ibid.*, p. 581.
[11]*Ibid.*, p. 588.
[12]*Ibid.*, Vol. II, p. 369

BY

HEWLETT & BRIGHT.

SALE OF

VALUABLE

SLAVES,

(On account of departure)

The Owner of the following named and valuable Slaves, being on the eve of departure for Europe, will cause the same to be offered for sale, at the NEW EXCHANGE, corner of St. Louis and Chartres streets, on *Saturday,* May 16, at Twelve o'Clock, *viz.*

1. SARAH, a mulatress, aged 45 years, a good cook and accustomed to house work in general, is an excellent and faithful nurse for sick persons, and in every respect a first rate character.

2. DENNIS, her son, a mulatto, aged 24 years, a first rate cook and steward for a vessel, having been in that capacity for many years on board one of the Mobile packets; is strictly honest, temperate and a first rate subject.

3. CHOLE, a mulatress, aged 36 years, she is, without exception, one of the most competent servants in the country, a first rate washer and ironer, does up lace, a good cook, and for a bachelor who wishes a house-keeper she would be invaluable; she is also a good ladies' maid, having travelled to the North in that capacity.

4. FANNY, her daughter, a mulatress, aged 16 years, speaks French and English; is a superior hair-dresser, (pupil of Guillac,) a good seamstress and ladies' maid, is smart, intelligent, and a first rate character.

5. DANDRIDGE, a mulatoo, aged 26 years, a first rate dining-room servant, a good painter and rough carpenter, and has but few equals for honesty and sobriety.

6. NANCY, his wife, aged about 24 years, a confidential house servant, good seamstress, mantuamaker and tailoress, a good cook, washer and ironer, etc.

7. MARY ANN, her child, a creole, aged 7 years, speaks French and English, is smart, active and intelligent.

8. FANNY or FRANCES, a mulatress, aged 22 years, is a first rate washer and ironer, good cook and house servant, and has an excellent character.

9. EMMA, an orphan, aged 10 or 11 years, speaks French and English, has been in the country 7 years, has been accustomed to waiting on table, sewing etc., is intelligent and active.

10. FRANK, a mulatto, aged about 32 years, speaks French and English, is a first rate hostler and coachman, understands perfectly well the management of horses, and is, in every respect, a first rate character, with the exception that he will occasionally drink, though not an habitual drunkard.

All the above named Slaves are acclimated and excellent subjects; they were purchased by their present vendor many years ago, and will, therefore, be severally warranted against all vices and maladies prescribed by law, save and except FRANK, who is fully guaranteed in every other respect but the one above mentioned.

TERMS:—One-half Cash, and the other half in notes at six months, drawn and endorsed to the satisfaction of the Vendor, with special mortgage on the Slaves until final payment. The Acts of Sale to be passed before WILLIAM BOSWELL, Notary Public, at the expense of the Purchaser.

New-Orleans, May 13, 1835.

Advertisements for slave sales were regular features of Southern newspapers. Not the least of the tragedies of slavery was its impact on children and parents who were sold to different buyers. (The Picture Collection, The New York Public Library)

After extended debate, Williamson of North Carolina moved that "In order to ascertain the alterations that may happen in the population and wealth of several states that a census shall be taken of free White inhabitants and 3/5th of those of other descriptions."[13] This was the infamous compromise accepted by the Convention that counted blacks as three-fifths of a human being for purposes of apportioning representatives in Congress. Ironically, not even to ensure the continued existence of slavery was Virginia willing to acknowledge a meaningless form of equality, the simple fact of being counted as one person.

Antislavery Sentiment

There was also considerable antislavery sentiment at the Convention.[14] The objections to slavery voiced by George Mason of Virginia were indicative of the sentiments of many delegates. He noted:

> "Slavery discourages arts and manufactures. The poor despise labor when performed by slaves. They prevent the immigration of Whites who really enrich and strengthen a country. They produce the most pernicious effect on manners. Every master of slaves is born a petty tyrant . . . It is essential in every point of view that the general government should have power to prevent the increase of slavery.[15]

Opposition to slavery emanated primarily from delegates who were worried about the social and economic impact of slavery on whites.

Convention delegates voted to make the slave trade liable to "equal tax with other imports," but they agreed to cease all importation of slaves by 1808. The first portion of this decision gave Constitutional protection to slavery, and the second part guaranteed that the slave trade would not undermine the position of the white majority. The taxation of the slave trade implied that most delegates regarded slaves as property. By 1808, it was assumed that the slave population would be sufficient to reproduce itself to meet the continuing needs of Southern agriculture.

While some delegates felt that slavery was a moral evil, the Convention produced a document that did little to improve the status of racial minorities. The delegates were uneasy about the ratification of the Constitution by citizens of the various states. To have outlawed slavery would have guaranteed the loss of Southern support. Yet there was a general reluctance to place the word "slave" in the Constitution. Hence, the compromise satisfied both sides. It was a victory for everyone except the slaves.

The inability of black Americans and other minorities to secure genuine freedom and equality can be explained in part by the implicitly racist perspec-

[13] *Ibid.*, pp. 369–379.
[14] *Ibid.*, p. 370.
[15] *Ibid.*, p. 371.

tives of the delegates that prevented them from prohibiting slavery and extending full citizenship to non-Europeans. Apparently, the framers of the Constitution felt that racial issues could be resolved by compromises such as the three-fifths provision and the decision concerning the importation of slaves. But those issues could not be reconciled any more than individuals could be compromised by dividing them into fifths. Citizenship is not a divisible status, and second-class citizenship is no citizenship at all. By failing to grant minorities the rights of full citizens, the framers relegated them to an inferior position for centuries.

The Founding Fathers: Racists or Not?

The failure of the Constitutional Convention to abolish slavery has led some observers to argue that the Constitution is a racist document. Perhaps the foremost advocate of this position was Frederick Douglass, a former slave and abolitionist leader prior to the Civil War. Douglass contended that "the Constitution was forged in full view of slavery and with an eye toward its perpetuation." In 1848, he noted that the slave trade was the only type of interstate commerce controlled by the states rather than by Congress. Hence, slaveowners were able to enact state legislation protecting the institution of slavery, which probably would have been defeated in Congress.[16]

By 1860, Douglass placed increasing emphasis upon what the framers actually accomplished in writing the Constitution rather than upon his interpretation of what they intended. He pointed out that the Constitution did not grant any class of people the right to enslave or to hold as property any other group. Thus he eventually concluded that the Constitution was not directly responsible for the perpetuation of slavery and the racism implied by that institution.[17]

With the passage of the Thirteenth, Fourteenth, and Fifteenth amendments, which outlawed slavery and granted former slaves the rights of citizenship, allegedly racist sections of the Constitution were repealed. Since racism is defined as "the predication of decisions and policies on considerations of race for the purpose of subordinating a racial group and maintaining control over that group,"[18] the obvious hostility of most delegates to the Constitutional Convention to any consideration of the rights of non-Europeans cannot explain the contemporary status of black Americans. An examination of the intentions of the framers concerning slavery would compel us to focus on issues that have been long since resolved. While the framers established a political system in which racist acts frequently are committed, extensive discus-

---

[16]*The Life and Writings of Frederick Douglass,* Foner (ed.) (New York, International Publishers, 1960), Vol. I, pp. 362–367.

[17]*Ibid.,* Vol. II, pp. 467–480.

[18]Stokley Carmichael and Charles Hamilton, *Black Power* (New York: Vintage 1967), p. 3.

sion of the constitutional treatment of slavery would divert attention from the most salient issues confronting racial and ethnic minorities in America.

Perhaps the most crucial problem for minorities arises from the unintended consequences of the American political process. The approach that the founders of the country used in coping with racial issues can be found not only in the literal provisions of the Constitution but also in the general intellectual climate that permeated the Convention.

Limiting Factions and Restraining Majorities

Perhaps the best expression of this climate is recorded in the writings of James Madison, and particularly in his essay (number 10)[19] in *The Federalist Papers* arguing for the adoption of the Constitution. Madison was primarily concerned with limiting the influence of groups or factions, which he defined as "a number of citizens, whether a majority or minority, who united behind some common impulse of passion or of interest adverse to the rights of other citizens or to the permanent and aggregate interest of the community."[20] He felt that factions could be curbed either by eliminating freedom or by establishing a federal republic that would mitigate against the development of a stable majority capable of dominating opposition groups. Since a majority could easily control minority interests by outvoting them, Madison was primarily interested in promoting political stability by restraining the power of a majority. He viewed factionalism[21] as a continuous kalaidoescopic process of grouping and regrouping that would prevent any single interest from dominating all other interests. As a result, groups will be essentially self-regulating because their activities will, by their mutual adjustment and accommodation, prevent any one group from exercising dominance over the others.[22] The American system of the separation of powers, which divides the national government into separate legislative, executive, and judicial branches as well as the process of checks and balances[23] that enables each branch to control the activities of other

---

[19]Alexander Hamilton, John Jay, and James Madison, *The Federalist Papers* (New York, New American Library, 1961) number 10.

[20]*Ibid.*,

[21]Our notion of factionalism differs from Madison's in that the citizens who are united by some common impulse of passion do not necessarily have to have interest adverse to the rights of others. They could simply be pursuing a common goal. As individuals and groups alter and develop their interest they move to join with others in an effort to form a majority. This process requires an almost continuous adjustment.

[22]Notice that Madison did not expect citizens to act out a commitment to the principles of freedom, equality, and justice. Instead, he designed a system in which individuals' pursuit of self-interest would provide for mutual checks and balances. This assumed, of course, that everyone would have the opportunity to participate.

[23]Checks and balances should not be equated with separation of powers. In designing the institutions of American government, the framers not only established three distinct branches of government, they also sought to insure that power would be divided among them. A major thrust of their design, therefore, was to prevent the concentration of power in any one branch.

branches, is highly consistent with Madison's political framework. By dividing authority among separate institutions within the federal government and between the states and the national government, Madison hoped to quarantine the influence of powerful factions. Such factions might be successful in capturing control of one state or branch of government, but they would be unlikely to gain control of the entire political apparatus.

Madison understood that groups participate in politics to further their own goals; but, when their goals are inconsistent or contradictory, compromise became the only means of resolving their differences. The dispersion of authority implied by Madison's views, therefore, necessitated compromise, which was the means by which the Constitutional Convention attempted to settle racial controversies. As long as important segments of the population were able to achieve significant influence in at least one branch of government, they could be virtually assured that their interests would be reflected in any final determination of an issue.

Madison's view of the political world, however, failed to encompass a persistent minority that was excluded from participating in government. Since racial minorities did not constitute an integral part either of Madison's theory or of the political process at the time the Constitution was written, they were denied the opportunity to engage in the exchange of influence to gain the support of other groups. Both the prevailing philosophy and the institutional arrangement of American politcs, therefore, precluded blacks, native Americans, and subsequent ethnic minorities from gaining the resources necessary for the effective pursuit of political goals.

The tendency of the founding fathers to neglect the problem of racial minorities stemmed not only from their insensitivity to the rights of non-Europeans, but also from their preoccupation with the task of restraining majorities rather than promoting the interests of minorities. Instead of creating numerous vehicles for the expression of minority demands, they sought to maximize political stability rather than opportunities for social change. The product of their efforts was a political system that has frequently seemed to sacrifice minority interests to the preservation of existing institutional arrangements.

ALTERNATIVE NOTIONS

The Concurrent Majority

Because the framers were primarily concerned with the maintenance of political stability, they failed to devote serious attention to the task of creating institutional mechanisms for the promotion of minority interests. This shortcoming became obvious some 50 years later during the controversy that preceded the Civil War. In one of the few distinctive American contributions to political theory, John C. Calhoun addressed this problem by drawing a distinction between the existing form of majority rule and the doctrine of the "concurrent majority":

> "One regards numbers only, and considers the whole community as a unit, having but one common interest throughout; and collects the sense of the greater number of the whole as that of the community. The other, on the contrary, regards interests as well as numbers, considering the community as made up of different and conflicting interests . . . and takes the sense of each, through its majority or appropriate organ, and the united sense of all, as the sense of the entire community. The former of these I shall call the numerical or absolute majority; and the latter, the concurrent . . . majority."[24]

Calhoun was a Senator from South Carolina who was primarily concerned with protecting the interests of Southern slaveholders. His theory was designed to uphold the doctrine of states' rights and to permit Southern states to nullify federal laws that conflicted with the will of the majority within those states.[25] He feared that the interests of slaveholding states would be overridden by an antislavery majority in the North. But Calhoun's theory could also have been applied to racial and ethnic minorities. If the doctrine of the concurrent majority were based upon ethnic or racial communities, the implementation of laws would require consent from minority ghettoes as well as from the dominant white majority.

The implications of Calhoun's ideas illustrate both the ironic tendencies in American politics, which permitted the theories of a racist slaveholder to be used for the protection of minority groups, and the fundamental issues raised by the presence of distinctive minority interests in a society predicated on the will of the majority. The dynamics of the controversy over slavery demonstrated that minority interests that provoke deep-seated emotions among major segments of the population could not be resolved by the principles of compromise and accommodation, implied by Madison's view of politics.

The Constitution did not provide a means by which the interests of a disaffected minority could be resolved. Calhoun's doctrine of the 'concurrent majority"[26] was not implemented, and the aspirations of racial and ethnic

---

[24]Richard M. Current, *John C. Calhoun* (New York: Washington Square Press, 1963), p. 52.

[25]The tensions between state and national government has been an enduring source of conflict in the American political system. Initially, states were particularly jealous of their rights and powers as they understood them in the Constitution. Over the years, however, power has increasingly gravitated to the federal government. The doctrine of "Nullification," which would have permitted States to make federal laws invalid within their boundaries, was advocated by Southern States prior to the Civil War but has never been implemented.

[26]Employing the notion of the concurrent majority in contemporary America would have some interesting consequences. For example, laws passed in Congress primarily aimed at native Americans could not be passed without their consent. Also, blacks in the nation's urban ghettoes would be able to exert a measure of community control. Revenue sharing initiated during the Nixon administration would be altered drastically because communities would have direct say-so over how monies were spent.

minorities have persisted as a woeful reminder of the inadequacies of the American political process.

In the American Constitution, the rights of racial and ethnic minorities were not specifically protected by an explicit commitment to political principles, such as a statement prohibiting discrimination on the basis of race, color, or creed. The assumptions and values that permeated the era in which the Constitution was drafted implied that each group would be responsible for preserving its rights by participating in the political process. Even the guarantees of the first 10 amendaments, or the Bill of Rights, did not contain an explicit recognition of the special problems of minority groups. Protection of the rights of racial minorities was not provided in the Constitution until the passage of the Thirteenth, Fourteenth, and Fifteenth amendments, which outlawed slavery, provided for equal protection under the laws, and established the right to vote respectively. Those amendments were adopted almost 100 years later

Japanese-Americans await evacuation to concentration camps in Owen's Valley, California. (Library of Congress)

after the country had endured a civil war; and many of these rights were not endorsed by the Supreme Court for another century. Moreover, as the experience of thousands of Japanese Americans who were sent to concentration camps on the West Coast during World War II indicated, the guarantees of the Constitution may not provide sufficient protection for a beleaguered minority when it is attacked by an aroused and determined majority.

Pluralism

Even though American political traditions have encompassed little protection for minority rights, many commentators on United States politics have assumed that such protection exists. Perhaps the most prominent interpretation of American politics has been the so-called "pluralist" approach. According to Robert Dahl:

> "The theory and practise [sic] of American Pluralism tends to assume, as I see it, that the existence of multiple centers of power, none of which is wholly sovereign, will help (may indeed be necessary) to tame power, to secure the consent of all, and to settle conflicts peacefully. . . . Because even minorities are provided with opportunities to veto solutions they strongly object to, the consent of all will be won in the long run."[27]

This view is based on the argument that different individuals or groups are responsible for exercising decisive influence on different political issues. It has been challenged by other researchers who have contended that communities and the country are run by a small and cohesive "elite" that constitutes a "power structure."[28] The latter position denies that rank-and-file citizens play any critical role in the decision-making process; but the pluralist position has not demonstrated that racial or ethnic minorities comprise an integral element in the multiple centers of power that allegedly determine policy outcomes. There has been a lack of empirical evidence showing that blacks, Asians, chicanos, Puerto Ricans, and native Americans play a critical or determinative role in the formulation of political decisions. Even if it could be proven that minorities have a veto power, pluralist theory does not incorporate a means by which minorities can go beyond the negative functions of a veto group and participate in positive efforts aimed at promoting or advancing their political

[27]Robert Dahl, *Pluralist Democracy in the United States:* Conflict and Consent (Chicago: Rand McNally, 1967), p. 24.

[28]For a statement of this view see Floyd Hunter, *Community Power Structure* (Chapel Hill: University of North Carolina Press, 1953) or C. Wright Mills, *Power Elite* (New York: Oxford University Press, 1956).

interests. Pluralism may simply represent a more recent attempt to justify the stability of existing political institutions without recognizing the need for the creation of means by which oppressed minorities can seek to press their claims in the struggle for political influence.

Allowing deprived and dispossessed minorities to engage in vigorous competition for governmental resources may occasionally produce instability; but establishing channels through which this conflict can be expressed may be indispensable to the preservation of a democratic regime. Pluralism has reflected a basic satisfaction with the existing system, but it has also diverted attention from the absences of effective vehicles for the expression of minority demands.

THE POLITICS OF MODERATION

The American political process apparently was founded upon the assumption that the structures established in the Constitution would promote the interests of all segments of society. But it failed to offer protection for minorities that were denied the opportunity to participate in government. Moreover, even after the Civil War extended the political rights of minorities, they were still at a serious disadvantage. Since minorities had little to offer other groups seeking benefits from government, there were few incentives for those groups to join with racial and ethnic minorities in the pursuit of major political goals. As a result, black citizens and other similarly disadvantaged groups were doomed to pursue a political course of action that entailed isolation, ostracism, and discrimination rather than compromise and conciliation. They became the lepers of the political process. Many other interests refused to join forces with minorities in the fear that the prejudice aroused by association with political outcasts would endanger their own objectives.

Incrementalism

Even when minorities have successfully enlisted the support of those few groups that were willing to assume the political risks of joining them, the pages of American history reveal that change has been an excruciatingly slow process. The spirit of compromise that was implicit in the Constitution has dictated a strategy of incrementalism.[29] For all portions of society, political gains usually are achieved through small advances rather than through sweeping victories. The preoccupation of the framers of the Constitution with the problem of maintaining political stability produced a form of government in which the prospects of securing immediate progress are sharply limited. The frag-

---

[29]By incremental we mean that political gains are usually achieved gradually and in relatively small amounts rather than suddenly or in massive quantities.

mentation of authority in the political process has bestowed a major advantage to interests seeking to preserve the existing distribution of resources. As a result, powerful interests frequently discover that they must be satisfied with minor achievements. And deprived groups often are forced to confront the frustration of repeated efforts that prove to be unsuccessful to the attainment of their goals.

Many segments of the population have learned that the most effective political strategy involves the pursuit of limited objectives that have a minimal impact on other groups in society. Hence, they are able to avoid provoking a sustained and determined opposition. At the same time, this process prevents a continuously dominant majority from ignoring the rights, interests, and privileges of contending forces in the political system. The incremental character of political institutions in America, therefore, simultaneously fulfills the interest in preventing the development of an aggressive opposition to influential segments of society as well as resolving the fears of the framers who wished to control the power of dominant groups.

The gradual nature of political change in America has profound consequences for racial and ethnic groups. Groups with extensive resources do not require continuous acquiescence to their demands; they can afford the luxury of partial rather than total success. The outcome of the political process is seldom a crushing defeat or a complete victory for well-established interests. Rewards are distributed by marginal advancements rather than dramatic gains. But the cumulative effects of these gains are sufficient to bestow major power upon entrenched interests.

By contrast, racial and ethnic minorities can obtain little if any relief from the incremental allocation of rewards. They have few resources, but great needs. Their needs demand decisive improvements rather than small gains. As a result they are forced to seek objectives that have a major impact on other interests and that frequently provoke a sustained and determined opposition. Disadvantaged groups are forced to play the game of politics according to a set of rules that is contrary to their basic needs and interests.

Blacks, Chicanos, and Native Americans

Since black Americans and other minorities were prevented from voting or participating in politics for almost a century after the Constitution was written, they did not share in the distribution of political rewards in America during an early period of economic expansion. As a result, a major gap developed between the resources available to racial or ethnic minorities and the influence afforded interests representing the dominant white majority. The incremental character of American politics has perpetuated this social and economic deprivation. Groups such as black and native Americans have achieved impressive progress in the twentieth century, but they have remained in an inferior position relative to white America. This problem is illustrated by the increases made by black and white Americans during the period from 1960 to 1970, which was a decade of intense civil rights activism.

Table 1 reveals the economic status of blacks, Chicanos, and native Americans compared with the total United States population. Native Americans have occupied the bottom rung of the socioeconomic ladder in this country as evidenced by the fact that approximately 40 percent were unemployed and almost three-fourths were in poverty. Significantly, however, all three groups occupied positions well below the level of the entire American population.

Although these statistics provide glaring evidence of the social problems confronting minorities in America, they also contain damning proof of the failure of the American political system to respond to minority needs and demands. The focus of this book, therefore, is directed at the institutional obstacles that confront minority efforts to improve their status in society rather than at the social and economic conditions that have resulted from centuries of political denial and neglect. By gaining a comprehensive understanding of the operation of the American political system and of the difficulties encountered by minorities within it, students of American politics can be equipped with the background and skills necessary to attack persistent social maladies.

While the effort to achieve political gains for black Americans has been the most persistent and absorbing struggle in American politics, many of the problems and strategies that have dominated black politics also have characterized the political strivings of other minorities.

"Native Americans for centuries and Mexican Americans for over a century have been the objects of scorn and ridicule, of prejudice and discrimination, of abuse and violence. . . . The protest and anger of these communities was effectively stifled for decades, and it was not until the 1960's that the Chicano and Native American once again physically protested in an organized manner the discrimination, abuse, and violence inflicted upon them by the dominant society. Impressed by the American public's initial support for black civil rights and by the apparent concessions made to blacks . . .' some Native Americans and Chicanos began to emulate the black mode.."[30]

The political movements of racial and ethnic minorities have displayed distinctive variations, but perhaps even more important have been their similarities. As a result, conclusions derived from the experience of blacks and comparable groups in American politics can, with much validity, be transferred to other minorities.

In pursuing their political objectives, racial and ethnic minorities have explored all of the routes to political change available to them. Their efforts to acquire benefits from government not only have included conventional and

---

[30]La Garza, Kruszewoko, and Aroniega (eds.), *Chicanos and Native Americans: The Territorial Minorities* (Englewood Cliffs: Prentice-Hall, 1973), p. 5.

time-honored forms of activity such as voting, working within political parties, exerting influence on legislators, attempting to gain the support of chief executives, and seeking to redress grievances in the courts. But they also have encompassed seemingly unconventional and highly criticized techniques such as protests, demonstrations, and violence. Yet, the unceasing struggle of black

Poverty among native Americans is widespread and has an especially devastating effect on children. (Bob Adelman/Magnum)

TABLE 1
Economic Status of Selected Groups in the United States, 1970 [a]

Group	Median Family Income	Percent below Poverty Line	Percent Unemployed
Blacks	$6500	33%	8.2%
Chicanos	7200	35	8.0
Native Americans	3600	75	40.0
Total U.S. Population	8600	25	5.0

[a] From *Beleaguered Minorities: Cultural Politics in America* by S. J. Makielski, Jr., W. H. Freeman and Company. Copyright © 1973.

and other minorities to improve their position in society has failed to elicit the rewards that it was designed to achieve. In large measure, one of the principal reasons for the inability of minorities to fulfill their objectives can be attributed to the barriers posed by the constraining influence of political institutions.

In general, political structures have seemed to contribute more to the maintenance than to the achievement of needed social change. The most appropriate point of departure for the examination of racial conflict in American politics, therefore, is the study of political institutions rather than public attitudes toward racial issues. This investigation of the means by which government has sought to cope with the problems of racial and ethnic minorities provides an important insight into both the strengths and weaknesses of American political structures.

• POINTS TO REMEMBER

The issue of minority rights in a political system based on majority rule has presented American political leaders and institutions with their most severe test. The size of the black population poses a special problem because race in America tends to be a "single-cleavage" issue and a major confrontation along racial lines might threaten the stability of the body politic.

The salience of conflict between black and white America can be traced to the failure of the framers of the Constitution to resolve racial issues in the early days of the republic. This failure was prompted both by hostility of the delegates to the Constitution Convention toward the rights of non-Europeans and by the unintended consequences of the underlying theory of the American political process. Instead of creating broad and numerous vehicles for the expression of minority demands that might result in changes in the political system, the framers of the Constitution sought to maximize political stability.

Observers of American politics have long recognized the lack of mechanisms for the promotion of minority interests and have suggested a variety of solutions to the problem including the concurrent majority, the inclusion of egalitarian principles in the Constitution, and the so-called "pluralists" approach to American politics.

The necessity for all groups participating in American politics to build coalitions, compromise, and be satisfied with incremental change has produced special problems for the nation's dispossessed minorities. Although the effort to achieve political gains for black Americans has been the most persistent absorbing struggle in American politics, many of the problems and strategies that have dominated black politics also have characterized the political strivings of other minorities.

• SOME UNRESOLVED ISSUES: A DIALOGUE

Hahn: In this section, we have attempted to explore the theoretical foundations of the American political process. In reviewing the evidence, I am struck by two considerations. Initially, the founding fathers were preoccupied by the fear of political instability. As a result, they designed political structures that would promote stability rather than change. Second, they sought to create institutions that would prevent the people from ruling directly. After nearly 200 years of experience with this system, it seems clear that these institutions have been major obstacles to the achievement of needed social changes. I believe, therefore, that two alternative possibilities should be given serious consideration: (a) the creation of institutions that would facilitate rather than impede the processes of change and (b) the potential of the people to govern themselves more directly.

Holland: I agree. Clearly, something is "rotten in Washington." However, it seems to me that you are employing an assumption that the people, if given the opportunity, would have long ago resolved what we consider to be the nation's most troublesome domestic issue. I am, at best, reluctant to accept the notion that racial and ethnic minorities will fare any better in a system that *simply* facilitates change.

Hahn: You are correct in noting that I have assumed that the people of this country are capable of resolving the issue, if given the opportunity. But this is an assumption that can be tested empirically. I believe that our needs now include the design of institutions that emphasize change rather than stability as well as the confidence and the courage to experiment with new political arrangements.

Holland: The use of your word "emphasize" is important. A political system in which the emphasis is on change rather than on stability would aid us in resolving what we have identified as America's most troublesome political issue. Many political observers have noted that the American system is perhaps the most stable in the world. But the stability of discrimination and oppression is no virtue.

Hahn: I believe the orgins of many current political problems also can be traced to the inability of the founding fathers to resolve issues concerning the only two minorities that were discussed in the constitutional convention, namely, native Americans and black Americans. The framers attempted to handle these issues through compromise. But such fundamental questions cannot be compromised.

Holland: The failure of the framers at this crucial point in history affected not only native Americans and blacks but also other minorities in the United States. Asians, Puerto Ricans, and Chicanos especially have been victims of a political system that has remained largely unresponsive to their needs. Because these groups comprise smaller numbers than black Americans, they have received even fewer benefits from the political system. In general, it appears that the smaller the size of a minority, the greater the political problems encountered by that group. As a result, many of the generalizations derived from the experience of black Americans in American politics can be applied with equal—and perhaps even greater—validity to other minorities.

Hahn: I agree. It seems to me that any political process, whether it be the existing system or one that allows for increased governance by the people themselves, might also devote serious consideration to the creation of special government agencies or delegations within legislative bodies that would serve as vehicles for articulating the interests of racial and ethnic minorities. As American history has revealed, the absence of such mechanisms probably has contributed to centuries of bitter, shameful, and disruptive turmoil.

Holland: I agree. Though not specifically provided for in the Constitution, political parties have been a primary means by which American citizens have aggregated and articulated their demands. Since the manner in which parties operate is largely dictated by the structure of the body politic as determined by the Constitution, they have proven to be relatively poor vehicles for serving minority interests. Our next chapter explores the relationship between minorities and parties and interest groups.

2 POLITICAL PARTIES AND INTEREST GROUPS

PARTIES

One of the most fundamental means by which people seek to promote their political interests in a democratic society is through the activities of political parties. Although parties are not formally recognized in the American Constitution, they evolved soon after it had been ratified to fill a critical vacuum in the governmental process. Some organization was needed to mobilize the sentiments of voters, to nominate candidates for public office, to provide leadership in the policymaking process, and to perform other critical functions. Political demands are more likely to have an impact on government policy if they are promoted by parties rather than by separate individuals. The combined strength of political goals advanced by party organizations usually is greater than the impact of persons acting in their own behalf. Fundamentally, therefore, parties have evolved to facilitate the aggregation of political interests and to transmit them to decision makers.

Parties frequently consist of a coalition of diverse and conflicting viewpoints. In fact, one of the basic purposes of parties is to weld together the interests of divergent groups, including midwestern farmers, urban laborers, small businessmen, and white-collar professionals. As a result, racial and ethnic minorities might be expected to occupy a critical position in party activities. Yet, minorities seldom have been able to muster the influence within party organizations that they hoped to achieve. While minority groups played a major role in the nature and development of the American party system, parties have served as an imperfect vehicle for the satisfaction of minority demands.

Political Parties and the Civil War

The origins of parties in America can be traced to the administration of George Washington, but one of the most critical periods in their history was the decade preceding the Civil War. That era marked a period of major party realignment including the collapse of the Whig Party, the emergence of extreme political movements such as the anti-Catholic and anti-immigrant Know-Nothing Party,[1] and the birth of the Republican Party.

Although the major objective of the Republican administration of Abraham Lincoln was to prevent the secession of Southern states, the fundamental conflict of the Civil War and the events that preceded it concerned the role of black persons in a predominantly white society. The issues and events that precipitated the Civil War were largely responsible for the reorganization of the American party system. From this controversy, Republicans and Democrats emerged as the two major political parties.[2]

Black Suffrage

The most controversial issue of this period focused on the political rights of black citizens. During the postwar reconstruction era, the federal government sought to guarantee the rights of freed blacks by sending federal troops into the South. For a relatively brief period of time, black residents were granted the right to vote, and many black candidates were chosen to fill major positions in Southern state and congressional offices.[3]

Simultaneously, the issue of black suffrage generated intense controversy in the North. During the period from 1865 to 1868, at least 10 Northern states held referenda on the question of black suffrage; and the proposal was defeated by voters in at least nine of those states. Opposition to black suffrage was related to the same phenomena that has stimulated racial prejudice on other issues and in other areas of the country: the fear of many whites that black persons might compete for and reduce their opportunities for employment.[4] The results of the referenda, and other expressions of public sentiments during this time, indicated that the Civil War had not put an end to racial prejudice in any section of the country. Perhaps the ratification of the Fifteenth Amendment to the Constitution, which granted black citizens the right to vote, was

[1]The Know-Nothing Party was a Ku Klux Klan type of organization that sought to preserve the dominance of white Protestants. It derived its name from the fact that its members, when asked about the operations of the organization, professed to "know nothing." Though no longer active, religious prejudice remains as a salient fact of American life. It was not until 1960 that a Catholic was elected President, and in that election Catholicism was an important issue.

[2]This fact seems to have escaped many observers of American politics. The inability of the leaders and institutions to resolve the slavery issue through available mechanisms caused a major party realignment in America that has persisted even until today.

[3]From 1873 to 1877 there were a total of 14 black Congressmen (seven in each Congress). By 1877, with the disenfranchisement of blacks the number dropped to zero. See *Black Politics '72* (Joint Center for Political Studies: Washington, D. C., June 1972), p. 83.

[4]See Robert R. Dykstra and Harlan Hahn, "Northern Voters and Negro Suffrage: The Case of Iowa, 1868," *The Public Opinion Quarterly*, (Vol. 32 (Summer 1968), pp. 202–215.

stimulated by concern of some "radical Republicans,"[5] who feared that black voting might not be approved in the North, even while they were seeking to ensure it in the South. Racial intolerance and bigotry continued to exert a powerful impact upon the ability of minorities to gain the vote and to exercise other constitutional rights.

Black Disenfranchisement

After the withdrawal of federal troops and the end of the reconstruction era,[6] Southern whites sought, with a vengeance, to regain political control of that region. Their efforts were designed to prevent black residents from exercising the right to vote by a variety of tactics that included legal obstacles as well as terrorism and intimidation. Most of these endeavors, as well as other laws enacted to require racial segregation, reflected an attempt by conservative Southerners to avert the threat of a coalition between black residents and lower-class whites that they feared was being formed by the efforts of the Populist Party in the late nineteenth century.[7] Since blacks constituted a numerical majority in many areas of the South, the impetus for this drive may have been understandable. Yet, the zeal and determination displayed by Southern whites in seeking to preserve their political prerogatives by excluding black voters from the ballot box exceeded all other attempts to prevent the exercise of legal rights in American history.

Immigration and Party Allegiances

Perhaps the major social trend that disrupted the partisan loyalties generated by the war was the immigration of ethnic groups from foreign shores. Many immigrants, who had not been exposed to the traumatic events of the Civil War, tended to affiliate with the Democratic rather than the Republican Party.[8] As those groups gradually acquired increasing political influence and recognition, they became a major force that disturbed the prevailing dominance of the Republican Party in the North. Since many ethnic groups congregated in large cities, they played a major role in reviving party competition in some of the

[5]After the Civil War a group of Republicans in the Congress and elsewhere were so vehement in thier views concerning the punishment of the South that they acquired the label of "Radical Republicans."

[6]Reconstruction is commonly referred to as that period of time between 1865 and 1877 in which federal troops were stationed in the South to insure the rights of the freed slaves.

[7]C. Van Woodward, *The Strange Career of Jim Crow* (New York: Oxford University Press, 1955).

[8]This was the beginning of the era of the political machine that reformers some 30 years later labeled as a major corrupting influence in American politics. However, one might argue that such organizations acted as an effective means of interest aggregation.

most populous states in the country. While traditional party attachments gradually were jarred by new social trends and movements, the partisan loyalties engendered by the Civil War had a profound impact upon both voting behavior and the nature of party organization.

Party Identification

Those events exerted a profound impact upon the political allegiances of American voters that has persisted for generations. As extensive research has demonstrated, one of the most important factors that affect the voting behavior of the American public is party identification, or the tendency of voters to support either Republican or Democratic candidates.[9] While many other considerations such as the appeal of the candidate, the nature of the issues, and the socioeconomic status of the voter also impinge upon electoral decisions, party identification has remained the single most powerful determinant of voter preferences. Party identification usually has been transmitted from parents to their children. Approximately three-fourths of Americans mark their ballots for the same party that their parents supported.[10] Thus, the results of elections in any geographic area usually have paralleled the proportion of Republican or Democratic votes cast in prior elections and the traditional voting habits of that area.

Political Socialization

The discovery that political allegiances exert a strong impact on voting behavior has stirred political scientists to pursue two separate methods of assessing their influence. One attempt to trace the transmission of party loyalties between generations is reflected in growing research on political socialization. Those investigations have sought to examine the process by which children acquire political values at home, in schools, and from other sources. Although the results of those studies have contributed greatly to an increased understanding of political beliefs and attitudes, they are often unable to identify the initial origins of political opinions and party affiliations.[11] Research on political socialization can trace the means by which parents influence the political views of their children, but it is limited in its ability to delineate the ways in which the mother or father of the child acquired political opinions from their parents and from preceding generations.

[9]Angus Campbell et al., *The American Voter* (New York: John Wiley, 1960).
[10]*Ibid.*
[11]For a review of this see Herbert Hyman, *Political Socialization* (Glencoe: Free Press, 1959) or Kenneth Langton, *Political Socialization* (New York: Oxford University Press, 1969).

Historical Loyalties

The appraisal of partisan loyalties, therefore, ultimatley leads to the study of historical influences. Many areas of the country exhibit the same partisan orientations and voting habits over an extended period of time. Although sharp population mobility or the migration of new elements to the community may affect those patterns, some localities even seem to cling to traditional loyalties despite gradual shifts in the social and economic composition of the area. The strong influence of history probably tends to impede the process of change in American politics; but it seems undeniable that traditional forces exert a major—if not a decisive—impact upon American politics.

Among the historical influences that have exerted a continuing influence on American voting patterns, perhaps none was more important than the controversy regarding slavery and the war that was fought over that issue. The Republican Party was born during that period, and many voters subsequently cast their ballots ón the basis of their feelings about the war and their perceptions of party positions concerning it. Partisan allegiances inspired by the war tended to follow the regional boundaries that defined the conflict. For many years, the Civil War made the Republican Party the party of the North, and the Democratic Party, the party of the South.[12] While there were a few Democrats who opposed the war in Northern states and some critics of the war in areas of the South that have traditionally voted Republican, events surrounding the war—and the racial issues that they implied—established fundamental political patterns in the country for many generations. As a result, entire states began to develop an attachment to a single political party that inhibited effective competition between the parties. During much of the late nineteenth and early twentieth centuries, the predominant political characteristics of many—if not most—states could be characterized as one-party. The opportunities for the opposition party in a state to achieve political power were negligible.

FEDERALISM AND PARTIES

Party Organization

It has become almost a truism in political science to observe that partisan politics in America is not the politics of two national parties nor of three branches of government; but it is the politics of 50 states, countless communities, and hundreds of parties. The organizational charts of major political

---

[12]V. O. Key, *Political Parties and Pressure Groups* (New York: Thomas Crowell, 1947).

parties in America comprise a confusing and chaotic diagram. In theory, both parties are led by a national chairman, who is selected by a committee consisting of party leaders and national committeemen and committeewomen from each state. Actually, the chairman often is chosen by the Presidential nominee of the party, acting in his role as titular head of the party, immediately after his nomination. Moreover, there is no formal membership in American parties; and candidates are not compelled to support either national or state party leaders. Both elected officials and voters regard themselves as party members only in the general sense that they tend to be aligned or identified with a particular party. American political parties tend to be diffuse and amorphous organizations that lack the ability to discipline or to control their followers.

State Politics

One of the major explanations for the disarray of the parties probably can be attributed to the American system of federalism,[13] which sought to avoid the centralization of national power by allocating much authority to separate states. Since party organizations and activities generally are controlled by state laws and regulations, party concerns tend to be centered at the state instead of the national or local level. Representatives to national party conventions are organized in state delegations, and electoral votes in Presidential campaigns are cast as a unit by states. Furthermore, one of the major responsibilities of political parties involves selecting candidates and promoting their election to state and local offices. The ability to swing the electoral votes of a state to a party nominee for President may be a dramatic event to voters across the country, but the principal focus of party attention often is concentrated on legislative, gubernatorial, and congressional positions, which form important resources for the distribution of rewards to party activists and supporters. As a result, perhaps the most salient government jurisdiction to political parties is the state rather than the community or the nation.

The institutional framework within each of the major parties probably can be characterized as 50 separate structures. This configuration has important implications for minority groups. Initially, the autonomy of state organizations in political parties has enabled particular states to repudiate the will of the national party. In national elections, Democratic leaders in the South even refused to allow the name of the national party nominee to appear on the ballot. Because of their disagreement with the civil rights position endorsed by John F. Kennedy in 1960, Democratic voters in Alabama and Mississippi were denied the opportunity to vote for the presidential candidate of their party. The independence of state parties, which permitted them to employ this tactic

[13]Federalism is the division of political authority between a central government and state or local governments.

as well as the threat of withholding electoral votes from candidates who carried the state, has permitted state leaders to frustrate national party demands that they adopt a more favorable attitude toward minority rights.

The ability of racial and ethnic minorities to gain influence within political parties has been sharply affected by geographic considerations. Trends in economics and population mobility have caused many minority groups to concentrate in distinct regions of the country such as blacks in the South, Chicanos in the Southwest, Japanese- and Chinese-Americans on the West Coast, native Americans in the Western and plains states, and Puerto Ricans in New York; but their residential patterns have been scattered to prevent them from achieving dominance within any of those areas. As a result, it is unlikely that minorities, either as separate groups or acting in unison, can acquire sufficient resources to emerge as a powerful national force. Political parties are not organized as a hierarchy with a chain of command that links the national

Shirley Chisholm, Democratic Congresswoman from New York, waged a vigorous campaign for the presidency in 1972. Here she chats with potential political supporters. (Lee Goff/Magnum)

level to state and local organizations. Hence, even if a minority did succeed in achieving influence in a particular state or community through intensive effort and mobilization, the effect of that gain might not be felt either at the national level or in any other state. Political interests that are based in specific localities and that lack a broad foundation of support across the country may tend to dissipate the impact of minority influence within state or local organizations without exerting a decisive impact on the national parties.

Minority Candidates

The geographic concentration and dispersion of minorities, as well as the relative size of minority populations, also can have a crucial effect on the electoral success of minority candidates in various areas of the country. In some of the less populous states, native Americans, Chicanos, and other minority candidates who are capable of attracting the support of white voters have succeeded in gaining high public office. In a few areas with strong party organizations, a formula has developed by which minority candidates are granted the opportunity to run for minor positions in a manner similar to the approach used by old-fashioned political machines that allocated candidates among European ethnic groups in order to present a party slate that included representatives of all major nationalities in the constituency. But the occasions on which minority candidates can achieve success as candidates for high public offices in predominantly white states seem to be relatively rare. Even in the election of Republican Senator Edward W. Brooke of Massachusetts, who defeated a liberal white opponent to become the first black member of the United States Senate since the Reconstruction era, surveys of voter attitudes revealed that opposition to Brooke was closely related to racial intolerance and prejudice.[14] Although the states occupy a critical position in party organizations, minority politicians might face major obstacles in their efforts to attain influence within states by winning elective positions.

Minorities in Urban Politics

In general, black and other minority politicians seem to possess the strongest prospects of electoral victory in jurisdictions where they comprise either a majority or a sizable proportion of the voting population. In cities such as Gary, Newark, Cleveland, Detroit, Atlanta, and Los Angeles, black candidates for mayor enjoyed unprecedented success in the late 1960s and early 1970s. Yet, most of those outcomes could be attributed to a large black percentage

---

[14]Eugene Heaton and John F. Becker, "The Election of Senator Edward Brooke", *Public Opinion Quarterly*, Vol. 31 (Fall 1967), pp. 346–358.

of the electorate that made the elevation of their own candidates to the office of mayor virtually undeniable.[15] In a few cities, black candidates were aided by support from other minorities, low-income whites, and by the unpopularity of their opponents. In general, black politicians received only a small—and often

Bobby Seale, former leader of the Black Panther Party, plays it "straight" in his unsuccessful campaign for Mayor of Oakland, California. (Stephens Shames/Black Star)

[15]Harlan Hahn and Timothy Almy, "Ethnic Politics and Racial Issues: Voting in Los Angeles", *Western Political Quarterly*, Vol. XXIV, No. 4 (December 1971).

a miniscule—fraction of the white vote. Although some evidence appears to suggest that white voters may express an increasing willingness to endorse minority candidates as America gradually achieves social—as well as legal—equality, the political opportunities available to minorities probably are greater in areas where they constitute a major fraction of the population, which can be employed as a base of political support, rather than in predominantly white localities.

The probabilities that minorities can achieve major political influence at the three levels of government—federal, state, and local—suggest some interesting patterns. As black migration to urban areas continues and as whites increasingly flee to the suburbs, many of the nation's largest cities are in the process of becoming predominantly black. The perennial attraction of the inner city to the most disadvantaged groups in society probably will increase the minority share of the urban population. As minority groups gradually approach the stage at which they can claim a majority of the electorate, these voters will be able to advance candidates to high elective office. Hence, the greatest likelihood of racial and ethnic minorities gaining major public office is at the local level.

The growth of minority executives in the major American cities, however, may have little effect in expanding the role of minorities in political party organizations. Elections in many American communities, including some of the nation's largest cities, are nonpartisan contests in which candidates do not run as Republican or Democratic nominees. Mayors and other political leaders chosen without partisan support lack the organizational backing necessary to speak authoritatively in state or national party councils, and they may find that the top positions in urban areas do not provide a viable route to higher public offices.

Cities and States

Furthermore, minority officials in urban areas could face the possibility that their authority might be restricted by the states. Under a classic legal doctrine in America, known as "Dillon's rule," cities are considered creatures of the state; and they may only engage in those acts that are specifically authorized by the states as opposed to undertaking all actions except those explicitly prohibited by the states.[16] Although many restrictive implications of this principle have been circumvented by so-called "home rule" provisions to expand the independence of cities, it is not inconceivable that the tension of state and municipal governments could become the basks of a new confrontation between minority leaders in the cities and white legislators representing the remainder of the state.

[16]John F. Dillon, Municipal Corporations (Boston: Little, Brown, 5th edition, 1911).

The acquisition of political control by minority groups in major urban areas could involve serious difficulties for the leaders of these groups. Cities frequently are described as confronting more intense social, economic, and political issues than state or national governments. Those problems are magnified by the declining economic resources available to cities. As industries and affluent whites relocate in suburbs and medium-sized cities, major action areas will encounter a critical loss of a tax base and dwindling financial resources. The task of managing the complex and multifaceted problems of urban areas may become so onerous that it is beyond the capacity of any man or group of men to govern those areas. The election of black and minority candidates to major offices in cities could satisfy the *symbolic*[17] aspirations of voters, but it might have little impact on the ability of cities to resolve the numerous difficulties that beset them. The growth of minority power in urban areas could leave them with little more than an "empty prize," which imposes numerous responsibilities rather than major benefits.

A critical problem confronting state and local governments is the absence of adequate financial resources. Both appear incapable of raising necessary revenues either because of the lack of an adequate economic base or because of popular resistance to increasing taxes. Most of the problems confronting ethnic and racial minorities seem to require the expenditure of large sums of money to alleviate their grievances. As a result, state and municipal officials are turning more and more to the federal government for assistance in meeting their needs.

Minorities in National Politics

Clearly, many—if not all—of the urgent problems that plague racial and ethnic minorities are national in scope, and they appear to require national action for their solution. Hence, the political influence exerted by minorities on the federal government may be a crucial factor in the enactment of policies to improve their status in society.

For many years, commentators have urged that the votes of black citizens and other minorities should be employed selectively as a "balance of power"[18] to form a winning margin for the candidate in greatest need of those votes who may be sympathetic to the needs of minorities. In many presidential campaigns, the black vote, especially in northern cities, has been regarded as pivotal. In part, this belief has developed because of the critical concentration

[17]For a discussion of the role and use of symbols in American politics see Murray Edelman, *The Symbolic Uses of Politics* (Urbana: University of Illinois Press, 1967).

[18]If whites are evenly divided on a given candidate or issues, blacks, by voting together could be the decisive determiner of the election outcome. In this sense they would represent "the balance of Power." For a discussion of this issue see Henry See Moon, *The Balance of Power: The Negro Vote* (New York: Doubleday, 1948).

of black residents in major urban centers of the North. Since many cities containing a large number of black voters are located in highly populous states, those ballots might be considered crucial in shifting the electoral votes of the state to one of the presidential candidates.

Minority Turnout

The ability of minorities to organize a bloc of votes that can be delivered to provide a decisive margin of victory has been limited by several factors. Initially, they have tended to vote less frequently than white segments of the electorate. In 1960, for example, 46 percent of black adults failed to vote in the presidential contest between John F. Kennedy and Richard M. Nixon. Other ethnic minorities, as well as whites with low incomes, unskilled occupations, and other disadvantages, have had similarly low rates of participation in national elections.[19] In part, however, the turnout of minority groups at elections frequently has seemed to depend upon the salience of issues in the campaign. When civil rights issues have arisen, minority voters usually appeared in larger numbers at the polls. Yet, for a variety of legal, political, social, and economic reasons, minorities have had relatively low rates of continuous participation in elections.

Minority Voting Patterns

In addition, minority voting in presidential elections has been affected by partisan affiliations. Like other segments of the population, black and other minority voters have developed party attachments based upon a combination of factors including traditional loyalties, the impact of specific issues, and social and economic considerations. As the effects of the Great Depression worsened for black voters, they tended to shift their allegiances from the party of Abraham Lincoln to the party of Franklin D. Roosevelt. Thus, black voters joined Chicanos, Puerto Ricans, Catholics, Jews, and labor in a Democratic coalition, which is opposed by Republican voters that attracts disproportionate support from smalltown and suburban Protestants, businessmen, and professionals. Minority voters in the Democratic Party have gained some assistance from sympathetic or deprived white groups in the party, but their capacity to act as an effective "balance of power" has been reduced by their general commitment to a single party.

Perhaps most important, presidential nominees may find it possible to wage a successful campaign based almost exclusively on an appeal to white voters.

---

[19]A national survey, however, revealed that blacks with a strong sense of "group consciousness" tend to have higher rates of political participation than those who lack this sense of identity. See Sidney Verba and Norman Nie, *Participation in America* (New York: Harper and Row, 1973).

The combined voting strength of the white majority usually exceeds the electoral power available to racial or ethnic minorities both in large states and in the nation. Thus, presidential aspirants may not attempt to solicit minority votes, and candidates who fail to receive their support often are unsympathetic to the cause of minorities.

BLACK POLITICAL PARTICIPATION IN THE SOUTH

In order to maximize their political strength, minority voters often are compelled to fulfill a number of requirements that are not imposed upon the white majority.[20] Among those criteria are the following: (a) sufficient numbers to affect the margin of victory; (b) high voter registration and turnout; (c) optimal cohesion or unanimity in the choice of candidates; and (d) a divided vote among the white majority. Some indication of the special problems confronting racial and ethnic minorities in their efforts to satisfy these requirements— and to exert a decisive impact upon the outcome of elections—can be derived from an examination of the growth of black political strength in the South after the passage of the 1965 Voting Rights Act that sought to guarantee the right of black adults to register and to vote.

Black Registration in the South

As Table 2 indicates, black voters were remarkably successful in fulfilling the first two criteria. Not only was there a large bloc of black voters that could influence election results (between 1963 and 1964, the ratio of eligible black voters to eligible white voters in the South increased from .49 to .79); but black voter registration also increased dramatically. When black Southerners were ensured the right to vote by civil rights legislation, they were prepared to avail themselves of this opportunity at an unprecedented rate.

Black Voting in the South

Furthermore, black voters in the South manifested remarkable unanimity in the choice of Presidential candidates. In 1968 and 1972, black Southerners in various states cast more than 90 percent of their ballots for the Democratic opponents of Richard M. Nixon. Yet, their votes had a limited impact upon the outcome of presidential balloting in the South. In the two elections won by Richard Nixon, Texas was the only Southern state in which minority votes seemed to be decisive; in 1968, Hubert H. Humphrey was awarded the elec-

[20]Much of the material is drawn from Joe R. Feagan and Harlan Hahn, "The Second Reconstruction: Black Political Strength in the South," *Social Science Quarterly* (June 1970).

TABLE 2

Nonwhite Voter Registration by State for Examiner and Non-Examiner Counties in Five Southern States: 1963–1964 and 1967

	Post-Act Number Registered to Vote		Pre-Act Percentage of VAP Registered (1963–1964)		Post-Act Percentage of VAP Registered (1967)	
	Examiner Counties	Non-Examiner Counties	Examiner Counties	Non-Examiner Counties	Examiner Counties	Non-Examiner Counties
Alabama	127,416	121,016	15	23	59	45
Georgia	6,013	316,483	10	28	63	53
Louisiana	50,413	252,735	9	37	54	60
Mississippi	94,674	86,559	8	5	71	50
South Carolina	9,377	180,640	17	38	72	51
Totals	287,893	957,433	12	30	62	53

Source: U.S. Commission on Civil Rights, *Political Participation* (Washington, D.C.: Government Printing Office, 1968), pp. 222–224.

VAP—Voting-age population as of 1960 Census. These figures reflect the estimates of official and unofficial sources and vary in reliability.

From Joe R. Feagin and Harlan Hahn "The Second Reconstruction: Black Political Strength in the South," *Social Science Quarterly* (June 1970), p. 48.

toral votes of this state with the combined aid of black and Chicano votes. Although the size of the black vote was sufficient to provide a winning margin for John F. Kennedy in four Southern states in 1960 and for Lyndon B. Johnson in four states in 1964, subsequent black political gains were impeded by the popularity of candidates such as Barry Goldwater, George Wallace, and Richard M. Nixon among white voters. The growth of black political participation did produce a major increase in the number of black elected officials at the local level in the South, but it had little immediate effect upon presidential politics. In attempting to impose their demands upon the national government, minority voters have encountered numerous obstacles including the countervailing actions of opponents who have promoted candidates capable of attracting overwhelming support among white voters.

POLITICAL CAMPAIGNS

Party Nominations

The critical role of political leaders in the political process requires minorities to devote major attention to the selection of party candidates. In campaigns for presidential nominations, the choice of convention delegates is determined either by state party conventions or by primary elections. Although only a small number of states hold presidential primaries that stimulate active campaigning by major contenders for the nomination, the results of those primaries are examined carefully by party officials across the country to assess the relative popularity of likely candidates. Moreover, in their efforts to gain party endorsements, potential nominees often feel an obligation to increase the breadth of their appeal. Perhaps their principal objectives in seeking the nomination are to form a viable coalition of popular support and to demonstrate to party professionals that they are capable of attracting votes from all sectors of the population. This approach has both advantages and disadvantages for minority groups. Aspiring candidates often make a more active attempt to acquire support among racial and ethnic minorities in their quest for party nominations than at any other stage of the electoral process, but those efforts may be little more than symbolic gestures and they may not be followed by a corresponding emphasis on minority needs after they have secured the nomination.

Party Conventions

One of the most crucial events in the American political process is the national party convention held by both Republicans and Democrats every four years

1972 Republican National Convention. (Elliot Erwitt/Magnum)

prior to presidential campaigns. In a carnival-like atmosphere, parties engage in the vital business of selecting the men who will occupy the offices of president and vice-president of the United States. Frequently, candidates are forced to share the center stage of such gatherings with controversies about racial questions. In 1948, for example, an intense debate on civil rights issues prompted the defection of Southern "Dixiecrats" from the Democratic Party and the third-party candidacy of Senator Strom Thurmond of South Carolina for President. Although blacks and other minorities traditionally have been underrepresented among convention delegates, the need to display attractiveness of the party to minority interests has enabled them to play a growing role in party conventions. Even in 1968, there were 106 black delegates chosen by Southern states to participate in national conventions, 88 percent of whom were Democrats. As a result, national party conventions may become a more and more important forum for the discussion of issues affecting racial and ethnic minorities.

Political Contributions

In general, however, delegates who attend national party conventions tend to represent party "angels" and activists. While the former group consists of persons who have demonstrated their loyalty to the party by providing generous financial contributions, the latter group is composed of people who have displayed similar support by devoting a vast amount of time and energy to party work. The pressing need for money and the status accorded wealthy contributors in party deliberations, has had an impact on the role of minorities in political parties. The largest contributors to political activities generally have been financial spokesmen for the major business and financial interests of the country. Not only have campaign contributions usually favored Republican candidates, but few minority groups have been represented among large contributors to the Democratic Party. Since minorities have not achieved a position of economic power in American society, they have seldom been able to afford large political contributions. Although members of minority groups have sought to overcome this disadvantage by extensive campaign work and party activism, their efforts have provided little encouragement for the belief that they can offset the effects of financial donations. Since campaigns for major elective offices have become multi-million-dollar enterprises, the relative absence of economic resources among minorities has reduced their influence within political parties.[21]

The crucial role of entrenched interests among both Republicans and Democrats has prevented political parties from becoming an effective champion of minority demands. Parties are responsible for setting the agenda of

---

[21]Harlan Hahn, Larry Berg, and John Smidthauser, *Political Corruption in the U.S.* (Morristown, N.J.: General Learning Press, 1974, forthcoming).

political discourse and for determining the priority of various issues. Although parties may embrace new proposals after their popularity has been demonstrated, they are not apt to assume the initiative or to launch the consideration of controversial plans. They are rarely willing to risk their political fortunes by presenting voters with radical programs of experimentation and social innovation. While most white citizens have favored the continuance of existing institutions and policies, the attitudes of minority voters have reflected a mounting dissatisfaction with the status quo and a growing desire for widespread social change. Perhaps the principal impact of electoral campaigns has been to restrict the range of questions that might be considered legitimate topics of discussion. As a result, parties seldom have been significant instrumentalities for social and political change in America or for the dissemination and consideration of proposals that would benefit minorities.

Party Competition

Although parties have failed to serve as an effective vehicle for the satisfaction of minority grievances, many social scientists have argued that vigorous competition between the parties for the support of voters could function as an effective means of satisfying political demands especially among disadvantaged segments of the population. For many years political scientists criticized the dominance of state and local governments by one party on the assumption that intense competition between parties would produce higher levels of expenditure for welfare programs designed to aid the disadvantaged. In electoral districts containing evenly matched parties, candidates would be forced to compete for the votes of all segments of the population, including minorities, to maximize their electoral appeal. Party competition, therefore, was portrayed

"SUPERB REFLEXES."

"Superb reflexes." (From *Wright On!* Copyright © 1971 by Don Wright. Reprinted by permission of Simon & Schuster, Inc.)

as accomplishing the function that parties themselves had failed to perform.

Subsequent research, however, failed to reveal any association between the intensity of competition and levels of expenditure for welfare and other programs. In fact, Thomas Dye discovered that state governmental expenditures were more closely related to economic variables than to political characteristics.[22] States with high levels of per capita income spent more on welfare programs than states with low average per capita incomes regardless of the levels of party competition. The findings therefore raise grave doubts about the efficacy of traditional political action as a means of obtaining a reallocation of social and economic benefits for the nation's impoverished minorities.

The Impact of Minority Voting

Not only has party competition failed to provide policies that would benefit minorities, but the size of the minority vote also apparently has had a negligible effect upon the outcome of the policymaking process. A study of the impact of black voting in two Southern cities that had previously denied them the franchise revealed some important findings. While blacks made greater gains in the city in which they constituted a majority of the electorate than in the community in which they remained a minority, many important political objectives were frustrated in both communities.[23] Although democratic theory assumes that the vote is a principal mechanism by which citizens can achieve their political goals, there is serious doubt as to whether this classic tenet has been realized in the experience of minorities in American politics. The failure of political parties to satisfy the demands of minorities, therefore, creates a need to investigate other methods by which citizens seek to influence governmental policies.

INTEREST GROUPS

One method of expressing political sentiments that has traditionally received major emphasis in American politics is to organize interest groups. Since many social scientists have become disillusioned with the impact that individuals could exert on governmental policies through voting, they focused their attention on the collective influence generated by the activities of groups and organizations. Although Madison had warned that factions comprised a major threat to the democratic process, many subsequent observers began to regard groups as a major hope rather than a danger for the preservation of democracy.

[22]Thomas Dye, *Politics, Economics and the Public* (Chicago: Rand McNally, 1966).
[23]William R. Keach, *Impact of Negro Voting* (New York: Rand McNally, 1968).

Voluntary Organizations

Since the beginning of the republic Americans have displayed a tendency to band together in the pursuit of collective goals. In the 1830s Alexis de Tocqueville, one of the most astute observers of American politics in history observed:

In many parts of the South, blacks attempting to vote ran the risk of imprisonment and death. (Danny Lyon/Magnum)

"Americans of all ages and conditions and all dispositions constantly form associations. They have not only commercial and manufacturing companies in which all take part, but associations of a thousand other kinds, religious, moral, serious, futile, general or restricted, enormous and diminutive. The Americans make associations to give entertainments, to found seminaries, to build inns, to construct churches, to diffuse books, to send missionaries to the Antipodes; in this manner they found hospitals, prisons and schools. If it is proposed to inculcate some truth or to foster some feeling by the encouragement of a great example, they form a society."[24]

Since membership in voluntary organizations seemed to be widespread, it was natural to conclude that those groups offered a viable approach to the governmental process that was not available through other institutions.

The Group Approach

One of the first political scientists to develop this theme was Arthur F. Bentley. Writing in 1908 Bentley concluded that all of American politics could be explained by the activities of groups.[25] Since everyone had an opportunity to join groups and since groups formed a major point of access to the political process, the group approach has been used to assert the essentially democratic nature of American politics.

Fifty years later Bentley's characterization of the American political system was modified by David B. Truman, who emphasized the role of interest groups. He also stressed the importance of overlapping membership, or the tendency of persons to belong to several groups, as a means of preventing the development of a dominant interest that would override the preferences of less powerful portions of society.[26]

Criticism of the Group Approach

The argument that groups offer a meaningful opportunity to influence governmental decisions, however, is based on several assumptions of questionable validity, especially for racial and ethnic minorities. Initially, the claim that many Americans belong to voluntary organizations is not substantiated by empirical evidence. According to a survey conducted in 1968, only 31 percent of white adults and 29 percent of blacks belong to any voluntary organization at all and fewer than 23 percent of whites and 11 percent of blacks belong to more than

[24]Alexis de Tocqueville, *Democracy in America* (New York: Knopf, 1944), Vol. I, p. 191.
[25]Arthur F. Bently, *The Process of Government* (Bloomington: Principal Press, 1948, first printing, 1908).
[26]David B. Truman, *The Governmental Process* (New York: Knopf, 1953).

one group. Furthermore, persons of high socioeconomic status are more likely to maintain membership in groups or organizations than low status individuals, which means that poor and disadvantaged segments of the population have fewer group spokesmen than wealthy citizens.[27] As a result, groups do not seem to provide an effective means of promoting the objectives of minorities or of preventing the dominance of powerful interests. Relatively affluent persons also receive benefits because the leaders of organizations tend to occupy a higher social status than the rank-and-file members. Within each group a small core of activists tend to determine the policy positions endorsed by the group as well as the actions taken to promote those policies. This tendency of some individuals to dominate the behavior of groups was termed by Robert Michels "the Iron Law of Oligarchy."[28] David Truman acknowledged this pattern in the structure of groups, but he labeled this small cadre of leaders "the active minority." He stated that:

"Although the active minority is characterized by a higher rate of participation than any others in the group and although this rate may be highly stable in a group over a period of time, the roles of leader and follower involve a dynamic relationship."[29]

But unequal levels of activity that seldom fluctuate as different issues and events arise seem to be more characteristic of a static than a dynamic interaction. The internal organization of most groups provides little assurance that the platforms of influential groups are representative of the opinions of their less prestigious members.

Powerful Interest Groups

Arguments concerning the democratic nature of group activities are also predicated on the assumption that groups can be utilized by the members as effective instruments of social change. In fact, some of the most powerful interest groups in America, such as the American Medical Association (AMA), the National Association of Manufacturers (NAM), the Oil Lobby, and the American Bar Association (ABA) tend to be primarily interested in the maintenance of the status quo rather than the adoption of innovative policies. The changes that are sought by these organizations focus mainly on the acquisition of incremental benefits and the slight alterations in existing programs. Their

[27]Charles R. Wright and Herbert Hyman, "Voluntary Memberships in American Adults: Evidence from National Sample Surveys," in *Interest Group Politics in America*, Salisbury (ed.) (New York: Harper & Row, 1970), p. 76.

[28]Robert Michels, *Political Parties* (Glencoe, Ill.: Free Press, 1958).

[29]Truman, *op. cit.*, p. 155.

efforts are mostly designed to avoid provoking powerful or sustained opposition. As a result they have been able to thrive in the moderate climate designed by Madison for the American political system.

Lobbying

Powerful interest groups have achieved success primarily through lobbying activities directed both at policymakers and at the general public.[30] Within assemblies and administrative agencies, interest groups have focused their efforts largely upon attempts to persuade decision makers to adopt a favorable attitude toward positions espoused by the organization. This activity has ranged from supplying important public officials with arguments and information to both covert and overt forms of bribery. Interest group activities, however, have not been confined to formal governmental institutions. Lobbying organizations have also sought to influence and manipulate public opinion through the expenditure of large sums of money for campaign contributions and publicity designed to secure a favorable public image. The Watergate Investigations of 1973 revealed that major airline companies and other business interests illegally contributed enormous sums of money to the 1972 presidential campaign of Richard M. Nixon, and a proposal advanced almost 25 years earlier to provide medical assistance for the needy was defeated by a massive AMA public relations effort to portray its members as devoted family doctors even though many of them had become well-paid specialists who did not engage in the practice of general medicine. The resources provided by money and prestige, therefore, have bestowed disproportionate influence upon a small number of major interest groups in American politics. As a result, America has developed a theory of what Theodore Lowi has called "interest group liberalism," in which all segments of the population are assumed to be represented by powerful organizations.[31]

Not only has the American political system granted major advantages to certain influential interests but it has also seemed to impose serious penalties upon other groups and organizations. Decades of experience with American politics have indicated that the effectiveness of interest groups may be contingent upon two criteria: their pursuit of limited objectives and the availability of large amounts of money and prestige. Organizations formed by racial and ethnic minorities have lacked both of those attributes. The changes sought by such groups, of necessity, have implied a major redistribution of governmental benefits that often adversely affects the interests of others. Such objectives are difficult to achieve, and they are likely to arouse the sustained opposition of competing groups. In addition, minority interests have suffered from a serious

[30]Lester Milbrath, *The Washington Lobbyist* (Chicago: Rand McNally, 1963).
[31]Ted Lowi, *The End of Liberalism* (Chicago: Norton, 1969).

financial disadvantage in comparison with organizations formed among the dominant white majority; centuries of deprivation and discrimination have also impeded their efforts to gain their rightful respect from white officials and the public.

A brief review of the activities of major black interest groups illustrates the difficulties that minorities have encountered in attempting to pursue their political objectives through lobbying activities.

MINORITY INTEREST GROUPS

NAACP

Perhaps the most prominent interest group in the struggle for civil rights has been the National Association for the Advancement of Colored People (NAACP) that was founded in 1910 during a period characterized by progressive reform and by antiblack sentiment.[32] The organization was a coalition of black intellectuals and white liberals including Oswald Garrison Vallard, English Walling, and Mary Ovington. One of the first major lobbying activities of the NAACP focused on efforts to secure the passage of antilynching legislation that were led by W. E. B. Dubois, editor of *The Crisis,* the official magazine of the organization. When this effort as well as similar attempts to secure the passage of bills outlawing the poll tax failed, the NAACP turned its attention from legislative lobbying to court action. Beginning in the 1930s, legal suits initiated by the NAACP were responsible for historic Supreme Court decisions ordering an end to the white primary and the desegregation of public schools. Perhaps the best known NAACP lawyer of this period was Thurgood Marshall, who argued the famous case of Brown vs. The Board of Education and who later became the first black Justice of the Supreme Court in 1967 during the Johnson administration. The NAACP also has been instrumental in securing desegregation in public accommodations, fair housing laws in 19 states and 55 cities, and equal employment opportunities for minorities in industries with federal contracts. In addition to its efforts to extend civil rights, the NAACP played a major role in bringing interest group activity under the protection of the first amendment guarantee of the right to petition the government for a grievances, as a result of its legal battles with the state of Alabama that had sought to prevent the organization from operating within the state and to secure its membership list. Although official policies are formulated at an annual convention, the group can be best described as a loosely confederated organization in which local chapters have considerable autonomy. In many

[32]Langston Hughes, *Fight for Freedom: The Story of the NAACP* (New York: Norton, 1962).

respects, the victories of the NAACP have been impressive, but many members have criticized the organization for its failure to improve the relative socioeconomic position of black Americans. The securing of legal rights reflected major progress, but for millions of blacks who continue to experience poverty and deprivation, these rights have signified only a short step to a distant goal.

The Urban League

Soon after the founding of the NAACP another major civil rights organization emerged as a result of the migration of black workers seeking jobs in Northern industries during World War I. Unlike the NAACP, the Urban League was less concerned with legislative issues and more oriented toward providing services for blacks. The initial focus of the Urban League was to provide social workers who would locate jobs for the new migrants and act as a catalyst for community organization. Consequently the League also had a local rather than national orientation. In many major cities the League sought to promote interracial good will, but its dependence upon conservative white financial assistance and cooperation reduced it to little more than a charity organization in some areas. Gradually, however, under the leadership of the late Whitney Young, Jr., the Urban League made serious attempts to recast its image in accordance with the increasing militancy of the black public, and added efforts to secure better schools, improved housing, expanding health care, and an end to poverty to its traditional program of job placement. As a result, the League assumed an active role in pressuring the federal government to provide increased aid for the poor and to expand the ill-fated war on poverty begun in the Johnson administration. Despite the increased scope of its activities, the League was no more successful in bringing an end to poverty and discrimination than many other organizations that have sought to achieve this goal.

CORE

A third major civil rights organization was begun in 1942 when the Chicago Committee of the Fellowship of Reconciliation formed a separate committee on racial equality that eventually became the Congress of Racial Equality under the leadership of James Farmer and Bayard Rustin. Presaging subsequent movements, Rustin and Farmer began a nonviolent action campaign against segregation that included sit-ins, voter registration drives, and integrated bus rides in the late forties and early fifties. When these tactics achieved widespread popularity in the 1960s, CORE was in the forefront of many efforts at direct action. After 1964, however, the orientation of the organization shifted again. As one commentator observed,

"The fight to open middle class jobs and housing, and the concern with integration of public facilities—always more of a middle class than a working class issue in the Negro community—has given way to a drive to alleviate the plight of the lower class. Black power—economic and political—has replaced integration as the goal of CORE's activities. Non-violence has given way to the assertion of the right of self defense. Direct action has been largely replaced by community and political organization in the ghetto. The membership of CORE has become predominantly Negro and increasingly working class."[33]

Although CORE has pursued a somewhat more radical strategy than its predecessors, the organization has suffered from a characteristic inability to gage the temper of the black community. While they appeared to be too militant for many black citizens on some occasions, CORE failed to assume the leading edge of the black movement at other times. Hence, the organization has not occupied the role of the major spokesman that many hoped it would achieve.

SCLC

The drive for civil rights has not only been advanced by deliberate organizational efforts, but it has also been occasionally promoted by grass roots expressions of righteous indignation. A major organization that began in this way was the Southern Christian Leadership Conference (SCLC) that developed out of the Montgomery bus boycott of 1955–1956. Led by Dr. Martin Luther King, Jr., SCLC applied the philosophy of nonviolent civil disobedience, in a tradition that had been inherited from Thoreau and Gandhi, to the cause of minority rights.[34] SCLC was active throughout the South during the 1960s, in attempting to secure desegregation, jobs for black workers, and voter registration. Although the singular commitment to the philosophy was both a source of strength and weakness for the organization, SCLC shifted its attention after the violence that began in 1964 from a war on legally sanctioned segregation to the flight against economic injustice and poverty. SCLC was planning a poor people's march on Washington that was led by King's successor, Ralph Abernathy. A long-standing uneasiness among many members of SCLC with an exclusive reliance on nonviolent direct action began to crystalize after King's death and led eventually to the formation of a separate organization in Chicago, Operation Breadbasket, headed by the Reverend Jesse L. Jackson. Since King's charismatic leadership had been the most important force uniting the organization, the prominence of SCLC began to decline after his assassination.

[33]Inge B. Bell, *CORE and The Strategy of Non-Violence* (Chicago: Random House, 1968).

[34]For an extensive discussion of Martin Luther King's views on nonviolence, see *Stride Toward Freedom* (New York: Harper & Row, 1958).

SNCC

Increasing civil rights activism created a national climate that encouraged the participation of all segments of the population. A leading role in this movement was assumed by young people who banded together in the Student Non-Violent Coordinating Committee (SNCC) a few years after the formation of the SCLC. Inspired by the sit-ins that had begun in 1960 in Greensboro, North Carolina, SNCC participated not only in direct action aimed at desegregation but also became heavily involved in voter registration and political organization in the South. Emerging from a cooperative endeavor by black and white young people, by 1966, under the leadership of Stokley Carmichael, the organization announced a policy of black power and excluded whites from its membership. As a result, SNCC abandoned many of its earlier tactics such as the attempt to seat the Mississippi Freedom Democratic Party at the 1964 Democratic national convention and shifted instead to the creation of groups with a more separatist orientation. Indicative of this change was elimination of the term "nonviolent" from the name of the organization. Although the growing militancy of the group produced some dissension and the loss of financial support, Howard Zinn noted:

> "The most obvious contribution of SNCC has been to move boldly into the center of danger and, while taking blows, enduring pain and poverty, leaving family and friends behind to force the nation to look at itself. Among civil rights organizations, it has remained unique in its youth, its willingness to immerse itself in the black communities of the Deep South, its distance from the circles of official power."[35]

Still, the youthful zeal of SNCC contributed an important page in the history of civil rights activism.

Other Interests Groups

Perhaps the most prominent characteristic shared by all major black interest groups has been their relative lack of success at traditional forms of lobbying in the executive and legislative branches of government. In fact, most of these organizations have tended to shift their resources into activities that appeared to promise more profitable results. The NAACP focused its attention on litigation in the courts. The Urban League has become primarily a local service organization, and CORE, SCLC, and SNCC adopted the tactics of nonviolent protest. One of the few organizations that achieved major progress through the actions of legislative lobbyists was a coalition of civil rights, religious, labor,

[35]Howard Zinn, *SNCC: The New Abolitionsts* (Boston: Beacon Press, 1964), p. 237.

and other groups that united to promote congressional enactment of the 1964 Civil Rights Act. Other minorities have had similar experiences. Among the few groups that have combined legislative lobbying and direct action are the American Indian Movement (AIM) and the United Farm Workers (UFW), a predominantly Chicano group led by Cesar Chavez. The most noteworthy activities of AIM have included the occupation of Alcatraz Island, the takeover at Wounded Knee, South Dakota, and a massive sit-in staged at the Bureau of Indian Affairs in Washington, D. C. Similarly the most successful efforts of the UFW include national boycotts of table grapes and lettuce and intense organizational efforts among migrant farm workers. Apparently the influence generated by traditional lobbying action has been an almost exclusive prerogative of groups representing the dominant white majority, a fact that has compelled minority interests to resort to other tactics.

BLACK SEPARATISM

Minorities not only have withdrawn from traditional forms of interest group activity but they have also displayed an increasing alienation from the political system that has been reflected in a growing acceptance of separatism as a political doctrine. A survey of the residents of a ghetto neighborhood in Detroit that had experienced major violence in 1967 revealed an intense disenchantment with the values and beliefs of white society among the one-fifth of the respondents who felt that racial progress could only be achieved by refusing to cooperate with whites. Separatists not only were more likely to approve violent displays of protest, but they were also more likely to reject traditional forms of political participation and policies, such as the antipoverty program, than blacks who maintained a belief in the desirability of integration. In fact, when asked how they would respond to a robbery, separatists reported that they would ignore or disregard the theft.

> "In many respects, the growth of black separatism has appeared to reflect an increasing loss of faith in established sources of legal and political authority. By advocating rapid social change, even if it entails violence or graft, separatists have confronted white society with an almost revolutionary program that probably could not be accomplished without a radical restructuring of existing political institutions. The problems posed by the demands of black separatists, therefore, have created some serious and agonizing challenges for white Americans and their political leaders."[36]

Many black Americans who endorse separatist values do not belong to an organized group, but those attitudes have also found organizational expression.

[36]Harlan Hahn, "Black Separatist," *Journal of Black Studies*, Vol. I (September 1970), p. 52.

The Garvey Movement

One of the first major separatist organizations in America was the Universal
Negro Improvement League (UNIL) founded in 1919 by Marcus Garvey.[37]
Arguing that blacks could never gain equality in America, Garvey launched the
Black Star Line to return blacks to their African motherland. His plan had a
powerful emotional appeal both to many blacks who were dissatisfied with their
status in the United States and to white supremists such as the Ku Klux Klan.
By 1926 the UNIL claimed a membership of more than six million although
the actual enrollment in the organization may have been considerably smaller.
While Garvey's program ran afoul of financial difficulties, his appeal to racial
pride had a strong impact that may have been a forerunner to subsequent
separatist groups.

The Black Muslims

The return of Garvey to his native Jamaica in 1927 left a major void in the
opportunity available to blacks with separatist sentiments to express their
views through a formal organizational channel. This gap may have been par-
tially filled in the 1930s when an itinerant salesman known as W. D. Ford
appeared in the black community of Detroit describing the religion of Islam
as the true faith of blacks. Ford attacked Christianity as the religion of the white
devil that would be destroyed in a future that was with blacks. After founding
an Islam temple in Detroit, he disappeared and Elijah Muhammad emerged as
the leader of the Black Muslims.[38] The Muslims adopted a belief in total
isolation from whites and economic independence, which included the produc-
tion of their own food and clothing. Although bound by strict rules of conduct,
the Muslims attracted a growing number of adherents. One of the most persua-
sive proponents of the Muslim faith was Malcolm X who was converted to the
religion in a Massachusetts penitentiary. Drawing upon his experiences on the
streets of Harlem, Malcolm X had a profound effect upon many lower-class
blacks who flocked to the religion. After a split with Elijah Muhammad in 1964,
Malcolm X was killed by an assassin. While there is considerable doubt as to
whether the Muslims will be able to attract the vast majority of black Americans, their appeal has been strong and their numbers have been increasing.

Revolutionary Action Movement

Impatience with traditional civil rights organizations and activities have been
another source of separatist groups. The Revolutionary Action Movement

[37]E. D. Cronin, *Black Moses* (Madison: University of Wisconsin Press, 1966).
[38]C. Eric Lincoln, *The Black Muslims in America* (Boston: Beacon Press, 1973).

The success of the Muslims can be traced in large measure to their insistence on individual dignity, self-pride, and hard work. (Roger Malloch/Magnum)

(RAM), for example, arose from the frustrations of Robert Williams who, while serving as president of the Union County, North Carolina, NAACP, after witnessing several acts of police brutality and receiving personal threats, advised blacks to arm themselves and "to meet violence with violence," an action that inspired the founding of RAM and the Choice of Williams as its president. Although he was forced to flee the country, efforts to extradite him to North Carolina to face a charge of kidnapping subsequently failed.

The Black Panthers

A Black Panther Party was organized in Lownes County, Virginia, by SNCC workers in 1965, but this group bore little resemblance to an organization bearing the same name centered in Oakland, California. While at Merritt College, Bobby Seale and Huey Newton organized the Panther Party as an attack on what they regarded to be social and economic suppression in America. By stressing their opposition to the police, the alleviation of hunger, and armed defensive reaction against the "enemies of liberation," the Panthers sought to devise a program that would appeal to those at the bottom of black society. To spread their program among black prisoners and others who regarded themselves as victims of unjust law enforcement, the Panthers enlisted the services of Eldridge Cleaver, an ex-convict who subsequently fled the country.[39] After numerous organizational difficulties and bloody encounters

[39]Eldridge Cleaver, *Soul on Ice* (New York: McGraw-Hill, 1967).

with the police, the Panthers declined and Bobby Seale adopted conventional political tactics in running for Mayor of Oakland in 1973.

Although separatist groups have never been able to attract a major share of black or other minority populations, their existence serves as a reminder of the difficulties encountered by minorities in attempting to promote their aspirations through group activity. In the face of the structural barriers posed by the American political system, increasing numbers of racial and ethnic minorities may be attracted to organizations that seek to provide an alternative to traditional efforts to influence the decision-making process.

• POINTS TO REMEMBER

Though parties are not formally recognized in the American Constitution, they emerged soon after it had been ratified and provided the principle means by which political interests are aggregated and transmitted to political decision makers. Party identification has been the single most important factor in determining the outcome of political elections and the issues that emerged during the Civil War concerning slavery have exerted enormous influence on contemporary party loyalties.

Because of the influence of federalism, partisan politics in America is not the politics of two national parties nor of three branches of government; but it is the politics of 50 states, countless communities, and hundreds of parties. Since political parties are not organized as hierarchies with chains of command that link the national level to state and local organizations, minorities that succeed in achieving influence in a particular state or community still might not have the effect of that gain felt at the national level.

The increasing concentration of minorities, especially black Americans, in the nation's urban centers has precipitated the election and appointment of minority officials. But the acquisition of political control by minority groups in major urban areas has entailed serious difficulties that have been magnified by declining economic resources.

The notion that black voters, because of their concentration in urban centers, represent a balance of power in national elections is weakened considerably because to maximize their political strength, minority voters often are compelled to fulfill a number of requirements that are not imposed upon the white majority. These include sufficient numbers to effect the margin of victory, high voter turnout, optimal cohesion or unanimity on the choice of candidates, and a divided vote among the white majority.

Black Americans have played an increasingly important role in the national conventions of the Democratic Party. But the pressing need for money and the status accorded wealthy contributors in party deliberations has sharply limited the influence minorities have on the party's selection of candidates and on the resolution of issues involving race.

Some researchers have argued that in electoral districts containing evenly matched parties, candidates would be forced to compete for the votes of all segments of the population, including minorities, to maximize their electoral appeal. Thus, party competition was portrayed as accomplishing the function of satisfying minority grievances in a way that parties had failed to do. Subsequent research has not supported this finding.

The idea that interest groups offer a meaningful opportunity to dispossessed minorities to influence governmental decisions is largely unfounded. The resources provided by money and prestige have bestowed disproportionate influence upon a small number of interest groups that have been able to thrive in the moderate climate designed by Madison for the American political system. The relative lack of influence generated by traditional lobbying activities of groups like the National Association for the Advancement of Colored People, The American Indian Movement, and the United Farm Workers has led to increasing alienation from the political system and to a growing acceptance of separatism as a political doctrine.

• SOME UNRESOLVED ISSUES: A DIALOGUE

Holland: I find it sadly remarkable that the major party realignment in the United States precipitated by the events that caused the Civil War took place without the direct participation of that segment of the population, Black America, which in many respects was responsible for it. The Republican Party after the war demonstrated that it had no particular sensitivity to the rights of non-Europeans even though those rights represented a major issue in the war. The outcome of this tragedy was predictable. Black Americans found themselves aligned to a political party that did not serve their interests.

Hahn: In many respects, it seems plausible that we are in a similar era of party realignment. In fact, it is difficult to believe that the two major landslides in presidential elections for opposing parties and the resignation of a president and a vice-president in a scandal-ridden administration can fail to produce major changes in political institutions. As a result of these events, there is a profound and increasing sense of alienation emerging in the American public. Most citizens are aware that the influence that they are capable of exerting on government policies is greatly exceeded by the political force of large campaign contributors and powerful interest groups. Perhaps the tragedy of these events, however, is that they again appear to be occurring without any conscious recognition of the fundamental problem concerning the role of racial and ethnic groups in American society. The political objectives of minorities remain unfulfilled; and the failure to satisfy their interest is certainly an underlying source of the discontent that swept the country in the late 1960s. But if major changes in political structures do occur it seems likely that they will transpire without an amelioration of the needs of the disaffected minorities.

Holland: The election of Tom Bradley as Mayor of Los Angeles and Edward Brooke as Senator from Massachusetts has led some political observers to note that it is indeed possible for minority candidates to appeal to electorates that are predominantly white. While it is undoubtedly true that the election of persons such as Bradley and Brooke represent important symbolic advances, one must also keep in mind that both individuals, in order to become acceptable to the dominant white majority, have been generally prevented from adopting a strong position of advocacy for black interest. Similar problems undoubtedly will plague members of other minorities aspiring to high political office.

Hahn: Essentially, it seems to me that two alternatives are emerging. One approach involves the formation of an aggressive coalition encompassing all minorities, perhaps aligned with disadvantaged segments of the white population. The second alternative would envision the emergence of separatist movements not only among black Americans but among other minorities as well. Such movements would pose a serious threat and a challenge to the ethnocentrism and the self-righteous superiority that has prevailed in white society. But it would also imply a society torn by ceaseless conflict and tension. Of the two alternatives, I would of course prefer the former; but, unless fundamental changes are made in the existing political process, I would be sadly forced to conclude that the latter may be more likely.

Holland: The only problem with your dychotomy rests with what we already know about coalitions. As Carmichael and Hamilton have pointed out, coalitions are based on exchanges and payoffs. That is, it is assumed that each group has something to give to the other. A coalition of groups that are on the bottom of the social-economic ladder raises the question in my mind as to what they have to exchange save for their own social economic misery. The history of such coalitions have indicated to me a pattern of failure.

Hahn: As long as the political system is controlled by economic interest, including wealthy contributors and powerful organizations, I would agree. But in a political system in which votes count more than dollars, I believe that minorities would be able to utilize the strength of their numbers to mutual advantage in the pursuit of political resources.

3 LEGISLATIVE REPRESENTATION IN AMERICA

One of the most crucial features of democratic government is its representative institutions. According to a popular view, the heart of the political process consists of transmitting public demands to political decision makers to be enacted into law. In this idealized form, public policy is regarded as a product of the will of the people, acting through their elected representatives. Since legislative bodies supposedly exist to translate public desires into government policy, it might also be assumed that they provide an appropriate vehicle for the satisfaction of minority grievances. Actually, however, legislative actions are shaped by a wide range of factors that affect the final outcome of policy decisions; and representative institutions may not comprise the most appropriate recourse for minority groups seeking to improve their position in society. The purpose of this chapter is to describe the legislative obstacles confronting racial and ethnic minorities by examining the nature and characteristics of representation in America.

REPRESENTATION IN AMERICA

In many respects, the creation of representative bodies reflects an accommodation to the problem of size. The classic tenets of direct democracy seem to suggest that all persons should be granted an equal opportunity to participate in the formulation of legislative policy.[1] In a large and diverse population such as the United States, it is impossible to fulfill this requirement. As a result, legislative assemblies including city councils, state legislatures, and the national Congress were established to act as intermediaries between the people and government policies.

Although the size of the population—even during the period in which the Constitution was written—seemed to preclude the direct participation of all citizens in the formulation of legislative decisions, the concept of representation posed serious questions to the Founding Fathers. Who will be repre-

[1]For a more extensive explanation see Alford DeGrazia, *Public and Republic: Political Representation in America* (New York: Knopf, 1951).

sented? How will representation be defined? What are the consequences of different methods of representation?

Forms of Representation

Answers to these questions are complex. Even if representation is extended to all citizens of a democratic society, there are many ways in which representation can be defined. In several foreign countries, for example, legislative seats are allocated to occupational groups.[2] This practice is justified on the grounds that the economic interests exemplified by various occupations denote meaningful cleavages in society; and policies that emerge from a clash between powerful interests such as labor and management provide an accurate reflection of the balance between opposing forces in the country.

The same rationale probably could have been applied to racial or ethnic minorities. Since the conflicting goals of minority groups and the white population have constituted one of the most basic and persistent divisions in American society, it might have been argued that legislative seats should be assigned to those groups according to their proportion of the population or on some other basis. This form of representation would have permitted racial polarization to manifest itself in the outcome of conflict within legislative chambers, but it seemed inconsistent with the maintenance of political stability. Many observers have feared that the allocation of legislative seats to racial and ethnic minorities might hinder their progress either by producing intense conflict that would stalemate the legislative process or by enabling the white majority to ignore the demands of small and distinctive minorities.

Proportional Representation

Perhaps one method that might have been adopted to increase minority representation in America was the system of proportional representation, which was proposed as part of a program of municipal reform in the early twentieth century.[3] Although this type of election assumed many complicated and technical forms, the basic principle of proportional representation was the allocation of legislative seats in proportion to the number of choices received by political parties or candidates. By removing the requirement of a winning majority as

[2]This has been done in Spain, Portugal, and Italy. See Austin Ranney, *The Governing of Men* (New York: Dryden Editions, 1971).

[3]Proportional representation is an electoral system that gives each political party the number of seats in proportion to the percentage of votes cast for them. In a plurality system such as ours, a party receiving 40 percent of the votes cast as compared with 60 percent for another party could fail to win a seat. However, with proportional representation that party would be guaranteed 40 percent of the seats. For a further discussion of this subject see C. G. Hoag and E. H. Hallett, *Proportional Representation* (New York: Macmillan, 1962).

a precondition of electoral success, proportional representation seemed to offer major advantages to minorities. But it also tended to encourage the growth of a multiplicity of parties or groups that hoped to achieve legislative representation simply by gaining a fraction—rather than a majority—of the vote. As a result, the endemic fear of factionalism and extremism prompted the repeal of proportional representation in a few American cities that experimented with this proposal.

Representation by Area

The basic form of representation outlined in the Constitution is founded upon the principle of area. In the United States Senate, constituencies are defined by state lines; and, for the House of Representatives, congressional district boundaries are drawn according to population requirements. The same principle is followed in state and local governments. State legislative districts are established to provide representation for equivalent numbers of residents in different sections of a state; and members of city councils are elected either by the entire community on an at-large basis or by wards comprising distinct neighborhoods or segments of the population. At all levels of government, therefore, representation is basically determined by population and geographic considerations rather than by social, economic, or racial characteristics.

Single-Member Districts

This method of representation has important implications both for minority groups and for the general operation of the American political process. Initially, the election of legislative representatives by a simple majority within single-member districts[4] has tended to promote the development of a two-party system; it has also modified conflict and restrained third-party movements. The relative absence of proportional representation and multimember districts has provided minor parties with few incentives to nominate candidates for legislative offices. Thus, statements on controversial issues such as minority rights frequently have reflected compromise by major-party nominees, each seeking to attract the support of moderate voters, rather than positions inspired by the prodding of radical third-party candidates. The single-member district, majority-election system has impeded the attempts of racial or ethnic groups to achieve representation. Minority groups that comprise less than half of a legislative district often have been consistently outvoted by the dominant

[4]A single-member district, of course, means a district or geographic area represented by only one elected legislator. Districts that elect more than one representative are called multimember districts.

white majority; and the election of a single representative has prevented them from concentrating their efforts, and their votes, on a favored candidate among contestants for several offices. The type of representation adopted in legislative bodies in America has seemed to provide more advantages for the white majority than for racial or ethnic minorities.

Residential Segregation

In addition to the barriers posed by constitutional provisions, however, the legislative representation of minorities in America has been limited by other variables. Perhaps the most important of the factors affecting the representation of blacks and other minority groups has been the widespread practice of residential segregation.[5] As millions of black Americans emigrated from the rural South to industrialized Northern cities in a continuous migration after World War I, they congregated in separate and sharply defined sectors of the community. The settlement of minorities in urban ghettos not only was stimulated by the natural tendency of persons with common experiences and problems to locate in similar areas; but, more important, it was the product of blatant discrimination. Through a variety of techniques including exclusionary zoning, prejudicial real estate practices, financial obstacles, personal pressures, and the threat of violence, black and other minority residents were confined to specific areas of the community.

Minority Representation

Although the concentration of minorities in distinct subcommunities might seem to offer a potential basis of organized political strength, they seldom were able to gain adequate legislative representation. In some cities, minority votes were diluted in at-large elections to choose city councilmen who would allegedly represent the community as a whole; and, in other cities with ward representation, ghettos were combined with adjoining white neighborhoods to form predominantly white constituencies.[6] Similarly, minority representation in state legislatures and in Congress was restricted by the actions of state legislators who merged ghetto communities with white areas to ensure white control in legislative and Congressional districts. In only a few cities such as Chicago, where organizational requirements compelled party leaders to recog-

[5]Karl E. Taeuber and Alma F. Taeuber, *Negroes in Cities* (Chicago: Aldine, 1965).

[6]Frequently, whether a city has at-large or district representation will determine whether minorities will be represented in the city council. For example, in the late 1960s in Tallahassee, Florida, when it became clear to white segregationists that blacks would soon constitute a majority in one of the elective wards, they pushed to change the representative system to at-large elections.

Richard Nixon reluctantly met with the Black Caucus in Congress to discuss legislation affecting the nation's racial and ethnic minorities. (Walter Bennett/Time-Life Picture Agency)

nize the growing importance of minority votes, were black politicians successful in gaining major elective offices prior to World War II.[7]

Apportionment

Traditional methods of legislative districting undoubtedly have played a major role in the underrepresentation of minorities. Political leaders, for example, often sought by a practice known as "gerrymandering"[8] to maximize the prospects of victory for members of their own party. In the historic case of *Gomillion v. Lightfoot*,[9] the Supreme Court held that legislative districting could not be employed as an instrument of racial discrimination. Although this decision nullified attempts to maintain white control of the city council in Tuskegee, Alabama, by creating council districts that would dilute the impact of black voters, it did not require affirmative efforts to ensure that minorities are granted equitable representation in legislative assemblies. In 1963, however, in *Baker v. Carr*,[10] the Supreme Court concluded that the failure of state legislatures to reapportion districts in accordance with changes in the distribution of the population was a denial of "equal protection of the laws" because it failed to provide equitable legislative representation. As a result of this case

[7]Harold Goswell, *Negro Politicians* (Chicago: Chicago University Press, 1967).
[8]Gerrymandering is the practice of drawing political boundaries in such a manner as to favor one group over another. The name is derived from a comment that a district in Massachusetts that favored the party of Governor Eldridge Gerry looked like a salamander.
[9]*Gomillion v. Lightfoot*, 364 U.S. 339 (1960).
[10]*Baker v. Carr*, 369 U.S. 186 (1962).

and subsequent decisions, legislators have been compelled to observe the standard of population equality in drawing boundaries both for congressional and for state legislative districts. Judicial decisions on apportionment were not directly concerned with the problem of aiding minorities, but they did make an important contribution by establishing equality as a benchmark of legislative representation.

Although the practice of basing representation on geographic areas could appear to be arbitrary, it also may signify an effort to achieve equality in the allocation of legislative spokesmen. Any attempt to assign representatives according to economic, racial, or similar characteristics not only raises complex questions concerning the weight to be attached to those attributes, but it also seems to imply that some segments of the population are more deserving of representation than others. Even though the allocation of legislative seats to racial or ethnic minorities might be proposed as a means of rectifying prior injustices, it may conflict with the basic premise that all men have equal political rights and are equally entitled to legislative representation. The use of population and geographic area as criteria of representation could be an important means of institutionalizing the principle of equality as a critical value in American politics.

Minorities and Legislative Representation

One of the most crucial problems confronting minority groups in their efforts to secure effective legislative representation involves the selection of candidates whom they will support. Ethnic or racial minorities can promote their political objectives either by seeking to elect representatives from their own ranks or by supporting white candidates who are sympathetic to their needs and aspirations. Although the choice between the two alternatives may be determined by several considerations including the relative strength of minority groups within a legislative constituency and the availability of trustworthy white candidates, there appear to be basic difficulties associated with either strategy.

The decision to advance the candidacy of a member of ethnic or racial minorities raises the critical issue of the difference between *symbolic* and *actual* representation.[11] For many decades, ethnic groups that immigrated to America from Europe encountered strong resistance in their struggle for political recognition. Their efforts to wrest political control from the indigenous white majority became a primary focus of attention, and it frequently seemed to overshadow other considerations such as the enactment of legislation designed to benefit ethnic groups. Many voters appeared to be more concerned with the

[11]Murray Edelman, *The Symbolic Uses of Politics* (Champaign: University of Illinois Press, 1967).

symbolic importance of elevating a member of their own ethnic group to major elective offices than with substantive policy goals.

Minority Legislators

Minority leaders who succeed in winning public office still must confront the problem of working within legislative assemblies dominated by representatives of the white majority. They often are regarded, both by legislative colleagues and by the voters who elected them, merely as articulate spokesmen of minority interests rather than as influential participants in the policymaking process. Hence, the demands imposed upon minority legislators could place them in an irreconcilable dilemma. They may be compelled either to acknowledge that they cannot satisfy the desires of their constituents or to face the wrath of voters for failing to fulfill their expectations. Black and other minority politicians have responded to this problem by adopting different styles of representation.[12] Yet, minority representatives in a predominantly white legislature may find themselves forced to play a frustrating and isolated role.

White Representation of Minorities

On the other hand, the election of legislators from the dominant white majority also poses serious problems. For decades, black residents of the South, who frequently comprised a majority of the population in various legislative and congressional districts, were prevented from voting by legal barriers or by intimidation. Southern blacks often found themselves "represented" by legislators who opposed their interests and who secured election by denouncing them in the most vehement and bigoted terms. As a result, black voters developed a profound distrust of white representatives that has affected their attitudes in the North as well as the South. Since many black citizens in the South regarded their elected representatives as political enemies rather than as legislative spokesmen, they were naturally anxious to elect black leaders to public office.

There is, however, another factor that might limit the ability of whites to serve as effective representatives of minority voters. Most politicians are shaped by the environments from which they emerge. White legislators are influenced not only by the dominant white millieu in which they were raised but also by their experience in achieving elective office. During their careers, representatives acquire values and associations with other people that continue to affect their behavior after they enter the legislature. In a homogeneous and predominantly white constituency, those contacts usually reflect the beliefs and orientations of the white majority.

[12]James Q. Wilson, *Negro Politics: The Search for Leadership* (New York: The Free Press, 1960).

Influences on Legislators

During a typical day, busy legislators at the local, state, and national level usually find themselves scanning newspapers and reports, reading and answering mail from constituents, meeting with lobbyists and interest groups, conferring with officials in the executive branch, attending committee meetings, engaging in discussions with legislative colleagues, and talking with family and friends. The host of influences that compete for their time and attention make it difficult to isolate the forces that are most determinative in shaping their decisions. Yet, among the many influences that impinge upon their activities, the attitudes and opinions of trusted friends and acquaintances from their own constituency usually receive great weight. Many legislators appear to have developed informal and loosely organized networks of communication within their constituencies that they often regard as a more significant barometer of public opinion than surveys based on a random sample of the population. To the extent that those networks encompass representative spokesmen from minority communities, their viewpoints may be reflected in legislative behavior. For many white legislators, however, minority leaders who seek to change their positions may be regarded virtually as emissaries from another portion of society. No matter how attentively they listen, the limitations imposed by their values and experiences in the white community prevent them from comprehending or appreciating the demands of racial or ethnic minorities. Since most white legislators are not exposed to broad segments of minority communities during their careers, minority interests have relatively little influence with those representatives.

CONGRESSIONAL PERCEPTIONS OF GHETTO VIOLENCE: A CASE STUDY

One indication of the extent to which elected representatives heed the opinions of white constituents can be derived from an examination of legislative reactions to the violence that swept urban ghettos during the 1960s.[13] Table 3 presents the percentage of Congressmen who identified various factors as "of great importance" in causing the violence.

Although Northern Democrats were somewhat more sympathetic to the plight of ghetto areas than Southerners or Republicans, most Congressmen tended to blame the violence on aberrant individual behavior rather than on social problems. The three most common explanations of ghetto violence

---

[13]Harlan Hahn and J. R. Feagin, "Rank and File Versus Congressional Perceptions of Ghetto Riots," in *Social Science Quarterly* (September 1970), pp. 361–373.

offered by Congressmen were "joblessness and idleness, especially among young Negroes," a "lack of responsibility among Negroes," and "outside Negro agitators." This orientation corresponded with the prevailing opinions of rank-and-file white citizens who generally cited "outside agitators," "looters

TABLE 3
Congressional Evaluations of Riot Causes (1967) [a]

| | | Percentage Replying "Of Great Importance" [b] | | | |
	N	All Congressmen	Northern Democrats	Southern Democrats	Republicans
Joblessness and idleness, especially among young Negroes	(259)	68	87	54	62
Lack of responsibility among Negroes	(257)	47	33	55	55
Outside Negro agitators	(259)	46	17	62	59
Neglect of social and economic problems by state and local governments	(241)	41	69	31	27
Irresponsible news media coverage of riots	(254)	39	33	55	36
Supreme Court crime decisions	(256)	33	5	56	41
Poor administration of existing federal programs in these areas	(254)	31	18	23	43
Poor police-community relations	(252)	27	44	28	15
White indifference to Negro needs	(254)	26	51	21	10
Insufficient federal aid in such areas as education, job training, antipoverty, housing, etc.	(250)	26	58	12	8
Irresponsible training techniques in Community Action Programs	(237)	22	13	25	28
Communist agitation	(241)	20	8	38	20
Negro resentment against Congressional inaction or restrictions on Great Society legislation and House exclusion of Adam Clayton Powell	(248)	5	7	6	4

[a] Data presented with permission of Congressional Quarterly, Inc.
[b] Question: "What importance would you attribute to the following factors mentioned by various persons as playing a significant role in the build-up to the riots?"
From Harlan Hahn and Joe R. Feagin "Rank and File versus Congressional Perceptions of Ghetto Riots," *Social Science Quarterly* (September 1970), p. 367.

and other undesirables," and "black power or other radicals" as the principal sources of the violence. But such opinions conflicted with the views of an overwhelming proportion of black Americans and of the residents of riot-torn ghettos who ascribed the violence to inadequate housing, employment, education, and other persistent minority problems. Perhaps most important, factors that paralleled the attitudes of ghetto residents, such as white indifference to Negro needs and insufficient federal aid, were mentioned as possible causes of the violence by only a small proportion of the Congressmen.

The same factors that shaped public and Congressional perceptions of ghetto uprisings also seemed to affect their reactions to various proposals to prevent the recurrence of violence. The percentage of Congressmen who considered various remedies for ghetto violence "of great importance" is recorded in Table 4.

In general, legislators in Washington placed the greatest confidence in efforts to avoid violence through strict law enforcement, an emphasis on personal morality, and the transfer of vaguely defined responsibilities to state and local governments. Extensive social and economic reforms received little favorable attention from Congressmen. Their viewpoints paralleled the attitudes of most white Americans, but they were in sharp contrast to black citizens and ghetto residents, who urged the adoption of increased government programs to ameliorate the conditions that had produced the violence. The response of federal lawmakers to the violence that erupted in major cities seemed to reflect an effort to follow the trends in public opinion that emerged in the white community rather than to heed the voice of ghetto residents.

Congress and Minorities

The attitudes of white Congressmen have important implications for minority groups. Although representatives in Washington placed great emphasis on state and local efforts in their search for solutions to ghetto violence, most of the responsibility for improving the status of racial and ethnic minorities in America has devolved from the federal government, which is the only level of political authority possessing the resources needed to make a significant impact on their problems. State and local action on fair housing legislation and similar measures has been an important concern to minorities, but controversies over racial issues usually have revolved around the national government. As a result, minorities have focused their attention on Congress rather than on state legislatures or city councils.

Representational Roles

Many investigations of Congressional representation have emphasized the conflict that often seems to develop between the legislator's duty of represent-

TABLE 4

Congressional Evaluations of Remedies for Riots (1967) [a]

	N	Percentage Replying "Of Great Importance"[b]			
		All Congressmen	Northern Democrats	Southern Democrats	Republicans
Greater state and local efforts (unspecified)	(257)	74	86	66	68
Emphasis on traditional church and family values	(254)	73	54	85	80
Private sector involvement through such devices as public low-income area development corporations	(235)	66	69	44	74
Greater penalties for rioters and those who incite to rioting	(249)	61	44	77	65
Larger, better-paid police forces	(263)	54	49	64	52
Greater expenditures for police anti-riot training	(258)	42	43	38	43
Legislation to avoid Supreme Court decisions relating to arrest, interrogation of prisoners, etc.	(252)	33	7	46	47
A massive "Marshall Plan" for the cities using federal funds	(239)	26	60	14	4
Gun control legislation	(243)	23	49	18	6
Increased federal aid for urban problems. . .through block grants to the states	(231)	17	11	6	27

[a] By permission of Congressional Quarterly, Inc.

[b] Question: "What importance would you attach to each of the following proposals to prevent recurrences of the rioting?"

From Harlan Hahn and Joe R. Feagin, "Rank and File versus Congressional Perceptions of Ghetto Riots," *Social Science Quarterly* (September 1970), p. 372.

ing the views of his constituents and his responsibility to exercise his personal judgment on major questions of public policy. Congressmen frequently have been depicted as torn between their roles as a "Washington representative," or a servant of the needs and wishes of the voters who elected them, and as a "member of Congress," or a legislator capable of acting in accordance with his enlightened opinion on political issues. A careful study of the relationship between public opinion and congressional votes, however, found that racial questions were among the few controversies that reflected a close association between legislative voting and the attitudes of constituents. On most social welfare and foreign policy issues, there were low correlations between constituency opinion and voting behavior. Only in the area of civil rights did congressmen seem to vote in accordance with the views of a majority of the residents of their districts.[14]

Constituency Influences

The research, therefore, contained some important implications for racial and ethnic minorities. Congressmen apparently were more closely attuned to public opinion concerning issues of minority rights than other political controversies. Many voters have regarded racial attitudes as an intensely personal matter, and legislators have probably felt compelled to devote careful attention to their viewpoints on this subject. Perhaps most important, the evidence provided little encouragement for minorities seeking to influence the behavior of white legislators. As long as a majority of white Americans remain opposed to the political aspirations of minority groups, it seemed unlikely that Congressmen would ignore the wishes of their constituents and align themselves with minority interests. On legislative issues of major importance, including those affecting minority rights, the decisions made by Congressmen probably has been strongly influenced by the advice of the informal network of confidants within their districts and by the knowledge that they have developed of the values and life-styles of the people whom they represent. Legislators are a product of the constituencies that elect them and their approach to political issues has been molded in numerous ways by personal experiences within those districts. Since an overwhelming number of congressmen represent predominantly white constituencies, the values and beliefs that they acquired before entering Congress as well as the pressures exerted upon them by the voters have tended to limit their responsiveness to minority demands.

THE INTERNAL OPERATION OF CONGRESS

Fundamentally, however, the relationship between voters and their elected representatives constitutes only one aspect of the legislative process that has important implications for minorities. To understand the wide range of factors that may influence the adoption of policies affecting minority interests, we must examine the internal operation of legislative institutions. Since most issues concerning racial and ethnic minorities involve broad social problems that have implications for the nation as a whole, this discussion is focused on the policymaking process in Congress.

[14]Warren Miller and Donald Stokes, "Constituency Influence in Congress," *American Political Science Review* Vol. 57 (March 1963), pp. 45–56.

The Personnel of Congress

The 435 legislators who comprise the House of Representatives and the 100 lawmakers in the Senate reflect a diversity of backgrounds and interests. Perhaps their most obvious common characteristic, however, is that they tend to be white males. When the 91st Congress convened in 1970, for example, there were only 11 women and 10 black legislators, including one woman, in Congress. Although the number of minority Congressmen comprised a major increase over a preceding decade, they have not been sufficiently numerous to exert a critical impact on legislation. Congress has remained a predominantly white, male institution; and decisive influence in both the Senate and the House is exercised by members possessing those attributes.

Congressional Terms of Office

Both the functions of Congress and the policies that eventually emerge from the legislative process are profoundly affected by several characteristics of the institution. The Constitution, for example, prescribes that members of the House of Representatives must be elected biennially to serve a two-year term, while Senators serve a six-year term, staggered so that approximately one-third of the Senate is chosen at each biennial election. Congressmen are more preoccupied with—and devote greater attention to—the task of gaining reelection than Senators. Senators also usually represent larger and more heterogeneous constituencies than members of the lower house. Senators, therefore, frequently appear to be less parochial and less concerned about voter reactions than Representatives.

Congressional Norms

In addition, the actions of Congress are strongly affected by numerous formal and informal rules that govern congressional operations. Congressmen who develop a close working relationship with their legislative colleagues are more likely to accomplish their goals than those who acquire a reputation as mavericks. In the Senate, an informal set of "folkways" have evolved that prescribe an appropriate mode of behavior for Senators. Some observers even have concluded that Senators who subscribe most closely to those informal norms, and especially senior members from the South, constitute an "inner circle" that controls the Senate and that often has blocked the enactment of civil rights legislation.[15]

[15]Donald Mathews, *U.S. Senators and Their World* (Chapel Hills: University of North Carolina Press, 1973).

Congressmen who seek to maximize their legislative influence may be advised to specialize in a specific area of legislation. Lacking extensive knowledge about the wide range of subjects that they must consider, legislators frequently refer to a colleague who has developed the status of an expert on a particular subject. The attainment of expert status makes it necessary for legislators to engage in a great deal of hard work, which is another value highly prized in Congress; and it may require a Congressman to sacrifice not only his time and energy but also some of his interests in broader and more controversial legislative issues.

Legislation Affecting Minorities

The pressures for conformity and specialization exert a strong influence upon Congressmen interested in promoting legislation that would benefit racial and ethnic minorities. Many of the most crucial acts of Congress can be found in detailed and technical measures relevant only to small segments of the public rather than in questions that attract newspaper headlines and extensive discussion. Although Congressmen could perform a constructive role by considering how minority groups would be affected by proposals in their field of specialized knowledge and expertise, this legislation contributes to the advantage of groups seeking incremental gains rather than widespread social changes. The emphasis on specialization may inhibit legislators from advocating massive programs to aid minorities and from engaging in general debates concerning minority problems. As a result, the informal norms of congressional behavior often prevent Senators and Representatives from focusing attention on broad questions affecting minority rights.

Congress in Session

For the average visitor to Washington who sits in congressional galleries to watch Congress in action, the scene of legislative decision making may be unimpressive. Debate on the floor of Congress usually is perfunctory and poorly attended. Congressmen move back and forth on the floor, engaging in small talk, and dashing to their offices to meet with legislative advisors and constituents.

Congressional Committees

The real business, if not the actual governance of Congress, is conducted in committees. As Woodrow Wilson observed almost a century ago, Congress in committees is "Congress at work."[16] In the House of Representatives, there

---

[16]Woodrow Wilson, *Congressional Government* (New York: Meridian Books, 1959).

are 20 standing committees; and in the Senate, there are 15. The most prestigious committees in the House include the Rules Committee, Appropriations, and Ways and Means. In the upper chamber, this respect is accorded several committees including Foreign Relations, Appropriations, and Armed Services. Major legislation concerning minority rights, including the Civil Rights Acts of 1960 and 1964, usually has been considered by the Judiciary Committees of the House and Senate, respectively. In 1974 the Judiciary Committee in the House of Representatives again achieved national prominence in its consideration of impeachment proceedings against Richard Nixon. All bills introduced in the House and in the Senate are referred to committees. The committees may recommend the bill for adoption with only minor changes, defeat the measure by a majority vote, completely rewrite the legislation in a new form, or ignore the proposal and prevent its consideration by Congress. Although the full membership of the House or the Senate may overrule the decision of its committees, members of Congress are reluctant to interfere with the prerogatives of committees. Perhaps more than any other group within government or in the general public, committees can determine the fate of legislation.

Committee Assignments

The membership of committees, therefore, often is a vital factor in the consideration of legislative proposals, including bills that have an important impact on minority interests. In the House, Democrats are assigned to committees by a Committee on Committees consisting exclusively of Democrats on the Ways and Means Committee. Although Republican committee members formally are assigned by a Committee on Committees consisting of one Republican member of each state delegation, assignments actually are determined by a subcommittee appointed by the Republican Party leader. In the Senate, on the other hand, Republicans are appointed to committees by a Committee on Committees, and Democratic assignments are made by a Steering Committee chosen by the Democratic floor leader. Although elevation to the most influential committees frequently is determined by the number of terms that a legislator has served in the Senate or the House, little effort is made to maintain a balance of geographic areas, racial and ethnic characteristics, or ideological positions in the selection of committee members. Hence, the concentration of a large number of Congressmen who are hostile to minority interests on a particular issue often is a major barrier to the enactment of legislation for minority groups.[17]

[17]Because of the overriding dominance of the race issue and the Democratic Party in the South, many Southern politicians have been able to build enough seniority to qualify for the chairmanship of important committees in Congress. This has had the effect of getting civil rights legislation through Congress all the more difficult.

Subcommittees

In addition, the nature of legislative proposals often may be affected by the membership of subcommittees, which are often delegated responsibility for the initial consideration of bills. In 1959, the study of civil rights legislation by the Senate Subcommittee on Constitutional Rights of the Judiciary Committee, which listed three Southern Senators among its six Democratic members, resulted in the deletion of a crucial provision of federal assistance for school desegregation and in the recommendation only of a 15-month extension of the U.S. Civil Rights Commission and of a requirement that voting records be made available for three years for examination by federal agents. Although attempts were made to strengthen the bill when it was brought to the Senate floor in the following year, the unrepresentative character of committee and subcommittee membership frequently has been a major source of frustration to the proponents of legislation extending minority rights.[18]

Committee Chairmen

Perhaps the most powerful positions in the legislative process are held by the chairmen of the standing committees of Congress. According to the principle of seniority, committee chairmanships are automatically bestowed upon the member of the dominant party who has served longest on the committee; and Congressmen from the opposing party with the longest records of committee service are called the ranking minority members. Frequently, the consideration of a bill by the full committee provides an opportunity for the reconciliation of party differences. In 1959, for example, the report of the House Judiciary Committee on civil rights measures represented a compromise between two bills offered by Democratic Chairman Emmanuel Cellar and by William M. McCulloch, the ranking Republican on the committee; and, in 1964, the bipartisan agreement reached by members of the committee was credited with strengthening the civil rights bill by reducing the likelihood that harmful amendments would be approved on the House floor. In most circumstances, however, the greatest influence in determining the outcome of legislative controversies resides with committee chairmen. Chairmen can give some proposals prompt and favorable consideration to enhance the success of acts that they favor; they can inject their own preferences into legislation by amending or rewriting bills; and they can influence other members to defeat measures that they oppose.

[18]For an extensive discussion of the 1960 and 1964 Civil Rights Acts see Daniel Berman, *A Bill Becomes a Law* (New York: Macmillan, 1966).

The Seniority System

The choice of committee chairmen by the seniority system often vests great authority in members of Congress who have been successful in gaining continuous reelection. Congressional districts or states that elect representatives or senators who eventually become committee chairmen tend to be sections of the country that are relatively unaffected by the influx of new migrants, such as racial and ethnic groups, by vigorous party competition, or by other political and economic trends that could upset the social equilibrium of the area. As a prominent political scientist once concluded, the seniority system

> "Stacks the cards against those areas where competition for votes is the keenest, where the two-party system is the liveliest, where political currents run fresh and free. It stacks them in favor of the politically stagnant districts—those made 'safe' for the incumbent by . . . restrictions on voting, by the monopolistic position of one party, by the ascendancy of a major interest group, by city or rural machines."[19]

Committee chairmanships traditionally have been dominated by Midwestern Republicans and Southern Democrats. In the Eighty-sixth Congress, which debated the Civil Rights Act of 1960, for example, approximately two-thirds of the committees were chaired by Congressmen from the South. Regions of the Northeast and the West that have experienced extensive social changes usually have been underrepresented in the leadership structure of Congress, and only a few minority Congressmen have attained the position of committee chairmen. During the 1960s, Congressman William Dawson of Chicago served as chairman of the House Government Operations Committee, and Representative Adam Clayton Powell from New York chaired the Education and Labor Committee until his ouster by the House of Representatives. Most committee chairmen not only have been elected by predominantly white districts, but they also have represented areas that were relatively immune to major political changes and movements. The seniority system, therefore, has seemed to inject a strong status-quo bias in the congressional process to the disadvantage of racial and ethnic minorities.

Committee Delays

Committee chairmen can postpone a vote on major bills by a variety of tactics including the infrequent scheduling of hearings on the measure in which testimony is invited from other Congressmen, officials from the executive branch, lobbyists, and spokesmen for powerful organizations. In 1964, Senate

[19]James M. Burns, *Congress on Trial—The Legislative Process and the Administrative State* (New York: Harper and Brothers, 1949), p. 59.

attention to the Civil Rights Act was facilitated by referring the section of the bill banning discrimination in public accommodations to the Commerce Committee, which was favorable to the measure, rather than to the auspices of Senator James O. Eastland, chairman of the Judiciary Committee, which had never voluntarily reported a civil rights measure. While the Commerce Committee completed its report within 22 days in which 47 witnesses testified and 81 statements were received, the Judiciary Committee held hearings for only 11 days during which it heard only one witness. Even though large segments of the Congress and the public are interested in the legislation, committee chairmen can prevent its consideration by extending public hearings on the matter, by failing to call a vote in the committee, or by engaging in other evasive and delaying tactics.

Investigative Committees and Legislative Oversight

The ability to hold legislative hearings designed to provide Congressmen with increased information about legislation is only one of several committee functions that could be used to aid minorities but that have often been employed to obstruct legislation extending minority rights. Although the power of either standing or specially appointed committees to conduct investigations could be utilized to discover discriminatory practices in government programs, it has occasionally been used by chairmen such as the late Senator Joseph McCarthy of Wisconsin to villify witnesses and to gain personal publicity.[20] Under the provisions of the Legislative Reorganization Act of 1946, committees also are charged with the responsibility of overseeing the activities of administrative agencies. This authority could be employed to ensure that minorities are receiving equal treatment under government programs, but it has often been used to restrict activities to aid minority groups. Perhaps the most direct influence of congressional committees upon executive agencies is exerted through the budget process. Each year, subcommittees of the House Appropriations Committee review the administration's budget and hold hearings on agency requests for funds. Although the appropriations process could result in financial increases for programs that would benefit minority groups, it has often produced significant reductions in the funds available for this purpose.[21]

The Rules Committee

After committee action has been completed, all bills in the House of Representatives—with the exception of those reported by the Appropriations and the Ways and Means Committees—must be submitted to the Rules Committee,

---

[20]Richard Rovere, *Senator Joe McCarthy* (New York: Harcourt, Brace, 1959).
[21]Richard Fenno, *The Power of the Purse: Appropriations Politics in Congress* (New York: Little, Brown, 1966).

which has broad authority in controlling the House agenda.[22] This Committee has the formal responsibility of determining the amount of debate that will be permitted on a bill and the number and kinds of amendments that may be offered on the floor. As a result, it has extensive power over the fate of legislation. Perhaps most important, the Rules Committee often has formed a major obstacle to the passage of legislation in behalf of minority groups. For many years, the Rules Committee was chaired by Congressman Howard W. Smith of Virginia, who consistently sought to obstruct the consideration of civil rights bills by failing to call committee meetings on such legislation. In 1957, for example, Smith prevented the committee from meeting on a civil rights measure by visiting his home district allegedly to inspect a barn that had burned on his farm, an action that prompted the Speaker of the House to comment, "I knew Howard Smith would do most anything to block a civil rights bill, but I never suspected he would resort to arson."

The Discharge Petition

Perhaps the most important power available to committees and their chairmen arises from their ability to neglect or to prolong the consideration of legislation. One of few methods of removing a bill from a committee in the House of Representatives is the "discharge petition," which requires the signatures of a majority of the members of the House to send the bill to the floor for a vote. Although only two bills have become law after they were released from committee by a discharge petition, this tactic can be used as a threat to speed committee action on legislation desired by many Congressmen. Chairman Smith, for example, was finally forced to announce that he would hold hearings on the Civil Rights Act of 1960 after the discharge petition was only 29 signatures short of the number required to take the bill from the Rules Committee.

The Filibuster

In the Senate, other techniques, which are closely related to the history of racial issues in America, have been evolved to prevent a vote on legislation. Although the control of debate rests with the majority leader, he does not have the power to limit or to curtail the discussion of bills on the Senate floor. Senators may engage in speeches for hours, and they are permitted to yield the floor to other colleagues interested in defeating the measures. Bills can be killed in the Senate literally by "talking them to death." For centuries this tactic, which is called the filibuster, was employed so frequently by the opponents of civil rights measures that it became known as a "Southern strategy." The only means of terminating a filibuster is cloture, a procedure allowed by Senate Rule 22 that requires a petition signed by at least 16 members and a favorable vote by two-thirds of the Senators present. While the Senate tradi-

[22]James Robinson, *The House Rules Committee* (Indianapolis: Bobbs Merrill, 1963).

During Senate filibusters, cots are often set up near the Senate floor so that senators can be available for roll calls. This is the scene in February 1960 as some Senators rest during the filibuster over the Civil Rights Act. (Wide World Photos)

"You ain't heard the last of me!" (Cartoon by Burck in *The Chicago Sun-Times*)

tionally has been reluctant to end debate, passage of a cloture motion was a major factor permitting Senate approval of the Civil Rights Act of 1964, one year after it had been submitted to Congress by President Kennedy.

Legislative Amendments

After a bill has been cleared for serious consideration by Congress, it frequently is subject to amendment on the floor. In the house of Representatives, the ability to amend a bill may be restricted by the guidelines established by the Rules Committee under which the measure is considered by the House. Senators, however, enjoy a virtually unlimited right not only to debate but also to amend bills. During the controversy over the Civil Rights Act of 1964, for example, the Senate voted on 107 proposed amendments, which did not result in any significant changes in the legislation.

Party Voting

The most important determinant of voting, both on major amendments and the final passage of bills, is party membership.[23] Congressmen are more likely to vote along party lines than on the basis of any other consideration. Although Senators and representatives occasionally may ignore the wishes of their party because of constituency pressures or for other reasons, party affiliations usually exert a strong influence on legislative decisions. In general, party votes, in which a majority of participating Democrats oppose a majority of Republicans who cast ballots, occur on approximately half of all roll-call votes held in Congress. Hence, the partisan composition of Congress and the positions of the parties are of major importance to citizens interested in securing the passage of legislation to benefit racial and ethnic minorities.

The Conservative Coalition

Another significant factor affecting the outcome of legislative decisions, especially on bills concerning minority interests, is the so-called "conservative coalition" of Republicans and Southern Democrats who frequently coalesce in opposition to Northern Democrats. Evidence of this coalition, as exemplified by roll calls in which a majority of Northern Democrats are opposed by a majority of Southern Democrats and a majority of Republicans among those voting, usually appears in about 20 percent of all congressional votes. Although the strength of the conservative coalition may be weakened by special

[23]David Mayhew, *Party Loyalty Among Congressmen: The Difference Between Democrats and Republicans* (Cambridge: Harvard University Press, 1966).

circumstances such as the 1964 election that increased the number of Northern Democrats in Congress, the combined power of Southern Democrats and Republicans generally has been sufficient to produce a victory for those forces in about one-half to two-thirds of the votes on which the coalition has emerged. In addition to many civil rights issues, the conservative coalition has voted together on many bills of major importance to minority groups including aid to depressed areas, minimum wage laws, federal aid to education, public housing, urban renewal, medical care for the aged, taxation, and other domestic welfare questions. In the final stages on Congressional decision-making, therefore, the "conservative coalition" often has been a formidable barrier to the passage of legislation designed to improve the status of minorities in American society.

Conference Committees

The tortuous route that a bill must traverse to become a law tends to promote delay and compromise rather than the speedy approval of legislative proposals. Before legislation can be sent to the President for his signature, both houses of Congress must pass the bill in identical form. As a result, the presiding officers often find it necessary to' appoint a joint conference committee to reconcile the disagreements between House and Senate versions of a measure. This committee consists of five members representing each party in both houses, and it usually includes powerful committee chairmen and other important congressmen. The necessity of obtaining the consent of a majority in both the House and Senate to the report of the conference committee, or to identical provisions of a bill, increases the pressures on each legislator for conformity and accommodation. Congressmen must seek legislative goals by conciliation rather than by a determined insistence upon the approval of their own views. In addition, the procedure tends to augment the influence of prominent congressional leaders.

Party Leaders

Perhaps the most influential members of Congress are the party leaders in the Senate and the House.[24] In many important respects, the outcome of a legislative session may be determined on the opening day of each Congress when the parties are responsible for organizing the two legislative chambers. The proportion of party members in each house determines who will be selected as the Speaker of the House, President pro tempore of the Senate, important committee chairmen, majority leader, minority leader, and party whips.

[24]Randal Ripley, *Party Leaders in the House of Representatives* (Washington, D.C.: Brookings Institution, 1967).

Of particular importance are the majority and minority floor leaders of both houses, who are chosen by party caucuses. The majority and minority leaders often function as legislative managers, overseeing the conduct of congressional business and shaping the agenda that determines the order in which bills receive consideration by each house. Their responsibility is to act as the chief congressional strategists for the parties. Assisting the floor leaders are the party whips, who have the duty of ensuring the attendance of party members at crucial votes and of informing those members about the wishes of the party leadership. Since party positions have great influence in congressional voting and since legislators must depend upon their leaders to gather party support for measures that they favor, Congressmen are understandably reluctant to resist the persuasion of party leaders. As a result, majority and minority leaders occupy a pivotal role in the passage or defeat of legislation.

An indication of the crucial position of party leaders in the legislative process is reflected by their efforts to secure the passage of civil rights bills in 1960 and 1964. In fact, the responsibility for originating the Civil Rights Act of 1960 can be attributed to Lyndon B. Johnson, then Democratic majority leader of the Senate, who honored an earlier promise to introduce this legislation by February 15, 1960, by amending a civil rights bill to an obscure act to authorize the leasing of an army building to the Stella, Missouri school district. As majority leader in 1960, Johnson played a vital role in steering this measure through the Senate; and, as President, he cooperated with his successor, Senator Mike Mansfield of Montana, in performing a similar task for the Civil Rights Act of 1964. Furthermore, the influence of the majority leaders in promoting the approval of civil rights bills, as well as other measures pertaining to minority groups, often has been extended by close cooperation with the minority leader. In both 1960 and 1964, for example, the active support of Republican minority leader, Everett M. Dirksen of Illinois, was crucial in obtaining Senate action on legislation to protect the rights of black Americans.

The Speaker of The House

Perhaps the single most powerful figure in Congress, however, is the Speaker of the House of Representatives, who is elected by the majority party of the House and who presides over that body. Prior to 1960, the Speaker served as the chairman of the Rules Committee, appointed both the members and the chairmen of all standing committees, and enjoyed unlimited discretion in recognizing members on the floor. Although his powers were curtailed in a revolt by insurgent Congressmen against Speaker Joe Cannon during the progressive era, the Speaker continues to have a major effect on the House agenda by referring bills to committees and by directing activities on the floor. A forceful Speaker, therefore, can exert a strong impact on the actions and decisions of the House of Representatives.

The Vice President

The presiding officer of the Senate is the Vice-President, who exercises less control over legislative affairs than the Speaker. Although the Vice-President is able to cast a ballot in behalf of the administration in the case of a tie vote in the Senate, his most important duties seem to focus on generating public support for the proposals and the party of the person who occupies the White House.

Since World War II, the role of the Vice-President and congressional leaders has expanded not only because of their own efforts and activity but also because of their proximity to the presidency. Four of the seven Vice-Presidents who served from 1945 to 1974 were former party leaders in Congress, including Alben Barkley, Lyndon Johnson, Hubert Humphrey, and Gerald Ford; and four Vice-Presidents—Harry S. Truman, Lyndon Johnson, and Richard Nixon, and Gerald Ford—succeeded to the presidency either by election or by the death of an incumbent President, or by Presidential resignation. This pattern has suggested the faint outlines of a route of succession to the presidency similar to the ladder from law enforcement or legislative offices to gubernatorial positions that has developed in many states.[25] In addition, party leaders—including spokesmen for the opposition as well as leaders of the party of the administration—frequently have been invited to confer with the President concerning both the preparation and the presentation of his legislative program. Congressional leaders have emerged as powerful figures that must be recognized by the general public, by other members of Congress, and by the President.

The importance of party leadership positions and the vice-presidency was illustrated by the dramatic events during the Nixon Administration. After the resignation of former Vice President Spiro Agnew in 1973 and the resignation of President Nixon in 1974, Gerald Ford, a former Republican minority leader in the House who had been appointed by Nixon to fill Agnew's unexpired term, became the first President to achieve that office without going before the national electorate. Ford's ascent was allowed by the Twenty-Fifth Amendment, adopted in 1967, which permitted the President to appoint a new Vice-President with the consent of Congress and which stipulated that the Vice-President shall become the chief executive upon the death or resignation of the President. These developments may cause Americans, including members of the dominant white majority as well as members of various racial and ethnic minorities, to focus increasing attention on the men or women who are selected as party leaders in Congress or as Vice-Presidents.

[25]The discovery that there are avenues of succession to gubernatorial positions was discovered by Joseph Schlesinger *How They Became Governor* (East Lansing, Michigan: Governmental Research Bureau, Michigan State University, 1957).

• POINTS TO REMEMBER

Since legislative bodies supposedly exist to translate public desires into government policy, it might also be assumed that they provide an appropriate vehicle for the satisfaction of minority grievances, but the obstacles confronting minorities have proved considerable. The basic form of representation outlined in the Constitution is founded on the principle of area. At all levels of government, therefore, representation is basically determined by population and geographic considerations rather than by social, economic, or racial characteristics. The absence of proportional representation and multimember districts has retarded the growth of third parties and made it difficult for minority groups to achieve representation.

The concentration of minority groups in the nation's central cities should have provided a basis for electoral strength. But because of gerrymandering and the use of at-large elections, the minority vote has been diluted. But even when minority candidates are elected, they must confront the problem of working within legislative assemblies dominated by representatives of the white majority. Since most legislators represent predominantly white constituencies, the values and beliefs that they acquire before entering Congress as well as the pressures from voters have tended to limit their responsiveness to minority demands.

The congressional maze through which bills must pass before they are sent to the President has given entrenched interests hostile to extending civil rights to minorities the opportunity to frustrate such legislative proposals. Some of the more important aspects of this maze include the emphasis on conformity and specialization, committee assignments based on seniority, the tradition of filibustering in the Senate, and the crucial role played by party leaders in both houses.

• SOME UNRESOLVED ISSUES: A DIALOGUE

Holland: One of the major reasons for the relative lack of minority representatives in the House can be found in the Constitutional provision for single-member districts. Each legislative district is allowed one representative and whoever captures a plurality of the votes wins the election. This makes it possible for any given minority to constitute 49 percent of the population in a district and still be unrepresented in Congress. Oddly enough, this has been both a source of strength and weakness. As the nation has moved further in the direction of residential segregation, some legislative districts have populations that are made up of a particular minority.

This has insured not only the election of minority candidates, but it also has meant that they have been able to build up seniority for strategic placement on important committees. On the other hand, blacks, Puerto Ricans, Chicanos, and Asians still do not have the number of Congressmen commensurate with their numbers in the general population.

Hahn: The foundation of representation upon single-member districts and states is only one example of the institutional barriers that have impeded the progress of minority groups. Another example is the reliance of opposing Congressmen on and candidates private campaign contributions both from powerful national organizations and from dominant economic interests in their districts. Changes in these two features of the political system could produce substantially different results.

The establishment of multimember districts or an alternative form of election, such as proportional representation, certainly would have a major effect upon the party system and upon representation of minorities as well as the dominant white majority. Similarly, elimination of private political contributions and the adoption of public financing of electoral campaigns might facilitate the flow of government funds to deprived minorities who desperately need such assistance rather than to powerful legislative interests who have become accustomed to receiving favorable treatment in Congress.

Holland: Care should be taken to note that almost any scheme of representation that facilitates racial and ethnic minorities is likely to benefit extreme right wing antiminority groups as well. That possibility notwithstanding, the need for change is still of paramount importance, and perhaps one of the most significant changes would be the alteration of the manner in which campaigns are financed. Since Congress is formally charged with the responsibility of initiating changes in our laws, perhaps we should focus attention on strengthening that body in a way that would allow for decisive political action aimed at providing solutions to our numerous political, social, and economic ills. Changes such as eliminating the seniority system, limiting debate in the Senate, reducing the power of committee chairman, and altering other mechanisms that impede the passage of legislation might be worth serious consideration.

Hahn: I believe that both reforms in the operation of Congress and major changes in political institutions should be given serious consideration. I proposed the alterations in the method of selecting legislators simply to underscore the importance of considering structural changes in the American political system rather than mere changes in political personnel. Too often Americans have believed that serious public problems can be solved simply by replacing incumbent officials with a new group of office holders when the real difficulty may result from structural defects. In addition to the two alternatives that I mentioned previously, I would like to suggest an additional thought. I personally believe that it should be as easy for the public to remove public officials as it is to elect them. The implementation of this idea would imply the adoption of provisions for the liberal use of the initiative, referendum, and recall, which have been established in many states and localities, as an amendment to the U.S. Constitution.[26]

Holland: The idea of a referendum has great deal of potential. For example, major campaign reform in California, very much on the order that we have called for, would probably not have been possible in 1973 had the referendum been unavailable to the citizens of that state. But I wonder if the other constitutional changes you suggest would have the effects you want. It seems to me that in states that have the recall, for example, the politics have remained essentially the same as in states that do not.

It could be argued that Nixon's resignation in 1974 was a form of recall by the American public; but his resignation left the adequacy of the constitutional provision for impeachment in question. The details of those issues are discussed in Section 9.

---

[26]The initiative provides that, upon receipt of a petition containing a specified number of signatures from qualified voters, the public may compel political issues to be considered by legislative bodies to be voted upon—and to approve or disapprove—a policy proposal. The recall offers a method of removing a public official from office prior to the expiration of his term by petitioning for a special election to decide his continuance in office.

4 THE AMERICAN PRESIDENCY

Growth of Presidential Power

Perhaps the single most influential person in American government is the President of the United States. Even though formal responsibility for the enactment of legislation is vested primarily in Congress, the legislative branch frequently is unwilling or unable to act without clear direction and support from the executive. Decisions and pronouncements made by the President can have a major impact on the lives of millions of people in the United States and abroad. As the nation's highest elected official, the President occupies the center stage of political attention both in this country and throughout the world.

A major reason for the growth of presidential power is that, unlike Congress and the judiciary, authority in the executive branch resides with a single individual. Collective decisions are intrinsically more cumbersome and time-consuming than judgments made by one person. While responsibility in legislative and judicial institutions is distributed among several actors, the President alone has the obligation and prerogative to lead his administration and the nation along the path that he chooses. Although progress toward his destination may be obstructed by other major and minor functionaries, his position atop the federal hierarchy gives him a commanding advantage in the exercise of political influence.

The Constitution provided few hints of the subsequent development of presidential power. The opening sentence of Article II simply asserts: "The executive power shall be vested in a President of the United States of America."[1] In large measure, the failure to delineate a specific and unambiguous role for the President arose from a sharp disagreement among the delegates to the Constitutional Convention concerning the appropriate functions of this office. While Alexander Hamilton was one of few delegates who seriously

---

[1] In the controversy over impeachment in 1974, the constitutional ambiguity regarding the responsibility of the President in exercising his executive power became a major issue in Congress. Although an impeachment resolution was reported by the Judiciary Committee in the House, the issue—and the Constitutional questions that it raised—became moot with the resignation of President Nixon on August 8, 1974.

proposed the establishment of a monarchy in America, the debate over a strong or a weak executive generated a severe schism among Convention participants. A proposal offered by New Jersey delegates called for a plural executive chosen by Congress for a single term, but this plan was opposed by advocates of a strong executive who anticipated the selection of George Washington as the first President.[2] Eventually the Convention approved a compromise. The provisions of the Constitution called for the selection of the President by the Electoral College, a body independent of Congress; and they left the specific powers of the presidency relatively undefined. As a result, subsequent Presidents have encountered few constitutional restrictions in the expansion of their powers. Despite the fears generated by the tyranny of King George III of England and the desire to establish a delicate balance between the three branches of government, they produced a document that seemed to promote a gradual shift of power toward the executive branch.

The aggrandizement of presidential power has developed primarily through the establishment of customs favoring a strong President rather than by changes in the formal structure of American government. After the choice of presidential candidates had become a matter of popular concern rather than a privilege of party caucuses in Congress, growing numbers of citizens looked to the President as the spokesman for public demands. This perspective was expressed by Andrew Jackson, Abraham Lincoln, and Theodore Roosevelt, who argued that the president should serve as the "tribune of the people" in initiating and implementing the will of the majority. While other presidents have been reluctant to exercise powers that were not explicitly authorized either by the Constitution or by laws, the success of presidents who assumed a strong role in the political process has left a major imprint upon American history. As Clinton Rossiter has noted:

> "... the outstanding feature of American Constitutional development has been the growth of the power and prestige of the presidency. This growth has not been steady, but subject to sharp ebbs as well as massive flows. Strong Presidents have been followed by weak ones ... Yet the ebbs have been more apparent than real, and each new strong president has picked up where the last strong one left off."[3]

Getting the Attention of the President

In the minds of the public, as well as government officials, the image of the active and aggressive President has triumphed.

---

[2]In this respect, the Framers proved to be rather short-sighted. Even though they trusted Washington, and assumed that he would not abuse the powers of his office, surely they were aware that others, in the years to come, would assume office who might prove to be considerably less trustworthy.

[3]Clinton Rossiter, *The American Presidency* (New York: Harper & Row, 1960), p. 82.

The increasing power of the President has made him the focal point both for citizens whose lives might be affected by his decisions and for interests seeking to obtain a share of government resources. As a result groups in American society are not only compelled to listen attentively to presidential announcements, but they are also forced to devote a substantial amount of energy in the effort to gain presidential attention. In fact, much of the activity of civil rights and minority groups has been devoted to attempts to secure a sympathetic hearing and support of the President. The accomplishment of this task has resulted in major successes for minorities including the establishment of the Fair Employment Practices Commission (FEPC) under Franklin D. Roosevelt; the order to desegregate the armed forces in the Administration of Harry S. Truman; Dwight D. Eisenhower's deployment of federal troops to insure school integration in Little Rock, Arkansas; the issuance of an executive order by John F. Kennedy to prohibit discrimination in federally supported housing; and the vigorous leadership provided by Lyndon B. Johnson for the 1964 Civil Rights Act.

These successes, have been paralleled, however, by numerous instances in which presidents have failed to support the demands of minorities, and other cases in which presidential neglect has prevented minority concerns from assuming their rightful place on the nation's agenda for political action. The failure of presidents either to recognize or respond to the aspirations of the disadvantaged not only may be prompted by a personal lack of sympathy but it also might be a result of constraints imposed by the voters who elected him and by his relationship with other political decision makers in American politics. A clear understanding of the role of the modern presidency, therefore, requires a careful examination of the limitations as well as the advantages provided by presidential support.

Presidential Election

A major interpretation of presidential behavior has been based upon support that candidates receive from different constituencies in the American electorate. The people do not vote directly for the President. The reluctance of the delegates to the Constitutional Convention to entrust the people with the task of selecting the nation's highest elected official resulted in the creation of the Electoral College,[4] which was not designed to be an accurate reflection of popular sentiment. Although members of the Electoral College usually have endorsed the preferences of voters in their states, all of the electoral votes for a state, which are determined by the number of Congressmen and Senators,

---

[4]Rather than voting directly for the President, the Constitution provides for each state to establish a slate of electors who constitute the electoral college. Citizens then vote for the slate of electors who, oddly enough, are not required to in turn to cast their votes as directed by the people. However, only a handful of electors have disregarded popular sentiments.

have been cast for the candidate winning a plurality of the vote in that state. Thus, it has been possible for a candidate to gain the presidency by winning a majority of the votes in the Electoral College while losing the popular vote count as Rutherford B. Hayes did in 1876.

Although this system has allegedly made presidential candidates more sensitive to the importance of minority voters in populous states, since 1936 many of these votes have been delivered automatically to the Democratic Party as a result of New Deal legislation that appealed to disadvantaged segments of the population.[5] Since some candidates have also found it possible to win presidential elections without extensive support from minority voters, neither the size of their votes nor the advantages supposedly provided them by the Electoral College have been sufficient to give them a decisive role in presidential decisions. For example, the policies of the Administration of Richard M. Nixon, which seemed to usher in a period of "benign neglect"[6] toward the aspirations of racial and ethnic minorities, frequently have been attributed to the lack of minority support for Nixon in the elections of 1968 and 1972.

Role as Leader of the People

Regardless of who voted for him or the method by which he was selected, the victory of a presidential candidate provides him with a mandate to serve as a spokesman for the entire country. Immediately after their election, Presidents are usually given the distinction in public opinion surveys of being the "most admired man in the nation." Similar approval greeted Gerald Ford in 1974 even though he had never been elected to the office of Vice-President or President. He has instantaneous access to the mass media to present his views to the American people; and by performing feats such as tossing out the first ball of the baseball season, lighting the Christmas tree on the White House lawn, addressing the annual conventions of powerful organizations and entertaining foreign dignitaries, the President symbolizes respected traditions of the nation's life. He embodies the collective aspirations of the American people.

In his role as leader of the people, the President has assumed the posture of a servant of the dominant white majority more often than as a champion of minority rights. When the public has become aroused in behalf of the extension of civil rights, as it did in the early days of the Johnson Administration,

---

[5]Depression relief under Roosevelt represented one of the few times in American history in which the government-sponsored programs that directly aided black America but that did not arouse the anger of the dominant white majority. The depression placed large numbers of blacks and whites on equal footing for the first time. It was an equality of poverty.

[6]The term "benign neglect" was made infamous by presidential adviser Daniel Moynihan who in a memo to Richard Nixon suggested that after all of the rioting and civil rights turmoil in the 1960s it was perhaps time for the government to ignore the problems created by racial issues in the hope that they would solve themselves without government interference.

Presidents have found it difficult to ignore or dismiss those sentiments. On the other hand, the failure of white opinion to support minorities, or expressions of intense hostility, frequently have been reflected in presidential action. Because of the deep-seated emotions aroused by the issue of race in American politics, Presidents have been reluctant to assume a leading role in the quest for freedom, equality, and justice. Public opinion not only has been a source of power for the Chief Executive, but it also has occasionally been a major constraint on presidential action. American Presidents have been compelled to devote close attention to the periodic reports on their popularity in samples of public attitudes. Popular support for the President often has shown dramatic variations. In January of 1973, shortly after a truce had been declared in the Vietnam War, approval of the Nixon Administration was recorded at 68 percent: one year later, after a series of shocking disclosures about improprieties in the White House, it fell to 24 percent, the lowest since President Truman's 22 percent after the firing of General Douglas McArthur in 1951.

Leader of the Party

In addition to his role as leader of the public, Presidents (and nominees for that office) serve as the titular heads of their political parties. Although this function frequently has appeared to give Presidents effective control over platforms and the general conduct of party business, it has been of limited value both to presidential hopefuls and incumbents. Candidates who do not occupy the office of the presidency frequently have sought to avoid taking strong positions on controversial issues in the fear that such action might disrupt the coalition on which they are hoping to build a winning campaign. (In 1964, however, one of only 25 Senators who opposed the Civil Rights Act was Barry Goldwater, who hoped to gain Southern support for his pending presidential campaign.) Similarly incumbents have often attempted to maintain the basis of support that brought them to power by refusing to align themselves with minorities in party councils. For example, President Lyndon Johnson declined to intervene in the effort to replace the white supremist Mississippi delegation to the 1964 Democratic national convention with the racially integrated representatives of the Mississippi Freedom Democratic Party (MFDP). Occasionally, however, issues of minority rights reached such intensity that they could not be prevented from emerging on party agendas, as in 1948 when a floor fight over the civil rights plank of the Democratic Party platform, led by Mayor Hubert Humphrey of Minneapolis, prompted the defection of Southern delegates who formed the Dixiecrat Party under the direction of Strom Thurmond.[7] In general, however, Presidents have used their role

[7]Strom Thurmond's opposition to extending the freedoms promised in the Constitution to blacks became so intense that he finally switched his membership to the Republican Party in 1971 because he felt that the Democrats had become too "liberal" on racial matters.

as party leaders to prevent divisive issues from threatening the party unity necessary to insure electoral victory.

Presidential Coattails

Candidates for public office at the federal, state, and local level have had little reason to challenge efforts of presidential nominees to maintain party cohesion. The popularity of presidential candidates and the fate of lesser party nominees have been intertwined. Successful aspirants to the White House often have been considered responsible for the election of candidates who might otherwise have been defeated without the benefit of presidential coattails. While American voters also have displayed a tendency to split their votes between candidates of opposing parties, the normal rule of thumb in American politics has encouraged candidates to link their campaigns to the national slate.[8] This dependence also has produced serious problems when presidential popularity has begun to ebb. During the 1960s when the national leadership of the Democratic Party adopted an increasingly favorable attitude toward civil rights, many Southern Democrats sought to disassociate themselves from this position; and in the following decade a national crisis of confidence in presidential leadership produced a similar reaction among Republicans who feared that the scandals of the Nixon Administration would jeopardize their careers. In the 1972 campaign the overly zealous activities of the Committee to Reelect the President, which resulted in an attempted burglary of the Watergate headquarters of the Democratic Party; compromised the position of Richard Nixon both as the leader of his party and of the nation; and forced him to resign.

Power to Make Appointments

There are relatively few Constitutional limitations on the exercise of presidential power. One restriction is reflected in the requirement that the President must obtain the advise and consent of a majority of senators on major administrative and judicial appointments. In addition, under the terms of the Twenty-Fifth Amendment, a Vice-President, appointed by the President must be confirmed by a majority vote in both houses of Congress. These requirements, however, have not enabled the Congress to exercise effective supervision over presidential appointments. The authority to make appointments is an important means by which a President seeks to insure the presence of persons in his administration who share his political values. But, care must be taken to avoid appointments that might offend influential members of the Senate or the general public.

[8]Candidates, by linking their campaigns to the national slate, hope that the voters will view their election and that of the President as one and the same. The opposite works as well. That is, when a presidential candidate's popularity drops, those running for lesser offices in the same party can be expected to "unhitch" their fates from that of the national ticket.

On occasion the need to make appointments palatable to the Senate has worked to the disadvantage of racial and ethnic minorities. In appointing Thurgood Marshall, a lawyer for the NAACP, to the Second Circuit Court of Appeals, President John F. Kennedy was forced to resort to a recess appointment that was formally submitted to the Senate for confirmation on September 23, 1961. Though marshall served on the court during the interim, favorable action on his appointment was delayed for one year by Senator James O. Eastland of Mississippi, who was chairman of the Judiciary Committee. Despite Eastland's objections, Marshall was later appointed by President Johnson to become the first black justice of the United States Supreme Court.

Submission of an appointment for confirmation gives the Senate a major opportunity to voice its objections to the personnel and philosophy of a presidential administration. During the first term of the Nixon Administration, for example, attempts to appoint two conservative Southern judges, Clement Haynesworth and Thomas Carswell, to the Supreme Court were rejected by the Senate. But those rejections were less significant than the nominees who were approved.

In 1968, Richard Nixon made the appeal for "law and order," with its implicit arousal of racial tensions, the major theme of his campaign for the presidency. In fact, two of his closest associates, vice-presidential nominee Spiro T. Agnew and campaign manager John Mitchell, were the most strident spokesmen for "law and order" and two of the most intensely disliked national figures in the minority community. Ironically, both Agnew and Mitchell as well as the President himself, subsequently left office charged with violating the law.

Presidential Resignation and Impeachment

The events that culminated in the end of the most corrupt and scandal-ridden administration in the history of the republic began at 2:30 a.m. on June 17, 1972 when five men were discovered in the offices of the Democratic National Committee. It was subsequently revealed that these men were in the employ of the Committee to Reelect the President headed by John Mitchell who left the office of Attorney General to direct Nixon's campaign again in 1972. Whether or not this burglary occurred at the direct orders of the President remains a mystery. But it is clear, as a result of an admission made by Nixon during his final week in office, that he did direct the Central Intelligence Agency (CIA) to halt an investigation by the Federal Bureau of Investigation (FBI) aimed at finding the sources of the money for the burglary. His confession was prompted by a Supreme Court decision that prevented him from invoking the claim of "executive privilege," which had been used by the President in an effort to keep confidential communications between him and his staff, to supress tape-recordings between Nixon and presidential advisors including H. R. Haldeman and John Erlichman. These actions, as well as the creation of a White House special intelligence unit (the Plumbers) raised some serious questions about the propriety of executive involvement in domestic espionage in a democratic society.

In addition to the burglary of the Watergate offices, it was discovered that a similar break-in occurred in the offices of Dr. Lewis Fielding, who had once been a psychiatrist to Daniel Ellsberg, who had given the press an official analysis of the Vietnam war prepared for the Defense Department. Ellsberg was tried for violating national security because he released documents that had been labeled "confidential"; but the disclosure of the illegal entry into the office of his psychiatrist forced the courts to dismiss the charges against him. Although the ability of the President to invoke claims of national security and executive privilege give him wide discretion in withholding information from the American public, the actions of the Nixon Administration also demonstrated that these powers could be abused.

Serious questions also were raised about the propriety of massive campaign contributions to the Nixon reelection effort. A spokesman for the Associated Milk Producers stated that his organization was prepared to donate more than two million dollars to aid Nixon's reelection. Other groups such as American Airlines, Braniff Airways, Goodyear Tire, Minnesota Mining and Manufacturing, Ashland Oil, and numerous other corporations pleaded guilty to making illegal contributions to the Committee to Reelect the President. Although it is difficult to prove conclusively that such contributions influenced administrative decisions, they created a general climate of moral decay in the Nixon era that contributed to his downfall. The necessity of resorting to private contributions in the conduct of expensive campaigns and the access of leading politicians to contributors who are eager to defray those costs, reflect serious structural weaknesses in the American political system that work both to the disadvantage of impoverished minorities and to the general public.

The potential for the abuse of presidential power was revealed by Nixon's efforts to force the Internal Revenue Service (IRS) to audit the tax returns of persons designated as political enemies and by his capacity to control and curtail the activities of the FBI and CIA. Many of these activities provided an impetus for the articles of impeachment that were prepared by the Judiciary Committee and adopted for presentation to the House of Representatives prior to Nixon's resignation.

The three articles of impeachment approved by the Committee focused on the obstruction of justice, the abuse of power, and contempt of Congress. In the first article President Nixon was accused of "engaging personally and through his close subordinates and agents, in a course of conduct or plan designed to delay, impede, and obstruct the investigation of such unlawful entry; to cover up, conceal, and protect those responsible; and to conceal the existence and scope of other unlawful covert activities." Similarly, the second article charged that he "engaged in conduct violating the constitutional rights of citizens, impairing the due and proper administration of justice and the conduct of unlawful inquiries, or contravening the laws governing agencies of the executive branch and the purpose of these agencies." By contrast, the third article of impeachment cited the president for failure to comply with subpoenas that had directed him to supply the Judiciary Committee with information to be used in its investigations of the impeachment issue.

The events leading to the resignation illustrate not only the potential for the abuse of presidential power, but they also illustrate the difficulty of removing a President from office. According to the United States Constitution, impeachment requires a majority vote in the House of Representatives; and in order to obtain a conviction a two-thirds vote is needed in the Senate, which sits as a jury with the Chief Justice of the Supreme Court presiding. Although articles of impeachment against Nixon were voted by the House, impeachment proceedings were never initiated on the floor of Congress because of his resignation. The only other attempt to remove a President from office was directed against Andrew Johnson who was impeached by the House but who escaped conviction in the Senate by one vote on May 26, 1868. Neither this effort nor the subsequent proceedings initiated against Richard Nixon fully resolved the ambiguities of the constitutional provisions that permit impeachment upon the "conviction of treason, bribery, or other high crimes and misdemeanors." The cumbersome, time-consuming nature of the impeachment process, as well as the national anguish that it evokes has raised serious questions about the adequacy of this constitutional mechanism for removing a president from office. The drama surrounding the resignation and the attempt to impeach Richard Nixon represented another chapter in the continuing struggle between the legislative and executive branches of government. Although Nixon left office as a discredited President and the reputations of the presidency undoubtedly had deteriorated, there seemed to be little opposition to the succession of Gerald Ford, who had never been a candidate in a national campaign. A few days after Ford took the oath of office, he appeared before Congress, where his claims to the presidency were greeted by widespread acceptance rather than resistance. Even in one of its gloomiest moments in American history the office of the presidency retained its strength and viability. For members of racial and ethnic minorities, as well as the dominant white majority, a crucial test of a President remained his ability to provide effective direction and guidance for Congress.

Legislative Leader

One of the most important roles played by the President has evolved from his position as the major initiator of legislative proposals. Although the technical requirement that only members of Congress can introduce bills prevented nineteenth-century presidents from assuming an active role in the congressional process, almost every President in the twentieth century has been regarded as the principal official responsible for determining the legislative agenda. Regardless of a President's personal opinion about the matter, both the public and Congressmen have developed expectations that virtually compel him to assume this responsibility.[9]

The central role of the President in the legislative process has been one of the principal factors that account for the intense efforts by nearly all segments of society to make the President aware of their demands. In the clamor to arouse the interest of the President some groups have a decided advantage over others. While a few organizations can rely upon existing resources such as economic influence and public prestige as a means of gaining accessibility to the inner circles of the White House, other groups have been forced to resort to tactics designed to dramatize their plight. During the energy crisis in the Winter of 1973–1974, for example, independent truckers threatened the nation's economy by suspending operations to underscore their demands for increased rates and a reduction in diesel fuel cost. In addition to securing presidential attention, groups also have been compelled to get his support to provide passage through the legislative maze. Though major legislative victories have occasionally been achieved without presidential approval and even over his strong objections, endorsements by the chief executive have been one of the most valuable resources available to groups in American society.

The importance of presidential blessings in determining the outcome of a controversy, however, often depends upon the intensity with which he seeks to advance his position. When a President decides to mobilize the full resources of his office in behalf of a proposal, his support may be worth the combined strengths of hundreds of private interest groups. The vigorous efforts of President Lyndon B. Johnson, for example, played a decisive role in the passage of the 1964 Civil Rights Act one year after it had been introduced by President Kennedy. By contrast, mild endorsement by a President who refuses to intervene actively in the legislative process might be of limited symbolic or publicity value.[10]

Presidential influence in the legislative process arises not only from prevalent expectations concerning his role as legislative leader, but also from close contacts with the leaders of his party in Congress. Although the success of a President's legislative program usually is enhanced when his party controls a majority in both houses of Congress, Presidents frequently have also sought to work closely with leaders of the other party both to gain bipartisan support for his proposals and to prevent the development of a determined opposition.

[9]The emergence of the President as the legislative leader is antithetical to the framers' attempt to establish a system of checks and balances. However, their failure to specify and delineate the power of the President made this development almost inevitable.

[10]There are numerous ways by which a President can camouflage his intentions from many American voters. Mild endorsement of legislative proposals and then failure to "line-up" the necessary votes on Capitol Hill is one of the most frequently used tactics.

Floor leaders of both parties frequently have been invited to the White House to discuss major legislative issues. Presidential effectiveness has depended both upon his willingness to cooperate with chairmen of important committees and other congressional influentials and upon continuing efforts by the President and his advisors to maintain a favorable relationship with Capitol Hill. The President and his staff often has sought the advise and support of members of Congress, and the success of these efforts has had a strong impact upon the fate of his administration. Presidents not only have left their imprint on Congress, but Congress often has exerted major influence upon presidential proposals. Chief executives frequently have been persuaded to modify their legislative objectives to make them more palatable to potential opponents on Capitol Hill.

Veto Power

In addition to the influence bestowed by custom and by public perceptions of the President as a legislative leader, a constitutional basis for this role is provided by his authority to veto acts of Congress.[11] Although a presidential veto can only be overriden by two-thirds vote in both houses of Congress, Presidents also have utilized the "pocket veto" to kill legislation by refusing to sign bills passed in the last 10 days of a session. Frequently the threat of a presidential veto has been as important as the actual exercise of this power. Just as consultation with Congress has often persuaded presidents to modify their proposals, the impending risk of a veto has induced Congress to dilute or eliminate legislative provisions that meet with strong presidential objections. The ability of minorities to attain their legislative goals has been frustrated not only by congressional inaction but also by presidential opposition. In 1971, for example, Richard M. Nixon employed this prerogative to promote his plans for dismantling the antipoverty program begun during the Johnson Administration, by vetoing a $6.3 billion, two-year extension of the Economic Opportunity Act.

Preparing the Budget

The ability of the President to exert decisive influence in Congress also has been enhanced by his crucial role in the budgetary process. Under the terms of the Budget and Accounting Act of 1921, the President is required to submit an annual budget to Congress that contains a comprehensive plan for the expenditure of federal funds. Perhaps more than any other document, the

[11]The strength of the power—and the resilience of the presidency—was demonstrated by the fact that during his last day in office, Richard Nixon still felt sufficiently confident to veto an important appropriations bill for the Department of Agriculture even after he had been personally discredited.

budget proposed by the President, as well as the appropriations ultimately approved by Congress, provides a succinct statement of national priorities and values. As Aaron Wildavsky noted:

> "The size and shape of the budget is a matter of serious contention in our political life. Presidents, political parties, administrators, Congressmen, interest groups, and interested citizens vie with one another to have their preferences recorded in the budget. The victories and defeats, the compromises and the bargains, the realms of agreement and the spheres of conflict in regard to the role of the national government in our society all appear in the budget. In the most integral sense, the budget lies at the heart of the political process."[12]

For many Americans, including racial and ethnic minorities, however, omissions from the federal budget, that reflect the resistance of dominant groups to the demands of the disadvantaged have been as significant as the figures contained in the budget that represent the bargains struck between powerful established interests.

Although numerous actors play major roles in the budgetary process, the President, by virtue of his taking the initiative in developing a comprehensive program of federal spending, occupies a pivotal position. In preparing his conception of the financial resources that should be conferred upon various competitors for governmental rewards, the President is greatly assisted by the Office of Management and Budget (OMB), which became a part of the Executive Office of the President in 1939.[13] In addition to its task of supplying the President with basic data upon which the budget is based, the Bureau also has a major responsibility for the planning and management of all facets of the federal bureaucracy and for determining whether or not proposed legislation is consistent with presidential policies. As a result of the legislative clearance function, the recommendations of the OMB concerning legislation as well as spending have a powerful impact upon governmental decisions. The values outlined in the federal budget seldom are subject to rapid shifts. Even if Congressional and presidential decisions imply a radical reordering of emphases, the budgetary process inhibits pronounced changes. Appropriations for various agencies and programs usually reflect a process of incremental growth in which small additional allocations of money are provided in accordance with increased cost and responsibility. Along with other aspects of the political system that have been characterized by modest change, the incremental nature of budget making has often seemed to penalize minorities, which have previously received few political benefits but which are deserving of substantial increases in governmental resources.

---

[12]Aaron Wildavsky, *The Politics of the Budgetary Process* (New York: Little, Brown, 1964), pp. 4–5.
[13]The Office of Management and Budget was formerly known as the Bureau of the Budget.

Executive Orders

The frustrations induced by the slow pace of change in the American society
have inspired deprived segments of the population, including minority groups,
to seek additional methods of avoiding the delays and uncertainties endemic
to the political process. One strategy of achieving dramatic gains has enlisted
minorities in efforts to persuade the President to issue executive orders prohibiting discrimination in practices covered by governmental policies. The first
executive order was issued by Abraham Lincoln on October 20, 1862, to
establish military courts in Louisiana. Subsequently the issuance of executive
orders such as President Harry S. Truman's edict to integrate the armed forces
has played a major role in the struggle for civil rights.

Perhaps the best known controversy over the use of presidential power
concerning the use of executive orders revolved around John F. Kennedy's
pledge to prohibit racially segregated housing. After promising, during
the 1960 campaign, to end housing discrimination "with the stroke of a pen,"
Kennedy was sharply criticized by civil rights organizations for failing to fulfill
that pledge. His delay, however, illustrated some constraints on presidential
power and the caution with which Presidents approach the use of their authority. Kennedy was interested in elevating the Housing and Home Finance Administration to cabinet status and in appointing its director, Robert Weaver,
the first black cabinet member in the nation's history. Since this plan compelled
him to seek congressional approval and the support of several Southern legislators, he felt that the immediate issuance of the order that was to become
Executive Order 11063 would jeopardize his objectives. JFK waited for an
opportune moment to honor his commitment. As Theodore Sorensen, Kennedy's domestic advisor, commented:

"He found the lowest-key time possible on the evening of November 20, 1962. It
was the night before he and much of the country closed shop for the long Thanks-
giving weekend. The announcement was deliberately sandwiched between a long,
dramatic and widely hailed statement on Soviet bombers leaving Cuba and another
major statement on the Indian border conflict with China.[14]

Kennedy's statement not only demonstrated the extent to which Presidents can
manipulate events for their own purposes, but it also revealed a widespread
belief that aggressive action on behalf of civil rights could only be taken when
the country was anesthetized by a major crisis. Although the issuance of orders
from the top of an institutional hierarchy frequently may constitute a more
effective means of changing attitudes and behavior, such as those reflected in
racial prejudice, than actions that are generated by grass-roots efforts to secure
a democratic consensus, presidents have been reluctant to pursue this strategy.

[14]Theodore Sorensen, *Kennedy* (New York: Harper & Row, 1965), p. 15.

When President Kennedy addressed the nation in the wake of the crisis over admitting two Negroes to the University of Alabama, he urged every American to "examine his conscience" about the rights of Negroes. (United Press International)

The apparent simplicity of executive orders has made this an attractive alternative to proponents of civil rights, but this approach to the nation's most troublesome domestic issue has also been afflicted by serious weaknesses. Although the Supreme Court has ruled that executive orders carry the force of law, they can be challenged either as an unconstitutional exercise of presidential power or as a violation of existing statutes. If either argument is successful, executive orders can be declared null and void. In addition, Presidents have refrained from promulgating executive orders concerning major policy issues in the fear that such action would be interpreted by Congress as an encroachment upon their legislative prerogatives. Excessive reliance upon executive orders, therefore, would destroy the harmonious relationship with Congress that is essential to the attainment of other presidential objectives.

Chief Law Enforcer

Presidential power not only has arisen from opportunities to exert leadership that have evolved from custom and tradition, but it has also emanated from obligations imposed upon the President by laws and the Constitution. Article II, Section III of the Constitution, for example, compels the President to assume the responsibility of taking "care that the laws be faithfully executed."[15]

One of the most dramatic challenges to the role of the President as chief law enforcer occurred in 1957 when Governor Orval Faubus sent the National Guard to Central High School in Little Rock, Arkansas, ostensibly to prevent disorders and violence. His action, however, had the effect of blocking school integration that had been ordered by the federal courts in compliance with the Supreme Court decision mandating school desegregation "with all deliberate speed." Both the vagueness of this directive and the threat posed by Faubus' action placed President Dwight D. Eisenhower in an awkward position. To implement the court decision and to protect his own authority, Eisenhower was forced to nationalize the Guard, and he ordered them to ensure the desegregation of the school. As Richard Neustadt has pointed out:

> "Eisenhower could no longer stay his hand in Little Rock without yielding to every Southern governor the right—even the duty to do what Faubus did. These consequences threatened, for the obvious reason that the instant challenge openly discounted the position of the president and bluntly posed the question, who is president."[16]

[15]The charge that Richard Nixon had violated his constitutional obligations to take care that the laws be faithfully executed appeared in each of the three articles of impeachment approved by the House Judiciary Committee on July 27, 29, and 30, 1974.

[16]Richard Neustadt, *op. cit.*, p. 31.

Eisenhower's decision demonstrated that vigorous executive action frequently has been necessary to overcome local resistance and to ensure the implementation of official policies. Perhaps more important, it revealed a reluctance by Presidents to pursue an aggressive course of action in behalf of minority rights. Only when presidential authority was challenged by the conduct of a lesser elected official, did Eisenhower intervene to exercise his constitutional responsibility to enforce the laws.

Commander-in-Chief

The authority of the President to direct national guard troops in Arkansas also was based upon his constitutional responsibility as leader of the nation's military forces. The actions of the President in his roles as Commander-in-Chief and as the principal architect of American foreign policy has sometimes worked the disadvantage of minority groups. For example, the United States exchanged the support of racist colonial policies in countries such as Mozambique for the right to maintain military bases in Portugal. Perhaps even more important to minorities, however, have been the domestic implications of the presidential role in foreign affairs. Presidential support for civil rights measures undoubtedly was stimulated by acts of discrimination perpetrated against black foreign diplomats. In 1957 President Eisenhower invited the finance minister of Ghana to dine at the White House after he had been refused service at a restaurant in Dover, Delaware. A series of similar incidents, especially along Route U.S. 40, which connected Washington and New York, provoked major embarrassment in the Kennedy Administration and increased presidential support for efforts to desegregate public accommodations. The desire to maintain a favorable image in the eyes of the world has forced America to avoid the exposure of acts of blatant prejudice; and perhaps it has contributed in some degree to the extension of minority rights.

White House Advisors

Although discussions of the role of the chief executive often focus on the personality and characteristics of the President himself, the office also has been shaped—for good or ill—by numerous White House advisors who act in the name of the President. The number of presidential aides and the functions they perform have varied according to the desires of particular presidents. Eisenhower and Nixon generally had about twice as many advisors as Kennedy and Truman. Some presidential responsibilities, however, have been institutionalized in specific organizational arrangements within the executive office. In the field of foreign policy, for example, advice to the President is provided by the National Security Council, which includes the President and Vice-President, the Secretaries of State and Defense, the Director of the Office of Emergency

Planning, and other officials invited by the President. A similar Domestic Council was created by President Nixon in 1970 to integrate government policy concerning domestic problems.

Perhaps the most important board concerned with internal issues in the executive office, however, is the Council of Economic Advisers, consisting of three professional economists who inform the President concerning the impact of governmental programs and policies on the nation's economy. The actions and decisions of this board, which was created by the Full Employment Act of 1946, often have had a major impact upon the country's ability to fulfill the terms of this law, which established the absence of unemployment as a major national priority. As a result, the Council of Economic Advisors has been of special concern to minorities.

The increased use of presidential advisors has been necessitated by the growing burdens of the office, but it has raised serious problems concerning presidential responsibility. In 1973 and 1974, criminal indictments were issued against numerous advisors to President Nixon as a result of the break-in of the offices of the Democratic National Committee in the Watergate building.

Although Nixon initially denied personal responsibility for the behavior of his confidants both subsequent hearings on his impeachment and his later confessions of partial blame that led to his resignation demonstrated the difficulty of separating actions of the President from actions of his close advisors. Presidential advisement has depended upon a relationship of trust and confidence, and violations of that relationship have raised serious questions that threaten to undermine not only the expanding role of advisors but also the Office of the Presidency itself.

MINORITIES AND THE EXECUTIVE BRANCH OF GOVERNMENT

The Cabinet

The administrative responsibilities of the President extend far beyond the White House. As the head of the executive branch of government, the President also supervises the activities of cabinet-level departments and the many offices that employ millions of people. The secretaries of major departments, including State, Treasury, Defense, Justice, Agriculture, Interior, Commerce, Labor, Health, Education and Welfare, Housing and Urban Development, and Transportation, form the Cabinet, that also meets to consult with the President on the general activities of the executive branch.

The President sits at the pinnacle of a huge federal hierarchy that has an enormous impact on American society. This vast bureaucratic structure is often unwieldy and difficult to control. But the size and scope of this administrative labyrinth make it one of the most crucial entities in the governmental process. Although the activities of almost all government agencies may have an indirect effect on the rights and privileges of minorities, only a few administrative offices have adopted this problem as a central focus.

Office of Economic Opportunity

One of the most ambitious and controversial attempts to cope with social and economic problems confronting minorities was contained in the antipoverty program launched by President Johnson. Appearing before Congress, Johnson defined the objectives of this program in unconditional terms when he stated, "I have called for a national war on poverty. Our goal is total victory." To fight this war, Johnson proposed legislation creating the Office of Economic Opportunity (OEO), which he located in the Executive Office of the President. In a memo to Sargent Shriver, first OEO Director, Johnson explained, ". . . if I have this program (OEO) in my office, all of the bureaucrats in Washington will be afraid to attack it . . . If we put it out in the bureaucracies, if we let you out there naked, they will cut you to pieces." Johnson feared that the normal inertia of the bureaucracy and its usual reluctance to embark on new ventures would prevent him from accomplishing his lofty aims; and he sought to protect the newly created program from legislative and administrative critics by linking it with the prestige of the presidency.

The OEO legislation provided for 2500 employees in 900 neighborhood offices located in 300 cities. Its aim was to give legal, social, and economic assistance to the poor. In the Nixon Administration, however, OEO was threatened by arguments that its functions could be handled more efficiently by other agencies. After the veto of an earlier bill extending the life of the antipoverty program, Nixon finally took action in 1973 aimed at dismantling the program. Although his actions were stymied by a federal court order, the turbulent history of OEO demonstrated the difficulty of protecting programs designed to aid the poorest and least powerful segments of society. Because of their leadership of the executive branch of government, Presidents have been in a position to act as an advocate for minority rights, but these attempts have been limited both by the resistance of the bureaucracy and by the succession of Presidents who are hostile to such programs.

Presidents, such as Richard Nixon, who have been elected without the support of minorities have had little reason to depart from a policy of benign neglect toward these groups.

Equal Employment Opportunity Commission

Administrative programs not only have been a critical instrument in efforts to improve the status of minorities, but they also have formed a basic means of securing compliance with policies designed to end discrimination. The 1964 Civil Rights Act, for example, established the Equal Employment Opportunity

Commission (EEOC) as an investigatory agency with the responsibility of handling complaints from minorities concerning discriminatory practices in hiring, pay scales, and promotions. Because the Act failed to provide EEOC with the powers necessary to force business firms to comply with federal regulations barring discrimination, the Commission could only smooth over job bias problems. Finally, in 1972, Congress passed legislation enabling EEOC to file suits in Federal District Court against employers who engaged in discriminatory practices. By that time EEOC had developed a backlog of 60,000 cases, and it sought to expand its staff to handle the anticipated influx of additional complaints. Although EEOC won several major victories, including a suit against AT&T which required that firm to spend approximately $38 million in promotion and salaries as backpay for discrimination, its efforts have been frustrated by the perennial bureaucratic problem of overlapping jurisdictions.

Other Agencies

In addition to EEOC several other federal agencies have been responsible for securing compliance with federal regulations barring discrimination. For many years the Civil Rights division of the Justice Department had the authority to file suits against private employers or labor unions, as well as state and local governments that were engaged in a pattern or practice of discrimination. The Civil Service Commission also has the responsibility of reviewing and approving the equal employment policies of all federal agencies. Finally, the Office of Federal Contract Compliance of the Labor Department and similar offices in other federal agencies have enforced the requirements that federal contractors undertake affirmative action to secure equal employment opportunities.

A part of this confusion was created by executive order 11246 in 1965, which "required federal contractors to take affirmative action to ensure that applicants are employed and that employees are treated without regard to their race, color, religion or national origin." Rather than requiring the federal government to demonstrate the existence of discriminatory practices, the active recruitment of minorities was established as a precondition for either securing or maintaining federal contracts. Because there is a tendency for each federal agency to establish its own standards of what constitutes an acceptable level of affirmative action and discrimination, both employers and labor unions have been able to avoid the requirements of the law by claiming a lack of understanding of its standards. Despite efforts to coordinate federal policy the ambiguity created by overlapping jurisdictions has impeded attempts to establish equal employment opportunity.

A similar problem has plagued federal efforts to achieve integration of the nation's public schools. Another federal office focusing on minority problems, which was established by the 1964 Civil Rights Act, was the Office of Civil

Rights (OCR) in the Department of Health, Education and Welfare. Although OCR was authorized to withhold federal funds from school districts that did not comply with court-ordered integration, its ability to fulfill this mandate has been repeatedly frustrated by a lack of consensus concerning standards of desegregation and by political pressures. Peter Libassi, who was OCR Director from 1966–1968, noted that effective desegregation required agreement on a standard of integration and the termination of arguments about it.

Perhaps the major controversy over this office has centered on the requirements of bussing to achieve desegregation. When Nixon was elected in 1968 he announced that since bussing went beyond any congressional mandate, he would oppose proposals put forth by the Office of Education approving bussing. This position was a major factor in forcing the resignation of OCR Director Leon Panetta in 1970. Since both the President and the Secretary of HEW expressed a willingness to negotiate with Southern districts concerning desegregation, Panetta found it impossible to pursue a vigorous campaign on behalf of compliance. Continuing disagreements about minimal standards of integration and a lack of support from key administration leaders have been major factors undermining attempts to implement federal policy concerning equal rights for minorities.

The Bureau of Indian Affairs

Although President Nixon displayed animosity toward programs designed to aid blacks and other minorities in America, he appeared to take a more conciliatory approach to the problems of native Americans. In a special message to Congress in 1970 the President announced a "new attitude toward Indians." Though greeted with skepticism by native Americans, Nixon sought to implement this position by proposing legislation to reorganize the Bureau of Indian Affairs (BIA) and by appointing Lewis Bruce, son of a Mohawk and Sioux, as its director. But the difficulty encountered by the people who sought to make the "new attitude" a reality served as evidence that BIA was as vulnerable to political pressures as other agencies created to advance the causes of the disadvantaged. The possibility of giving "self-determination" to native Americans over their 55 million acres of land was perceived as a serious threat by officials in the Department of Interior and Congress who had traditionally facilitated the use of that acreage by big business concerns interested in timber, strip mining, and grazing.

"... some of the chief usurpers of Indian resources have been Department of Interior agencies themselves, like the Bureau of Reclamation, which has diverted Indian water to non-Indian reclamation projects and built dams that flooded Indian lands, as well as the Bureau of Land Management. The Department—and indirectly the two Congressional committees concerned with its activities—therefore wears two hats. As trustee of Indian resources, it is bound by law to protect

Native American activists during the takeover of the Bureau of Indian Affairs. (United Press International)

tribal holdings; at the same time, its own agencies and various private interests (who, incidentally, have more votes and can contribute more campaign funds than Indians) must also receive sympathetic representation by the Department and its solicitors."[17]

The failure to fulfill the promises of a "New Deal for Indians" ultimately led to the takeover of the BIA in November, 1972 and the occupation of Wounded Knee, South Dakota in 1973 by leaders of the American Indian movement who sought to demonstrate their dissatisfaction with government policy toward native Americans. The obligation of the president to supervise agencies in the executive branch of government that are responsible implementing public policy is but one of the many duties conferred upon the chief executive. Perhaps equally important is his ability to retain the trust and confidence of the Congress and the American people. Although Presidents may, on occasion abuse their powers and fail to meet the standards imposed by society, the Office of the President has continued to occupy the most prominent position among the three branches of government. However, any assessment of the American political system would be incomplete without an analysis of the role of the judiciary, which we shall do in the next section.

• POINTS TO REMEMBER

The President's position atop the federal hierarchy and the growth in the power and prestige of the office, has given him a decisive advantage in the exercise of political influence. The formal wording of the Constitution, provided few hints of the subsequent development of presidential power.

As leader of the people, the President has been more sensitive to the dominant white majority rather than to the quest of minorities to achieve freedom, equality, and justice. Because of his obligation and power to be the leader of his party, initiate legislation, issue executive orders, be Commander-in-Chief, and chief law enforcer, and act as the major figure in submitting a budget to Congress, the President makes decisions that affect the lives of millions of citizens. Therefore, the people seeking to influence governmental decisions are forced to secure the attention and support of the President. Racial and ethnic minorities have been able to accomplish this feat with varying degrees of success, but generally presidents have been reluctant to act on their behalf both because they have been unsympathetic to minority causes and because of fear of reprisal from the dominant white majority.

[17]Alvin M. Josephy, Jr., "What The Indians Want," *New York Times Magazine,* March 8, 1973 (New York: New York Times Company), p. 70.

The President sits at the pinnacle of a huge federal hierarchy that has an enormous impact on American society. A few of the offices have a direct impact on the rights and privileges of minorities. Four of the most important of these include the Office of Economic Opportunity, the Bureau of Indian Affairs, the Equal Employment Opportunities Commission, and the Office of Civil Rights. Though apparently struggling in earnest to improve the relative social and economic position of the nation's disaffected minorities, these offices have encountered enormous opposition within and without the federal bureaucracy.

• SOME UNRESOLVED ISSUES: A DIALOGUE

Holland: We have noted in this section that the nation's attention is focused on the President. There can be little doubt that this is a source of strength. But it may not be apparent that it can also be a tremendous source of weakness. For example, every President from Calvin Coolidge to Richard Nixon, with the exception of Dwight David Eisenhower, has either died in office or left in a cloud of public disapproval. I am led to wonder if the modern-day President can retain the confidence of the American people over an extended period of time.

Hahn: Presidents not only have suffered from overexposure, but they have also become the target of a more general sense of alienation. Large segments of the American public have lost confidence in the entire political process as well as in the President. We should not forget that Americans traditionally have distrusted politicians, and they have regarded politics as a corrupting influence. Recently these sentiments have expanded to include major segments of the white populations as well as minority groups; more important, they have become increasingly articulate.

Holland: As can easily be imagined, the President's day is taken up with people and issues considered to be important both by his closest aides as well as himself. Getting the attention of the President is probably difficult for the vast majority of those groups who seek presidential favors for their particular cause. However, large campaign contributors and other "respected" groups in the society have a much easier time of it than do racial and ethnic minorities. In fact, one of the few ways for the nation's dispossessed to secure presidential attention is through the use of protest which, as we shall see in Section 7, creates as many problems as it solves.

Hahn: Traditionally Presidents have been regarded as a major source of political leadership; but, in the face of a rising tide of alienation, it seems possible that Presidents may not be able to take decisive action for minorities. In order to restore the confidence that the Office of the Presidency previously enjoyed, Presidents may be compelled to follow the wishes of the people rather than to lead them. Thus, I wonder if the increasing use of public pressure and the expression of discontent may become an even more viable method of securing favorable response from the executive branch of government.

Holland: Although minorities have fared better at the hands of the judiciary over the past few decades, there is still a tremendous need to have effective executive leadership, because as we shall see in the next section, the courts can adjudicate but they are not provided with the machinery to implement their decisions.

5 JUSTICE IN AMERICA

The judicial system, which extends from local tribunals to the United States Supreme Court, not only is an important means of controlling the acts of political leaders; but it also provides an opportunity for citizens to affect public policy. In addition to exerting their influence on political parties, legislators, and leaders of the executive branch of government, people can file suit in courts to seek a remedy for their grievances. As a result, many political controversies become legal questions that must be settled by court decisions. Although the issues raised by minority groups have not always been effectively resolved by judges, racial and ethnic minorities frequently have sought to achieve major goals by initiating legal action, and they have probably enjoyed more success in the courts than in any other political arena. The purpose of this section, therefore, is to review some of the major court decisions affecting the rights of minorities in the United States.

POWERS OF THE SUPREME COURT

Judicial Review

Perhaps the principal foundation of the decisive impact that courts impose on other branches of government is the doctrine of judicial review, which was not included in the written Constitution. In the historic case of *Marbury v. Madison* (1803),[1] however, Chief Justice John Marshall of the Supreme Court successfully argued that the Court had the authority to declare legislative and executive acts unconstitutional. The power of judicial review was not used in behalf of minorities for many decades; but, especially after the adoption of the Fourteenth Amendment in 1868, it has been a critical weapon in the arsenal with which minority groups have battled for their rights. Since the Constitution is a living document that must be applied to contemporary situations, the ability of the Court to interpret the meaning of the Constitution is an important prerogative in the American political process.

[1] *Marbury v. Madison*, 1 Cr. 137 (1803).

107

Judicial Activism and Self-Restraint

In deciding legal issues, and in exercising the power of judicial review, courts frequently are caught in a difficult dilemma. While there is little doubt that judicial decisions contribute to the formulation of public policy, many have urged the courts to play a stronger role in resolving political problems and others have advised judges to avoid exceeding their ability to enforce their decisions. The former view is usually identified with the proponents of judicial activism, and the latter position is associated with the advocates of judicial self-restraint.[2] Although increased judicial intervention in social issues generally has been related to the expansion of minority rights, two early cases in American history illustrate the dangers implicit in this approach.

In an attempt to resolve the controversy over land occupied by native Americans in the state of Georgia, the Supreme Court ruled in 1832 that the federal government "had exclusive jurisdiction over Indian lands and that the Cherokees were not within the authority of Georgia law."[3] The decision was contrary to the policies of President Andrew Jackson, and it reputedly prompted an angry Jackson to state, "John Marshall has made his decision, now let him enforce it." Since the Supreme Court does not possess an independent enforcement apparatus, Georgia was able to ignore the ruling and to force its laws on the Cherokees. Without the support of other agencies of government, the Supreme Court is powerless to implement its decisions.

The Dred Scott Case

Although the Supreme Court can refrain from hearing cases that do not attract the interest of at least four of the nine justices, it has occasionally sought to intervene to affect the outcome of critical political issues. In the Dred Scott case of 1857,[4] for example, the Court attempted unsuccessfully to resolve some of the major questions in the controversy that precipitated the Civil War. Dred Scott was a former slave who had been taken to Minnesota for four years and then returned to Missouri, where he argued in court that his residence in Minnesota had made him a free man. In a decision studded with racist assumptions and statements, Chief Justice Roger Tanney applied the doctrine of judicial review to an act of Congress, which might have granted Scott his freedom, and declared that "colored persons were natural objects of slavery." Reactions to the case revealed that the Supreme Court was incapable of ending the furor

[2]Judicial activism usually has implied a willingness to have the courts intervene in deciding controversial political issues; judicial self-restraint has been urged by people who fear that an aggressive role for the judiciary might undermine the authority of the court.

[3]*Worcester v. Georgia*, 6 Peters 515 (1832).

[4]*Scott v. Donald*, 665 U.S. 58 (1857).

over slavery. Although the decision sought to settle the issue by maintaining a sharp division between slave and free states, perhaps its principal effect was to stimulate growing demands for the abolition of slavery.

The Fourteenth Amendment

The major source of constitutional issues affecting the rights of minority groups has been the Fourteenth Amendment, which was adopted after the Civil War and which asserts:

> "No State shall make or enforce any law which shall abridge the privileges or immunities of citizens of the United States; nor shall any State deprive any person of life, liberty, or property, without due process of law; nor deny to any person within its jurisdiction the equal protection of the laws."

Only five years after the ratification of the Fourteenth Amendment, the Supreme Court ruled in the *Slaughter House Cases*[5] that "privileges or immunities" inhered in state citizenship and were not protected by the Fourteenth Amendment. Since this decision virtually nullified the effect of this clause, subsequent cases have revolved around the interpretation of the "due process" and "equal protection" provisions of the amendment

State Action and Private Behavior

In the aftermath of its adoption, however, the Fourteenth Amendment seemed to be of little value to the cause of minorities. Since the amendment provided that states could not deprive persons of their rights "without due process of law," the Supreme Court ruled in a series of decisions that discrimination was unconstitutional only when it was the product of state action rather than of people acting in their capacity as private citizens.

The Civil Rights Cases (1883)

In the *Civil Rights Cases* of 1883,[6] the Supreme Court voided the Civil Rights Act passed by Congress in 1875, which prohibited segregation in public accommodations, on the grounds that this legislation was directed at the behavior of individuals rather than at policies enacted by the states. Although Justice John Marshall Harlan dissented by arguing that "railroad corporations, keepers of inns, and managers of places of public amusement are agents or instrumentalities of the State," this decision was not reversed for more than 80 years

[5] *Slaughter House Cases*, 16 Wall 36. Ironically this interpretation of the Fourteenth Amendment which virtually guaranteed that blacks would not be protected by due process arose out of a dispute involving litigants who had nothing to do with the rights of black Americans.
[6] *Civil Rights Cases*, 109 U.S. 835 (1883).

when the Court had an opportunity to rule again on the issue as a result of the passage of the Civil Rights Act of 1964, which also outlawed discrimination in public accommodations.[7]

Plessy v. Ferguson

Perhaps the most notorious Supreme Court decision of the nineteenth century, however, arose from the case of *Plessy v. Ferguson*[8] in 1896, which tested a Louisiana law requiring railroads to provide "equal but separate" coaches on trains traveling within that state. Homer Plessy, who was seven-eighths white and one-eighth black by birth, was arrested for refusing to ride in the "colored car." Plessy argued that the Louisiana statute denied him rights guaranteed by the Thirteenth and Fourteenth amendments to the Constitution. Since racial segregation in this case was produced by state action rather than by individual practices, the Court was compelled to confront the issue of whether or not the Constitution permitted the states to enact discriminatory laws. The majority opinion of the Court held that such laws were not unconstitutional. Admitting that the purpose of the Fourteenth Amendment "was undoubtedly to enforce the absolute equality of the two races before the law," the decision by Justice Henry Billings Brown contended that "in the nature of things it could not have been intended to abolish distinctions based upon color, or to enforce social as distinguished from political equality, or a commingling of the two races upon terms unsatisfactory to either." He asserted that:

> "If the two races are to meet upon terms of social equality, it must be the result of natural affinities. . . . Legislation is powerless to eradicate racial instincts or to abolish distinctions based upon physical differences. . . . If one race be inferior to the other socially, the Constitution of the United States cannot put them upon the same plane."

Brown argued that "the case reduces itself to a question whether the statute of Louisiana is a reasonable regulation." Using the "established usages, customs, and traditions of the people" as a standard, the nineteenth-century Court concluded that it was reasonable.

The decision provoked a sharp dissent from Justice Harlan, who said, "Our Constitution is color blind." He contended:

> "Sixty millions of whites are in no danger from the presence here of eight million blacks. The destinies of the two races in this country are indissolubly linked together, and the interests of both require that the common government of all shall not permit the seeds of race hate to be planted under the sanction of law. What can more certainly arouse race hate, what more certainly create and perpetuate a feeling of distrust between these races, than state enactments, which, in fact, proceed on the ground that colored citizens are so inferior and degraded that they

---

[7] *Heart of Atlanta Motel v. United States,* 379 U.S. 241 (1964).
[8] *Plessy v. Ferguson,* 163 U.S. 537 (1896).

cannot be allowed to sit in public coaches occupied by white citizens?" Although decisions of the Supreme Court supposedly are confined to questions of law, the majority and minority opinions in this case revealed that the Court was engaged in more than a decision on legal or constitutional issues. By refusing to invoke the Fourteenth Amendment against discrimination that does not entail direct state action and by upholding state laws requiring segregation, the Court, in effect, established a social policy that was maintained for centuries.

THE SUPREME COURT AND MINORITY RIGHTS

For many years, black Americans found it difficult to persuade the courts that the provisions of the Fourteenth Amendment offered important protection of their rights. According to the principle of *stare decisis* ("let the decision stand"), judges have been reluctant to overrule or to reverse prior decisions on legal issues. Ironically, however, the guarantees of the Fourteenth Amendment were extended to another minority in *Yick Wo v. Hopkins* (1886),[9] which involved a San Francisco ordinance refusing a license to laundry owners occupying wooden buildings, a prohibition that had in fact affected only Chinese applicants. In this case, the justice was willing to look beyond the appearance of the law by examining its effects; and the Court concluded this action constituted arbitrary discrimination against a class of people that was a denial of equal protection. There were few Supreme Court decisions in the late nineteenth and early twentieth centuries that granted similar remedies to black citizens. Gradually, however, the foundations were laid for a major change in judicial attitudes toward minority rights.

Jury Trials

One of the first important areas in which the Supreme Court extended the rights of the Fourteenth Amendment to minorities was in criminal trials. Two cases involving jury service initiated this trend. In the 1880 case of *ex parte Virginia*,[10] the Court ruled that a county court judge acting in his capacity as a state official could not systematically exclude qualified black citizens from his list of potential jurors. Similarly, in the same year, the Court struck down a West Virginia statute that explicitly excluded blacks from serving on juries.[11] Although the same principle was not applied to a Southern county that had never allowed blacks to sit on juries, the two early decisions comprised impor-

---

[9] *Yick Wo v. Hopkins*, 118 U.S. 356 (1886).
[10] *Ex parte Virginia*, 100 U.S. 667 (1880).
[11] *Strauder v. West Virginia*, 100 U.S. 303 (1880).

tant precedents for subsequent cases protecting the legal rights of minorities in court.

The Scottsboro Trials

Perhaps the most publicized case involving the right to a fair trial arose from the conviction in 1932 of the so-called "Scottsboro seven," who were sentenced to death for an alleged rape of two white girls in a railroad car in Alabama.[12] In this case, the Court stated:

> "In light of the facts outlined . . . the ignorance and illiteracy of the defendants, their youth, the circumstances of public hostility, the imprisonment and the close surveillance of the defendants by the military forces, . . . and above all that they stood in deadly peril of their lives—we think the failure of the trial court to give them reasonable time and opportunity to secure counsel was a clear denial of due process."

Subsequently, the case was returned for a retrial, and the Supreme Court again reversed their conviction because no black residents within the memory of witnesses had ever served on a jury in that area.[13] In this case, the Court finally displayed a willingness to go beyond procedural formalities and to investigate local circumstances that denied black citizens the rights guaranteed them by the Fourteenth Amendment.

In later decisions, the Supreme Court has invalidated several attempts to prevent blacks from receiving a fair trial and to exclude them from juries, including one practice that entailed putting the names of prospective black jurors on yellow cards and potential white jurors on white cards. In general, if defendants were able to demonstrate that there had been systematic exclusion of black citizens from juries, the state was compelled to present detailed proof to the contrary or have the conviction reversed. While such decisions have strengthened the legal rights of minorities, they have not yet fulfilled the constitutional promise of equal justice under the law. As one commentator observed:

> ". . . Some of the most conspicuous gains the Afro-American made in the three decades after 1938 were won in court actions and in civil rights legislation, both of which—while they hardly improved his housing, his job, or his education in the ghetto—nudged him further down the road at least to the political and civil equality that the Constitution guarantees him. But, ironically, it was precisely in the field of law and administration of justice that he continued to be most frequently foiled. The southern courthouse continues to be the sign and seal of white power over blacks. The symbol is a bastion compounded of laws and ordinances against 'disturbing the peace,' frankly intended to keep the black community under

[12] *Powell v. Alabama*, 287 U.S. 45 (1932).
[13] *Norris v. Alabama*, 294 U.S. 587 (1935).

control; ill-educated justices of the peace, paid on a per-conviction basis; a lack of Negro lawyers; . . . a bail system calculated to keep accused Negroes in their segregated jails until they come to trial; poverty that keeps adequate legal counsel beyond a black's financial reach; courthouses where everyone except the janitor is white; . . . an etiquette, adapted from slavery days, that permits judges and attorneys to address a Negro witness as 'boy,' and to refer to the accused as 'this nigger.' "[14]

How "justice" was once dispensed to black Americans in the South. (Danny Lyon/-Magnum)

[14] *The Civil Rights Record—Black Americans and the Law, 1849–1970,* Bardolph (ed.) (New York: Thomas Y. Crowell, 1970), pp. 526–527.

Although his comments were directed at the treatment of black citizens in the South, many analogous statements could have been made about other minorities located in different regions of the country. As this writer concluded, "A trend to correct these ancient abuses is unmistakeable . . ., but it cannot as yet be characterized as more than a trend."[15]

Voting Rights

Another major field in which minorities achieved early progress concerned the exercise of voting rights. In 1915, the Supreme Court declared the so-called "Grandfather clause" unconstitutional by nullifying a state constitutional amendment in Oklahoma. This state granted the right to vote to all lineal descendents of persons who were entitled to vote on January 1, 1866; but it required all other persons, including black residents, to submit to a difficult literacy test before they could cast their ballots. Since the adoption of the Fifteenth Amendment in 1870 had granted the franchise to citizens regardless of "race, color, or previous condition of servitude," the Court had little difficulty in rejecting this attempt to curtail the right to vote.

The All-White Primary

Similarly, in the 1927 case of *Nixon v. Herdon*,[16] the Court found a Texas law prohibiting black voters from participating in Democratic Party primary elections to be unconstitutional. Since the Democratic nomination often was tantamount to election in many parts of the South, this decision seemed to form an important step toward strengthening the electoral influence of black voters.

Texas, however, responded by attempting to remove state action from the selection of party nominees. In *Nixon v. Condon* (1932),[17] the Court held as unconstitutional an action authorizing the Democratic Party executive to adopt membership rules, which resulted in the exclusion of black voters from the primary. Although white segregationists won a temporary victory in a 1935 case that did not involve state laws affecting primary elections, the Supreme Court finally struck down the all-white primary in the 1944 decision in *Smith v. Allwright*.[18] Primaries were no longer viewed as the elections of a private club; they were regarded as an integral part of the electoral process that required constitutional protection.

Subsequently, the Court has declared a variety of efforts to prevent minorities from voting an unconstitutional violation of the Fourteenth and Fifteenth amendments. Perhaps the most subtle of these attempts was reflected in *Terry*

[15]*Ibid.*, p. 527.
[16]*Nixon v. Herndon,* 286 U.S. 536 (1927).
[17]*Nixon v. Condon,* 286 U.S. 73 (1932).
[18]*Smith v. Allwright,* 321 U.S. 649 (1944).

v. Adams[19] (1953). This case involved an ostensibly private club, known as the Jaybirds, which barred blacks from membership and which conducted straw polls for party nominees to county offices. Although attorneys for the Jaybirds claimed that the polls merely represented an innocent form of entertainment, the club had compiled an amazing record for more than 60 years of predicting that their selections would be party nominees and winners in the general election. As a result, the Court found that the practices of the Jaybirds violated the guarantees of the Fifteenth Amendment.

Decisions of the Supreme Court have reflected an expansion of the concept of state action and the provision of increased protection for voting rights, but they have not eliminated all of the obstacles that were created to prevent minorites from achieving political influence. In many areas of the country, private threats and intimidation replaced public laws and practices as effective deterrents to voting. The greatest increases in the proportion of black adults registered to vote in the South, for example, occurred only after the passage of the Voting Rights Act of 1965, which created a corps of federal examiners to supervise election procedures; and most of those gains were recorded in counties visited by the examiners.[20] The history of minority efforts to express their political sentiments has indicated that extensive and continuing government efforts may be required to ensure the constitutional right to vote.

Housing

The principle of state action also played a prominent role in Supreme Court decisions concerning housing. In 1917, the Court's concern for property rights was used to invalidate two municipal ordinances preventing anyone from moving onto a city block inhabited preponderantly by the other race and requiring the consent of existing residents before a member of one race could move into an area zoned for the other race. In *Corrigan v. Buckley* (1926),[21] however, the Court refused to rule on restrictive housing conventions, which prevented white home owners from selling to minorities, on the grounds that these agreements involved private individuals rather than government action. This ruling was not disturbed until 1948, when *Shelley v. Kraemer*[22] effectively nullified discriminatory covenants by ruling that their enforcement required judicial intervention that was prohibited by the Fourteenth Amendment. In 1953, the Court coupled this decision with a ruling that held that violators of restrictive covenants could not be sued for damages.[23]

[19] *Terry v. Adams,* 345 U.S. 461 (1953).
[20] Joe R. Feagin and Harlan Hahn, "The Second Reconstruction Black Political Strength in the South," *Social Science Quarterly* (June 1970).
[21] *Corrigan v. Buckley,* 271 U.S. 323 (1926).
[22] *Shelly v. Kraemer,* 334 U.S. 1 (1948).
[23] *Barrows v. Jackson,* 346 U.S. 249 (1953).

Although the courts finally recognized that government action played a major role in the perpetuation of many forms of housing discrimination, their decisions did not end residential segregation. Many members of minority groups discovered that their ability to leave the ghetto, the barrio, or other similar enclaves has been restricted by financial obstacles and informal community pressures, which ranged from social ostracism to threats of violence. Despite court action and the passage of numerous federal, state, and local laws to end discrimination in housing, the segregation of minority groups from the white majority has remained the predominant pattern in most American communities.[24]

Public Accommodations

Perhaps some of the most significant Supreme Court decisions on minority rights have resulted from litigation concerning public transportation and accommodations. One of the first occasions on which the court confronted this issue was in the 1878 case of *Hall v. DeCuir*,[25] which involved a Louisiana act passed during the Reconstruction era that required desegregated facilities in public transportation. Under the terms of this law, a black woman, Mrs. De-Cuir, sued the owners of a steamboat on the Mississippi River for assigning her to the "colored" section of the vessel. Noting that the river "passes through or along the borders of ten different states," the Supreme Court ruled that the law was unconstitutional because it entailed the regulation of interstate commerce, or traffic between the states, rather than of intrastate commerce, or transportation within the state of Louisiana. The Court held that the nature of the conveyance required "uniformity" in its rules of governance, which apparently meant uniform racial segregation. Coupled with the finding in *Plessy v. Ferguson* that laws forbidding integration constituted a "reasonable" regulation of transportation within states, the Court decisions permitted racial segregation in both intrastate and interstate commerce.

The Expansion of the Commerce Clause

Gradually, however, the position of the Supreme Court shifted. For many years, the Court had relied upon a restricted interpretation of the "commerce clause," as well as other sections of the Constitution, to strike down legislation to aid disadvantaged groups. During the era of the Great Depression, however, President Franklin D. Roosevelt proposed a plan to appoint additional justices

---

[24]The Court can rule, but the Constitution does not provide it with the machinery to implement its decisions. In an important sense, the Court depends upon its image as fair and impartial arbiter of disputes to maintain its respect among American citizens. This reliance upon "good will" has been a major factor for the people who have advocated judicial restraint.

[25]*Hall v. DeCuir*, 95 U.S. 485 (1878).

to augment several aging members of the Court who had failed to retire. Subsequently, the Court began to approve increased government regulation of property rights and to expand the interpretation of the "commerce clause"[26] until it now encompasses many phases of social and economic activity.

Morgan v. Virginia

The issue of segregation in public transportation was presented to the Supreme Court again in 1946 when another black woman refused to move to the back of a Greyhound bus as was required by a Virginia law. In the case of *Morgan v. Virginia,*[27] the Court outlawed the racist form of musical chairs that had previously compelled black and white passengers to move to different seats when the bus crossed state lines. A majority of the justices held that interstate transportation required a "single, uniform to promote and protect national travel." Unlike the holding in *Hall v. DeCuir,* however, the uniform rule to which the Court was referring demanded integration rather than segregated public transportation.

In a series of subsequent cases, which were brought to the courts between 1955 and 1968, segregation was banned in a variety of public accommodations including swimming pools, beaches, hospitals, hotels, restaurants, and bars.[28] Perhaps the most important of these rulings, however, was the Supreme decision upholding the constitutionality of the Civil Rights Act of 1964, which prohibited discrimination in public accommodations. Although many unfortunate incidents of prejudice continued to be recorded, these cases provided black Americans and other minorities with some assurance that they could enter any public establishment and that they would receive the service accorded other patrons.

Education

Perhaps the most important Supreme Court decisions affecting minority rights were issued in the field of education. After the announcement of the "separate but equal" doctrine in the *Plessy* decision, the Court upheld racial segregation in the schools with undesirable consequences not only for black Americans but also for whites and other minorities. In 1908, predominantly white, sectarian Berea College, which had refused to discriminate in its admissions policies, lost

[26]Congressional authority to enact regulatory legislations has been based upon the phrase in the constitution that empowers Congress to "regulate commerce with foreign nations, and among the several states, and with the Indian tribes."

[27]*Morgan v. Virginia,* 328 U.S. 373 (1946).

[28]For a discussion of these cases see, *The Civil Rights Record: Black Americans and the Law,* 1849–1970, Bardolph (ed.), New York: Crowell, 1970).

its fight against a Kentucky law making it illegal to teach both black and white students unless the two races were kept at least 25 miles apart; the Court held that any institution operating with a state charter was subject to "reasonable" regulations of the legislature that had granted the charter.[29] Moreover, in *Gong Lum v. Rice*[30] (1927), the Court ruled against a Chinese-American in Mississippi who had challenged the state's classification of his daughter as nonwhite, because he wanted her to attend white schools.

Gaines v. Canada

Almost a decade later, however, Charles Hamilton Houston, professor of law at Howard University, who was appointed special counsel to the National Association for the Advancement of Colored People, began an assault on the concept of "separate but equal" in public education that eventually produced a decision of major advancement to the cause of minority rights. Houston's strategy focused on the effort to obtain equal educational opportunities for black students in graduate and professional schools. His first major victory was recorded in the 1938 case of *Gaines v. Canada.*[31] Lloyd Gaines was denied admission to the University of Missouri Law School because of a state law requiring segregation in public education. Although the state offered Gaines a cash grant that enabled him to attend law school in another state, the Supreme Court held that the refusal to admit him was "a denial of the equality of legal right." Gaines disappeared and was never admitted, but the precedent established by his case was an important step toward the realization of equal rights in education.

Graduate and Professional Education

In 1948, the Court required that a black student should be afforded immediate equality in legal training at the University of Oklahoma without waiting for a separate law school for blacks to be built.[32] While this decision prevented segregationists from using the promise of equal facilities as a stalling tactic, even more important was the opinion handed down by the Court in *Sweatt v. Painter* (1950).[33] A black student, Herman Sweatt, who applied to enter the University of Texas Law School, was told that he must accept admission instead at the law school of Texas State University for Negroes. In upholding Sweatt's challenge to the Texas law requiring the separation of the races in public education, the Court considered "those qualities which are incapable of

[29] *Berea College v. Kentucky,* 211 U.S. 26 (1908).
[30] *Gong Lum v. Rice,* 275 U.S. 78 (1927).
[31] *Missouri ex rel. Gaines v. Canada,* 395 U.S. 337 (1938).
[32] *Sepuel v. Board of Regents of the University of Oklahoma,* 332 U.S. 631 (1948).
[33] *Sweatt v. Painter,* 339 U.S. 629 (1950).

objective measurement but which make for greatness in a law school." The criteria of equality involved not only classrooms and buildings, but it also included intangibles such as "reputation of the faculty, experience of the administration, position and influence of the alumni, standing in the community, traditions and prestige."

Similarly, in *McLaurin v. Oklahoma State Regents,*[34] the Court removed the stipulations on the admission of a black student to the University of Oklahoma Graduate School of Education that compelled him to occupy a segregated seat in the classroom, to sit at a separate desk in the library, and to eat at a designated table in the dining hall. The Court stated, "Such restrictions impair his ability to study, to engage in discussions and exchange views with other students, and, in general, to learn his profession." Since McLaurin was studying to become a teacher, the Court also noted that the education of his own students eventually would "suffer to the extent that his training is unequal to that of his classmates."

Equality in Education

The series of Supreme Court decisions affecting graduate and professional education played a major role in undermining the concept of "separate but equal." By insisting upon a strict adherence to a literal meaning of equality, the Court made it physically impossible for segregationists to provide separate and equal educational facilities. But the petitioners who sought to overturn the segregation laws had another purpose:

> ". . . The engineers of the judicial challenges hoped that the courts would eventually find separate facilities inherently unequal, not only because of intangible privations and disabilities that might accrue to the disadvantaged race when they were sequestered in their own institutions, but also because the act of segregation carried with it implications of inferiority and disparagement of the minority race that produced emotional distress, psychic shock, and spiritual anguish. It was precisely that position which the highest court did, in the end, adopt."[35]

The early cases, therefore, were crucial in setting the stage for an historic Supreme Court decision on legal segregation by state action.

Brown v. the Board of Education

On May 17, 1954, the Court finally confronted the issue of segregation in public education directly, in *Brown v. Board of Education,*[36] a unanimous court

[34] *McLaurin vs. Oklahoma State Regents,* 339 U.S. 737 (1950).
[35] Bardolph, *op. cit.,* pp. 270–271.
[36] *Brown et al. v. The Board of Education of Topeka,* 347 U.S. 483 (1954).

held that segregation in the public schools was an unconstitutional deprivation of the equal protection of the laws guaranteed by the Fourteenth Amendment. In assessing the effects of segregation on students in grade and high schools, the opinion of the Court stated:

> "To separate them from others of similar age and qualifications solely because of their race generates a feeling of inferiority as to their status in the community that may affect their hearts and minds in a way unlikely ever to be undone. As a result, the justices concluded that "in the field of public education the doctrine of 'separate but equal' has no place. Separate educational facilities are inherently unequal."

Although the *Brown* decision was widely attacked as an unprecedented legal ruling and as an excursion into social philosophy, its findings that racial segregation tended to produce feelings of inferiority was no more a social argument than the Court's dictum in Plessy that the relationship between the races was characterized by inferiority that could not be eradicated by government regulations. Unlike the latter case that seemed to reflect prevailing racist assumptions of the late nineteenth century, however, the *Brown* decision was supported by extensive evidence, experience, and constitutional principles. Perhaps even more important, the 1954 case had been preceded by a series of holdings that seemed to make the final decision almost inevitable. As one constitutional

"You one of those extremists who thinks it's time for desegregation?" (From Herblock's *STATE OF THE UNION,* Simon & Schuster, 1972.)

authority noted, "the decisions were not an abrupt departure in constitutional law or a novel interpretation of the guarantee of equal protection of the laws. The old doctrine of separate-but-unequal, announced in 1896, had been steadily eroded for at least a generation before the school cases, in the way that precedents are whittled down until they finally collapse."[37]

Implementing Desegregation

In deciding the issue of public school segregation, however, the justices asked the litigants to return to argue the question of how the court might effectively issue a decree to accomplish desegregation. After this rehearing, the Court issued a second opinion in *Brown v. Board of Education*[38] in 1955 that included the infamous statement that the schools must begin desegregation "with all deliberate speed."[39] The Supreme Court left the primary responsibility for approving desegregation plans to the lower courts. The Court stated:

> "Full implementation of these constitutional principles may require solution of varied local school problems. . . . Because of their proximity to local conditions and the possible need for further hearings, the courts which originally heard these cases can best perform this judicial appraisal."

By failing to issue a decree requiring prompt acceptance of their decision, the Court permitted decades of litigation on these issues and numerous delays that prevented the integration of school systems in many areas of the country.

Attempts to Avoid Integregation

Although the attempts to evade or to postpone compliance with the desegregation decision assumed many forms, three of the most prominent efforts to circumvent the ruling included the closing of public schools; the so-called "freedom of choice" plans, which allowed students to attend any school in their district that they chose; and the apportionment of school districts to maintain segregation. In an early plan to avoid desegregation, Prince Edward County, Virginia, closed its schools and claimed that the Constitution did not require the county to provide a public education for its children. Instead, pupils were given tuition grants to attend private educational institutions. In response to a challenge of this policy initiated by black citizens, the federal court held:

[37]Paul Freund, *The Supreme Court of the U.S.* (Cleveland and New York, World Publishing, 1961), p. 173.

[38]*Brown vs. Board of Education of Topeka,* 349 U.S. 294 (1955).

[39]Extensive delays, litigation and controversy concerning desegregation of public schools prompted many observers to note that the Court had allowed the emphasis to be placed on "deliberation" rather than speed.

"By closing the public schools, the Board of Supervisors have effectively deprived the citizens of Prince Edward County of a freedom of choice between public and private education. County tax funds have been appropriated (in the guise of tuition grants and tax credits) to aid segregated schooling in Prince Edward County. . . . We do not hold these County ordinances are facially unlawful. We only hold they become unlawful when used to accomplish an unlawful end."

The Court held that the closing of public schools to preserve segregation was unconstitutional.[40]

The decision in the Prince Edward County promoted another attempt to resist the *Brown* ruling by maintaining a dual system of black and white schools and by permitting students to attend the school of their choice. While the so-called "freedom of choice" plan allowed white pupils to remain in the schools that they had formerly attended, it required black students entering white schools to face the overt hostility of classmates, teachers, and administrators. Through informal pressures and intimidation, segregationists sought to maintain the separation of the races in public education that had prevailed prior to the Supreme Court decision of 1954. In *Green v. School Board of Kent*

The court-ordered integration of public schools in Little Rock, Arkansas in 1956 was marred by violence against blacks. (Burt Glinn/Magnum)

[40] *Allen v. Prince Edward County School Board*, 198 Supp. 497 (E D Va. 1961).

County, Virginia[41] (1968), however, the Court held that the refusal to dismantle separate schools was an unconstitutional denial of equal protection and ordered the school board to "fashion steps which promise realistically to convert promptly to a system with a 'white' school and a 'Negro" school, but just schools."

De Facto Segregation

Perhaps the greatest controversy over the implementation of the school desegregation cases, however, arose concerning the geographic definition of school districts. Since the original decision focused on separate educational systems required by law (de jure segregation), it did not resolve the issue of segregated schools produced by residential housing patterns that divided black and white sectors of the community (de facto segregation). As a result, many Northern cities, in which blacks and whites lived in separate neighborhoods because of residential segregation, felt that they were relatively immune from the requirements of the Court rulings.

In an early case in New Rochelle, New York, however, the courts invalidated the gerrymandering of school districts that "had for more than thirty years drawn and redrawn district lines which would ensure the confinement of Negroes within one particular district."[42] Subsequently, the efforts to end de facto segregation in Northern schools produced numerous—and often conflicting—lower court decisions as well as a major public furor over "busing" and other methods to achieve integrated education. Although Title IV of the 1964 Civil Rights Act authorized the Department of Health, Education, and Welfare to withhold federal funds to school districts that failed to display adequate progress toward desegregation, neither the threat of this administrative action nor extensive litigation in the courts seemed able to settle the issue of integration in the schools decisively. In the face of determined local resistance, government appeared powerless to provide a conclusive answer to the questions raised by the constitutional requirement that all citizens must be granted "equal protection of the laws."

THE COURT SYSTEM

Although minority groups probably have received greater protection of their rights from the courts than from any other branch of government, the decades of evasion and delay following the Supreme Court decision that outlawed segregated schools illustrates one of the principal disadvantages of attempting to secure political objectives through judicial acts. Courts are empowered to adjudicate disputes arising from the laws and the Constitution, but they pos-

[41] *Green v. School Board Kent County,* Virginia 391 U.S. 430 (1968).
[42] Bardolph, *op. cit.,* p. 443.

sess little authority to implement their decisions. Hence, years after the historic decision in *Brown v. Board of Education,* many school systems remained segregated in defiance of the law of the land. Courts were forced to await patiently legal challenges, lengthy arguments, and procedural maneuvers before they could order desegregation in local districts. Moreover, they often found it necessary to obtain the support of the executive arm of government to enforce their rulings. The inability of the judiciary to ensure that its orders would be observed greatly limited its effectiveness as a route to the achievement of political goals espoused by minorities.

State and Federal Courts

Paralleling the difficulties faced by courts in securing the enforcement of their rulings are the problems encountered by litigants in attempting to have their suits decided by the judges. The judicial process is divided into two separate hierarchies, consisting of state and federal courts. In the states, the legal system extends from local or county courts, which handle the major share of all litigation; through state appellate courts, which hear appeals from the court of first instance; to the state courts of highest jurisdiction, which divide major questions involving the interpretation of state laws and constitutions. Since many of the important civil rights cases involved state laws, plaintiffs were required to exhaust the appeals available in state courts before they could enter the federal tribunals.

Federal courts are empowered to hear cases involving federal laws, treaties, and important constitutional questions, as well as disputes between specific parties stipulated by the Constitution and laws. In addition to specialized courts such as the Court of Claims, the Court of Customs and Patent Appeals, the Court of Military Appeals, and territorial courts, the United States courts are organized into district courts, which are located in all areas of the country; Courts of Appeals, which are usually composed of a panel of three judges; and the U.S. Supreme Court. Because the Supreme Court has no obligation to review cases appealed to it, defendants cannot be assured that they will have an opportunity to present their arguments to the highest court in the country, even if their constitutional rights have been violated.

Liabilities of Judicial Action

The problem of obtaining a definitive judicial decision on major issues affecting minority groups is compounded by several practices that are followed by both state and federal courts. In order to discourage the raising of peripheral federal issues, the courts have sought to settle cases, if possible, by state law. Furthermore, even if plaintiffs succeed in introducing a constitutional question, judges usually have attempted to decide the issue on the narrowest

On the few occasions when whites were tried for murdering blacks, especially civil rights workers, there was little need to take the trial seriously. This was true in 1964 in Mississippi when 21 whites were arraigned for murdering civil rights workers. (Bill Reed/Black Star)

possible grounds, and they have been reluctant to overrule previous court decisions. The principle of *stare decisis* ("let the decision stand") has forced the courts to follow the legal precedents established by earlier cases, and it has prevented them from reversing prior rulings. The task of moving a case through the courts is a costly, tedious process beset with many delays and defeats. Court procedures embody a conservative orientation that has produced a disadvantage to litigants who are dissatisfied with the processes of incremental change and who are seeking the adoption of broad standards protecting minority rights.

Advantages of Judicial Action

On the other hand, the judicial system has seemed to offer certain advantages to minority groups. Many observers have contended that minorities should seek to extend their rights through legal action because the courts are relatively insulated from public pressures. Federal justices are appointed rather than elected, and they hold office for life during good behavior. Although national surveys indicate that the public frequently may disagree with specific decisions, they are willing to grant the Supreme Court diffuse support for the interpretation of constitutional provisions. An independent judiciary possesses a broad mandate to decide major issues without consulting public opinion, and minorities frequently have sought refuge in the courts from the hostile attitudes of the white majority.

The judicial branch of government often provides a forum for the presentation of issues that might receive less consideration in other political institutions. Any citizen with a plausible case or a valid complaint cannot be denied access to the courts, regardless of the approval that he can generate among the general public. Some of the most important court decisions have been produced by cases involving unpopular litigants. Furthermore, individual rights are protected in the courtroom by a formal set of rules and procedures and by the adversary system, which is designed to ensure that opposing sides of an issue receive equal and objective consideration. Although the initiation of legal action often is an expensive and time-consuming process, minorities and other segments of the population lacking extensive political support usually can be assured of a fair and impartial hearing in the courts.

Perhaps most important, the courts comprise a vehicle through which minorities can pursue their objectives by asserting a principle rather than by attempting to gain political allies. The sections of the Constitution guaranteeing "equal protection" and "due process of law," and the meaning that was eventually given to those phrases by the courts, form a standard of justice to which minorities can appeal in their efforts to achieve equality and justice. Judicial action often does not require that minorities resort to the tactics of compromise and the formation of coalitions that usually shape political activity in America.

• POINTS TO REMEMBER—JUSTICE IN AMERICA

The Supreme Court of the United States, as established by *Marbury v. Madison*, has the authority to declare legislative and executive acts unconstitutional. But until recently in the history of American jurisprudence, the Court has been extremely reluctant to rule in favor of minority rights. The eighteenth- and

nineteenth-century courts were overwhelmingly against the extension of political and social rights to racial and ethnic minorities. In the Dred Scott Decision
of 1857, for example, Chief Justice Taney declared that "colored persons were
natural objects of slavery." Even after the passage of the Fourteenth Amendment of the Constitution, which specifically sought to give black Americans
equal protection under the laws, the Court still was unwilling to act as an
advocate for minority rights.

One of the first important areas in which the Supreme Court extended the
rights of the Fourteenth Amendment to minorities was in criminal trials in the
1880 case of an *ex parte Virginia*. But it was not until 1932 with the Scottsboro
boys that the Courts spoke with unmistakable clarity about fair trials.

Because judges are relatively insulated from the wrath of public opinion,
minorities have taken the judicial route to securing political rights more than
any other. The most important rulings have come in areas such as housing,
education, voting, the white primary, and public accommodations. While the
Court has been an important instrument by which minorities could precipitate
social change, it has been of limited value because courts lack the power to
implement their rulings. Thus, in the areas of segregated housing and education, the nation remains essentially divided along racial and ethnic lines.

• SOME UNRESOLVED ISSUES: A DIALOGUE

Holland: The recent history of the Supreme Court might leave the student
with the erroneous impression that the Court has essentially acted
as a bastion for the rights of racial and ethnic minorities. In actually, the pro-civil rights stance of the Court has been fairly recent
and there is some indication that it might be ending. From 1954
to 1974, the Supreme Court took a stand that sought to end
segregation in the nation's public schools. However, a 1974 decision involving the city of Detroit and its suburbs the Court ruled
5–4 gainst a bussing plan that would have ended the dual system
of education there. There is considerable doubt in my mind that
the civil liberties gained by minorities over the last 30 to 50 years
will be done away with, and there is no real indication that additional civil liberties will be granted.

Hahn: The resort to the courts is certainly less complicated and difficult
than the intricate prosesses of the formation of coalitions. But the
courts do not offer a panacea.

Holland: I agree. The student should recall that one of the limitations of
judicial action is the inability of the Court to implement its own

decisions. Therefore, securing a favorable court decision is only half the battle.

Hahn: I also feel that the inability of the courts to fulfill the political objectives of minorities is further evidence that insulation from public pressures does not necessarily produce desirable outcomes. Justices of the United States Supreme Court are not elected, and they are not directly accountable to the people. But they are not always sympathetic to the desires of racial and ethnic minorities. In fact, my personal belief is that the major gains of minorities usually have stemmed from intense and insistent public pressure.

Holland: Certainly, public pressure has been an important weapon in the civil rights arsenal; but I hasten to add that it is a weapon that is considerably more effective when it has the weight of law behind it. Therefore, going before the nation's highest tribunal and securing a favorable ruling can add an important impetus to the push to secure civil liberties. Admittedly, taking one's case before the Supreme Court in no way guarantees that you will either be heard or receive a favorable verdict. However, of the three branches of government, the Court has the greatest capacity to issue unpopular decisions.

Hahn: Let me caution you, however, that decisions in the interests of racial and ethnic minorities are not necessarily or always unpopular. Furthermore, important gains have been made by minorities who lack the weight of the law in demonstrations of protest and, in fact, have acted contrary to the law with outbreaks of violence.

Holland: While I would agree that rioters acted contrary to the "law" and that some protestor did not have favorable court decisions on their side at the time of particular protest, I would hesitate to characterize these activities as securing "important gains." These activities will form the focus of the three following sections of the book.

6 JUSTICE IN THE STREETS

Although decisions of the Supreme Court and other judicial bodies define the broad limits within which constitutional governments are required to operate, those judgments often appear to have relatively little impact upon the lives of ordinary citizens. In order to affect personal behavior, policies emanating from legislatures and the courts must be implemented by some other institution of government. As an agency that has wide authority to administer the law and close contact with all segments of society, police officers form one of the most important groups of public officials who assume this responsibility.

The crucial role of law enforcement agencies in the operation of American government illustrates an important facet of the relationship between the people and their political leaders. Politics consists not only of the process by which public demands are communicated to government, but it also encompasses the procedures by which public policies are transmitted to the people. The public must be granted numerous and extensive opportunities to influence political decision makers, *and* their decisions must be applied to social behavior in an effective and impartial manner. Since policymakers are forced to rely upon intermediaries to perform that function, the police occupy a uniquely important position in the political system. Even though law enforcement often is regarded simply as a public policy issue that is similar to other questions such as housing, education, and employment, it is also an important means by which government leaders seek to insure that the public respects their decisions. Hence, the conduct of law enforcement officers constitutes an important linkage between the public and political institutions.

Actions and decisions of the police often are of particular importance to racial and ethnic minorities. The question of minorities has reflected an effort to achieve justice as well as freedom and equality. While pronouncements of the Supreme Court and other major political bodies have been of crucial importance in promoting the progress of minority rights, their statements may have little meaning unless they are accepted by subordinate public officials and translated into specific social changes that affect the lives of minorities. As many leaders have pointed out, justice in the highest courts of the land does not necessarily mean that there will be justice in the streets.

POLICE AND POLITICAL AUTHORITY

The performance of law enforcement duties seems to entail some fundamental questions of social and political theory.[1] The functions of the police, for example, often form an integral element of Max Weber's classic definition of the state as an institution that preserves a legitimate monopoly on the exercise of physical force. Since governments occasionally are confronted by rebel or vigilante groups that seek to usurp the capacity of the state to enforce and administer laws, the police may play a crucial role in the protection of sovereignty. No doubt policy actions would also be ineffectual if citizens did not regard the laws of the state as morally justifiable or worthy of their loyalty and respect; and the conduct of law enforcement officers often is a basic factor in shaping public perceptions of political legitimacy and obligation. In addition, the responsibility of determining the legality or the acceptability of various forms of political expression, and especially unconventional activities such as protests and disorders, often rests with local law enforcement agencies. As the behavior of local sheriffs and the police in the North as well as in southern cities such as Birmingham and Selma have demonstrated, the resolution of this issue may be a critical question for minorities.

The police, therefore, act as a basic extension of public authority. They must assume both the advantages and the liabilities of popular assessments of political institutions. While a favorable image of governmental authority can encourage public compliance with law enforcement officers, policemen also are compelled to accept the burdens of hostile or antagonistic attitudes toward the state. In addition, police behavior can reflect upon governmental institutions. Public approval of police conduct may result in increasing confidence in government, but criticism of their behavior might contribute to the discredit of the state. To the extent that political institutions are regarded as legitimate, people may be willing to comply with the directives of police officers; but the flagrant abuse of police powers might tend to undermine public confidence not only in law enforcement officers but also in the political agencies that they serve.

Fundamentally, the definition of legal and illegal acts is one of the most basic decisions that governments are required to make. By outlawing a particular form of behavior, the state is essentially asserting that such conduct is intolerable or inimical to its basic interests. But the failure to enact legislation prohibiting any type of activity provides an activity with a form of social sanction and legitimacy. Perhaps even more important than the decisions of government authorities, however, are the judgments of policemen on the beat. Persons who are charged with the duty of enforcing or administering the law may not accurately understand the intentions of the political leaders who formulate

[1] Harlan Hahn, "The Public and the Police," in *The Police and Urban Society,* Hahn (ed.), (Beverly Hills: Sage, 1971).

those rules, or they may inject their own personal values and biases into their responsibilities. Although the actions of police officers are subject to scrutiny by the courts, this supervision has little impact upon incidents between policemen and citizens that do not involve violations of the law or the trial of a criminal suspect. For groups possessing relatively little political power such as minorities, therefore, the effort to attain equality in law enforcement may be as important as attempts to alter legal regulations.

Police Discretion

In discharging their responsibilities, law enforcement officers are granted wide discretion. Unlike other private and public organizations, in which executives at the top of the administration have greater latitude than subordinates in lower echelons of the structure, discretion in police departments tends to increase "as one moves *down* the hierarchy."[2] Departmental commanders have few effective means of supervising or controlling the activities of patrolmen in the field. Many critical encounters between citizens and patrolmen, as the representatives of public authority, are not monitered either by their superiors or by other institutions of government.

Furthermore the interaction between police officers and civilians often is hampered by several factors. The basic mission of law enforcement officers, which places a strong emphasis on "fighting crime," compels them to maintain a suspicious posture toward members of the public; and they frequently encounter people who are emotionally distraught or morally vulnerable. Almost by definition, contacts between policemen and the public are usually a result of deviant or abnormal behavior, or the police would not have been summoned to the scene. Law enforcement officers usually confront people in moments of crisis, and they consequently develop a discouraging perspective on human behavior that emphasizes personal weaknesses and foibles rather than man's capacity for kindness and ethical conduct.

Perhaps more important, however, policemen often tend to be sensitive to subtle cues in making their evaluations of personal behavior. The appearance or demeanor of a citizen frequently is one of the most crucial factors determining the action that the police will take in a particular situation. Although social characteristics such as dress, speech, and mannerisms play an important role in those decisions, policemen also use racial or ethnic characteristics as a basis for deciding the appropriate disposition of an incident. Although many policemen attempt to justify this procedure by citing statistical correlations between race, social status, and the rate of crime, the basic tenets of the legal process require that persons must be judged as individuals rather than as members of a social group to which they belong. By allowing such factors to influence their

[2]James Q. Wilson, *Varieties of Police Behavior* (Cambridge: Harvard University Press, 1969).

behavior toward citizens, many policemen have violated a fundamental axiom of justice in the exercise of their discretion. The law stipulates that all members of society must be treated equally and impartially, and police practices that fail to respect those standards by permitting social and racial characteristics to intervene in their perceptions of the public seriously undermine popular respect for both the law and law enforcement officers.

History of the Police

The history of the relationship between police officers and racial or ethnic minorities provides some important insights concerning the tension that has emerged between these two groups. Though law enforcement duties evolved from the "night watchman" system that had been organized in colonial America, municipal police departments were not established in major American cities until the mid-nineteenth-century, when the combined effects of population density and repeated incidents of ethnic or racial conflict made this act necessary. In many Northern cities, friction soon developed between police departments and ethnic groups that emigrated from European countries. Gradually, however, as those groups acquired increasing political influence, police departments became attached to the political organizations or "machines" that dominated many large cities. In 1915, Martin Lomasny, the political "boss" of Boston, authored a compelling rationale for this arrangement when he told reformer Lincoln Steffens, "I think there's got to be in every ward somebody that any bloke can come to—no matter what he's done—and get help. Help, you understand; none of your law and justice, but help."[3] Many white ethnic groups assumed a predominant influence in urban police departments that has persisted during much of the twentieth century. Perhaps more important, the experience of many European ethnic groups with police officers generally entailed the adjudication of minor disputes and the exercise of discretion on an informal basis that emphasized community services rather than the punitive application of the law.

Police in the South

By contrast, in the South, where the preponderant number of black Americans were located during the nineteenth and early twentieth centuries, relationships between the police and minority groups reflected severe antagonism and hostility. The energy and attention of law enforcement officers and of the entire legal system in the South during much of this era was devoted primarily to the punishment of relatively rare offenses committed by black residents against white victims. Crimes involving black victims generally were regarded as unworthy of police interest or concern. Black residents seldom summoned the

[3]Lincoln J. Steffens, *The Autobiography of Lincoln Steffens* (New York: Harcourt, Brace, 1931).

police for assistance in enforcing the law, and policemen made few efforts to solve crimes involving blacks that did not arouse the wrath of the white population.

In general, police officers shared in the predominant attitudes of the country that assigned black citizens to a position of legal and social inferiority. Law enforcement officers often failed to take any action to prevent the lynching of blacks in the South, and they frequently were accused of mistreatment involving black participants in race riots in Northern cities. Since the social structure during this period was based upon prejudice and discrimination, both police action and the law manifested signs of racial intolerance and bigotry.

Police in the North

Gradually, however, as growing numbers of black citizens migrated to the North and as they began to exercise other legal and political rights, their attitudes concerning law enforcement officers reflected some major changes. Perhaps the clearest manifestation of those shifts was evident in the increased willingness of ghetto residents to report crimes that may have been committed by other members of the black community. In fact, the dramatic growth in the urban crime rate since World War II even has been ascribed by some observers to the declining reluctance of black residents "to report crimes against themselves."[4] Although some black Americans continued to regard the police as agents of oppression that acted like an army of occupation in ghetto communities, others slowly began to perceive them as neutral enforcers of the law, and they began to call upon the police for protection against crime and other problems that afflicted them.

Police Professionalism

Simultaneously, police departments in many major cities were beginning to undergo a process of professionalization. One of the major principles of this movement entailed the assignment of police personnel in relation to the amount of crimes reported in different sectors of the community. Hence, the growing volume of crime reports from predominantly black ghettos tended to produce the assignment of increased police manpower to those neighborhoods, which also inspired a cyclical process. The mounting number of patrolmen assigned to minority communities produced an increasing number of arrests, and the growing volume of both arrests and reported crimes stimulated the allocation of even larger numbers of policemen to those areas. As one historian concluded in 1968, "Negro ghettos are . . . more thoroughly and intensively policed today than Irish, Italian, and other ethnic ghettos were two

[4]Daniel Bell, *The End of Ideology* (New York: Free Press, 1961), pp. 155–57.

"Go back to your homes and act like civilized human beings." (From *Wright On!* Copyright © 1971, by Don Wright. Reprinted by permission of Simon & Schuster, Inc.)

generations ago."[5] The presence of expanding numbers of police officers in minority ghettos enhanced the likelihood of uninvited and antagonistic contacts between the police and neighborhood residents. While minorities in northern cities received the benefits of expanded police protection, they were also increasingly exposed to incidents of police malpractice and harassment.

The movement toward police professionalization had numerous other consequences. Unlike the relationship between policemen and ethnic groups in the late nineteenth century, police officers in the twentieth century were trained to enforce the law strictly and to maintain a neutral and impassive attitude toward civilians. Policemen seldom intervened in the black community to provide assistance or support; their role was impersonal and punitive. Because of this orientation and other technological advances such as the patrol car and two-way communication systems, policemen became further divorced from the neighborhoods that they were assigned to patrol. As modern policemen acquired the salary of a white-collar occupation and the prerequisites associated with it such as a home in the suburbs, they found it difficult to understand the culture and the life-styles of inner-city areas. Seen through the windows of a patrol car, the habits and activities of ghetto communities seemed strange and disquieting. Thus, the drive toward police professionalization created an increasing number of barriers between police officers and ghetto communities.

Police Attitudes toward Minorities

Although overt manifestations of racial prejudice have declined among police officers as well as among other segments of the population, the police have displayed little sympathy toward the cause of minority rights. According to a survey conducted among policemen assigned to ghetto neighborhoods in 11 major American cities, 60 percent of those officers believed that black Americans were moving "too fast" in their efforts to achieve equal rights; and only 14 percent felt that their progress had been "too slow." In addition, 75 percent of the white officers assigned to those areas claimed that the activities of civil rights groups had made their work as policemen more difficult.[6] Additional evidence of discriminatory attitudes was disclosed by a Denver survey that revealed that one-third of the policemen in that city believed that black and Chicano residents required stricter law enforcement practices than the dominant white population. Policemen also have voiced strong objections to protest and expressions of discontent that have accompanied minority efforts to

[5]Robert Fogelson, "From Resentment to Confrontation: The Police, the Negroes, and the Outbreak of the 1960 Riots *Political Science Quarterly LXXXIII* (June 1968), pp. 217–47.

[6]Peter Rossi et al., "Between Black and White: The Faces of American Institutions" in *Supplemental Studies for the National Advisory Commission on Civil Disorders* (New York, Praeger, 1968), pp. 103–114.

achieve equality and justice. The survey of ghetto policemen in 11 cities revealed that while only 21 percent ascribed the outbreak of urban violence to the failure of political institutions to resolve persistent grievances, 84 percent felt that the riots were produced by nationalists or militants, 74 percent said that they were the work of criminal elements in the ghetto, and 33 percent claimed that "Negroes are basically violent and disrespectful."[7] Since law enforcement officers usually have focused on the process of locating a specific suspect for a crime, they also may have been inclined to attribute the blame for social problems to personal faults rather than to institutional or structural deficiencies and to deemphasize their role in protecting or expanding minority rights. The predominant values and attitudes of law enforcement officers have tended to widen the gap that separates policemen and racial and ethnic minorities. Although the professionalization of police procedures probably has promoted the adoption of relatively equitable practices in enforcing the law, it has not contributed to an increased understanding or cooperation between law enforcement officers and minority communities.

Perhaps most important, modern police practices have tended to discourage law enforcement officers from becoming familiar with the people whom they are assigned to protect. The survey of policemen who patrol ghetto neighborhoods in 11 major cities, for example, revealed that more patrolmen were familiar with local merchants and the organizers of unlawful enterprises such as crime syndicates, numbers rackets, and drug pushers, than with "important teenage and youth leaders," even though they perceived adolescents and young people as the principal antagonists of the police.[8]The failure of police officers to develop an informal acquaintanceship with the great bulk of residents who live in minority communities has deprived them of an important source of contact and understanding that could assist them in the performance of their duties.

Preventative Patrolling

A critical factor affecting the relationship between law enforcement officers and minority groups has been the practice of "preventive patrolling," which was adopted by many urban police departments. Just as professionals in other fields of endeavor have attempted to adopt interdictive measures, law enforcement officers have placed increasing stress on preventing crimes before they occur. This action usually has entailed the extensive use of "field interrogations," or the questioning of persons in "suspicious circumstances," which is usually undertaken at the initiative of the police officer. "Preventive patrolling" also has involved the use of "stop and frisk" procedures in which a suspect is detained for questioning on the street and subjected to a personal

[7] *Ibid.*, p. 110.
[8] *Ibid.*, p. 113.

search to determine if he is carrying concealed weapons; and it has tended to occur primarily in high crime rate areas, which are inhabited by low-income minority groups.

Police Brutality

The widespread use of "preventive patrolling" in ghetto areas has contributed to the growing resentment among minorities toward law enforcement officers.[9] Numerous surveys in minority neighborhoods have disclosed extensive criticism of police practices and frequent charges of police "brutality" or harassment. The proportion of black citizens who believed that "police brutality" existed in their communities, for example, was reported at 47 percent in the Watts area of Los Angeles, at 43 percent in Harlem, and at 49 percent in the Bedford-Stuyvesant section of New York. Another survey in Denver disclosed that 68 percent of the black residents of that city, 59 percent of the Chicanos, and only 46 percent of the white majority said that they had heard charges of "police brutality."[10] Although these charges often are difficult to document or to prove conclusively, such incidents have undoubtedly occurred. Perhaps even more important, large segments of minority groups believe that they do occur. Since people often act primarily on the basis of their beliefs, those accusations have placed policemen at a major disadvantage in ghetto neighborhoods. The charges of harassment and mistreatment promoted by practices such as "field interrogations," "stop and frisk" procedures, and "preventive patrolling," which tend by their very nature to place policemen and urban residents in antagonistic positions toward each other, undoubtedly have contributed to a decline in public confidence in police practices within minority communities.

The growing tension and hostility between police officers and racial and ethnic minorities have important implications for the governance of society. If people lack confidence in law enforcement officers, they may not be inclinded to inform the police about illegal activities. The inability of the police to obtain information, in turn, can impede their capacity to reduce crime. Hence, the failure of police officers to enforce the law justly and equitably could reduce the ability of the state to maintain its authority within minority communities.

Minorities and Crime

The loss of public trust in law enforcement officers might have serious repercussions not only for police and for the state but also for minority communities. Members of racial and ethnic minorities are frequently the victims of

[9]Harlan Hahn and Joe R. Feagin, "Riot-Precipitating Police Practices: Attitudes in Urban Ghettos," *Phylon*, Vol. 31 (Summer 1970), pp. 183–193.
[10]*Ibid.*, pp. 186–188.

crime; and, like other segments of the population, they must rely upon the police for protection against harm to their lives and property. In general, the burden of crime tends to fall disproportionately upon the poor. Crime seldom crosses racial lines. If the perpetrator of a crime is a black suspect, the victim is also likely to be black. In fact, the residents of low-income minority communities are more frequently the victims of crime than middle-class white neighborhoods. Since crimes tend to be *intra*racial rather than *inter*racial, prevailing white fears that illegal acts may be committed against whites by minority suspects seem to be unfounded. The crimes produced by a history of poverty and discrimination result in the greatest injury to minorities. Since minority groups are more likely than whites to be found at the lower end of the socioeconomic spectrum, they are forced to endure the greatest suffering and deprivation as a result of crime.

Crime Rates

Crime has emerged as a major national problem not only for the white majority but also for racial and ethnic minorities. Moreover, evidence indicates that the reluctance of citizens to cooperate with the police has been a crucial hindrance in efforts to reduce crime. A national survey of the victims of crime in 10,000 households, which provided the only accurate and reliable information on the crime rate in the United States, concluded, "As a whole, there appears to be twice as much major crime as is known to the police." This survey revealed that 51 percent of the victims of crime did not notify a law enforcement agency about the incident. Although low-income, black respondents were more hesitant about reporting property crimes, 55 percent of the crime victims who did not contact law enforcement officers stated that "the most important reason" for their inaction was the belief that "the police would not be effective"[11] Obviously, the police have been able to do little in solving crimes whose existence they were unaware of. The amount of public confidence vested in the police perhaps has been the single most important factor affecting the ability of law enforcement officers to fulfill their responsibilities.

The Fear of Crime

Both members of the white majority and racial and ethnic minorities have expressed an increasing fear of crime. The national survey of criminal victimization disclosed that one-third of all Americans felt unsafe about walking alone at night in their own neighborhoods; and in some communities of the country, such as Brooklyn, this fear has apparently gripped almost half of the

[11]Phil Ennis, *Criminal Victimization in the United States: A Report of a National Survey* (Washington: Government Printing Office, 1967).

population. Another survey of Boston and Chicago neighborhoods found that 61 percent of the residents reported that they had changed their personal habits, because of a fear of crime, by staying off the streets at night, avoiding being out alone, refusing to talk to strangers, installing new locks on their doors, or carrying weapons.[12] By interfering with the ordinary routines of everyday life and by generating a public hysteria about "law and order" that was often directed against minority groups, popular anxieties about crime have had a major impact upon American society. The increasing fear of crime apparently has tended to undermine popular confidence in public authority and in law enforcement officers. A national survey that asked respondents whether they felt the protection of their lives and property was a personal responsibility or an obligation that could be delegated to the police revealed that almost two-thirds of black Americans and more than half of the whites believed that they had "to be prepared to defend their homes against crime and violence" rather than leaving this duty to the police. Among whites, this reluctance to trust the ability of the police to provide adequate protection against crime was significantly related to several other characteristics including gun ownership, the opinion that policemen should use more repressive measures to control urban violence, and to the belief that ghetto rioting represented an effort by blacks "to take over the cities."[13] The implications of those findings not only disclosed the threat that the issue of crime might become the basis of increasing polarization between minority groups and the dominant white majority, but also implied the danger of armed attempts by whites to usurp police prerogatives.

Mounting public hysteria produced by the fear of crime ultimately may create severe problems for law enforcement agencies. For many years, the alleged growth of the crime rate has been cited by public officials as a major justification for the allocation of increased public resources to law enforcement agencies. Yet, police departments have little control over many factors that contribute to the crime rate, such as population growth as well as social and economic deprivation. Perhaps one of the major sources of crime, for example, is poverty; but this problem seldom has been mentioned by police officers as a major explanation for crime, and the activities of law enforcement agencies have had relatively little impact in improving the social and economic status of disadvantaged groups. Even though many of the principal reasons for the apparent increase in crime may lie outside the scope of police responsibilities, law enforcement agencies may be subjected to increasing public criticism for their failure to reduce or to eliminate illegal acts. Growing public concern about crime, therefore, could ultimately redound to the disadvantage of police departments.

[12]Albert Reiss, Jr., *Studies in Crime and Law Enforcement in Major Metropolitan Areas* (Washington: Government Printing Office, 1967).
[13]Joe Feagin, "Home Defense and the Police" in *The Police and Urban Society*, Hahn (ed.), *op. cit.*

Minorities and Police Protection

Public anxiety about crime has been reflected in minority criticism not only of police brutality and harassment but also of inadequate police protection. A survey of white and black attitudes in 15 American cities revealed that while approximately one-third of the black residents and only one-sixth of the whites complained about the use of insulting language, unjustifiable searches, and unnecessary physical force, a majority of the black inhabitants of those cities —and only about one-fourth of the whites—stated that the police did not arrive promptly when they were called for help.[14] This pattern also has been discovered in other communities. As the National Advisory Commission on Civil Disorders concluded, "Surveys have reported that Negroes in Harlem and South Central Los Angeles mention inadequate protection more often than brutality or harassment as a reason for their resentment toward the police."[15]

A major source of these complaints has been the widespread perception among minorities of differential police protection for various sectors of the community. The survey in Denver found that 56 percent of the black residents, 47 percent of the Chicanos, and only 20 percent of the whites believed that personal status affected how people were treated by the police; and most of the blacks and Chicanos felt that "rich and influential people."[16]

Perhaps the emphasis in many cities on "preventive patrolling," which has stressed aggressive efforts to stop and search suspects on major streets in areas with high crime rates, also has diverted police manpower from the investigation of the many complaints for minor crimes that occur in residential neighborhoods of minority communities. Moreover, such perceptions apparently have been a major deterrent to a public cooperation with the police. A study conducted in a Detroit ghetto disclosed that persons who perceived major inequalities in the amount of police protection granted to various sectors of the community also were less likely to contact the police in a variety of everyday circumstances.[17] The implications of this research revealed that efforts to increase police protection and to provide equitable protection for all areas of the city might promote an increased willingness to assist police officers in the performance of their duties. Since most crimes are solved on the basis of information provided by civilians, extensive public cooperation may be an essential prerequisite to the performance of law enforcement responsibilities. Efforts to arouse increased public trust in police activities in ghetto communi-

[14]Angus Campbell and Howard Schuman, "Racial Attitudes in Fifteen American Cities" in *Supplemental Studies for the National Advisory Commission on Civil Disorders* (New York, Praeger, 1968), p. 44.

[15]*National Advisory Commission on Civil Disorders: Report of the National Advisory Commission on Civil Disorders* (New York, Bantam, 1968), p. 162.

[16]Bayley and Mendelshon, *op. cit.* pp. 112–113.

[17]Harlan Hahn, "Ghetto Perceptions of Police Protection and Authority: *Law and Society Review.*

ties, therefore, may be one of the most important objectives confronting law enforcement agencies.

Minority Policemen

One method that has been proposed to promote cooperation between police-men and the public requires the recruitment of increased numbers of minority officers, especially in neighborhoods inhabited by the same racial or ethnic group. Although no evidence has indicated that those officers tend to be either more strict or more lenient with minority suspects, a survey of patrolmen in 11 major cities revealed that black officers in ghetto areas were acquainted with a larger number of local leaders and residents of the area than white officers.[18] Another study in Boston, Chicago, and Washington found that 89 percent of the black patrolmen and only 20 percent of their white colleagues claimed that it was easy to get to know people on their beats.[19] In most cities, however, the number of minority policemen has not reflected their proportion of the local population. The entrance of minorities into the police, and their promotion within departments, has been a relatively slow process. While the recruitment of minority officers might assist in the development of increased public under-standing between the police and the community, in most cities those officers have not been available in sufficient numbers to fulfill this responsibility.

Police and the Judiciary

Although the conduct of police officers plays a crucial role in the administra-tion of justice, many of their activities are at least theoretically subject to the supervision of local courts. Those judicial bodies have the responsibility of ensuring that police practices conform to the guidelines established in the American legal system. As a result of the historic 1966 decision of the United States Supreme Court in *Miranda v. Arizona*,[20] for example, policemen are required to inform persons at the time of their arrest of their right to remain silent, that anything they say can be held against them, and of their right to obtain an attorney, which will be provided by the state if they cannot afford one. In addition, the doctrine of the so-called "exclusionary rule" has pre-vented local courts from admitting evidence that was illegally seized by the police. As a result, the courts frequently have been regarded as a major agency of the government responsible for the control of police behavior.

The relationship between law enforcement agencies and local courts, how-ever, raises some critical questions concerning not only the accountability of

[18]Rossi, *op cit.*
[19]Reiss, *op cit.*
[20]*Miranda v. Arizona*, 384 U.S. 436 (1966).

police activities but also the effectiveness of the judicial system. In many courts, the guarantee of equality before the law may be undermined by several factors, including overloaded facilities, prolonged detention, the difficulty of acquiring bail, inadequate legal defense, variable sentencing practices, and similar problems.[21] Since courts frequently find that they cannot handle or process the large number of criminal cases that are brought before them, they are not in an effective position to supervise police activities. Moreover, approximately 90 percent of all criminal charges in the United States are determined by a plea of guilty. The initial decision by a police officer to arrest the suspect frequently constitutes a final determination of his fate. In such cases, as well as in a large number of other incidents that do not produce an arrest or that do not receive adequate investigation because of pressures on attorneys and the courts, the activities of policemen are not exposed to extensive judicial supervision or control. As a result, the judicial branch of government seldom occupies a position that would enable it to undertake a comprehensive assessment of the activities of law enforcement agencies.

Civilian Review Boards

Another attempt to secure the increased accountability of police actions was reflected in the movement to establish civilian review boards in major urban police departments. Although this proposal aroused intense opposition and hostility among law enforcement officers, it also failed to receive widespread public support. Since plans for the civilian review boards were specifically limited to the investigation of cases of alleged police misconduct or malpractice in encounters with civilians, they did not provide for a thorough examination or supervision of police practices. Hence, the impetus for the establishment of civilian review boards has appeared to suffer a major decline.

In both existing institutions and proposals for structural changes, therefore, have offered either a comprehensive solution to the problem of crime or an effective means of promoting increased confidence in the police. As an agency that has placed major emphasis on social control and on efforts to combat crime, the police frequently have appeared to assume the role of an opponent rather than a champion of minority rights. Although police departments might be able to improve their image in minority communities by placing increased emphasis upon community services rather than upon punitive responsibilities, law enforcement officers have exhibited little interest in securing this objective. At the grass roots level, therefore, the effort to secure "justice in the streets" has revealed another critical deficiency in the American political process.

[21]Leonard Downie, *Justice Denied: The Case for Reform of the Courts* (New York: Praeger, 1971).

• POINTS TO REMEMBER

Police officers form one of the most important group of public officials who
have the responsibility of implementing policies emanating from legislatures
and the courts. Since the state preserves a legitimate monopoly on the exercise
of physical force, the policy may play a crucial role in the protection of this
monopoly from groups that seek to usurp the power of the state. While the
actions of police officers are subject to scrutiny by the courts, this supervision
has little impact upon incidents between policement and citizens that do not
involve violations of the law or the trial of a criminal suspect.

The history of the relations between the police and various ethnic groups
is one of friction and hostility. In the South during the nineteenth and early
twentieth centuries, the legal system was devoted primarily to the punishment
of relatively rare offenses committed by black residents against white victims.
As black Americans moved to the urban centers and as police departments
underwent professionalization, the incidents of police malpractice and harassment of blacks rose dramatically. Police tended to perceive their role in black
communities as punitive and impersonal rather than helping or supportive. In
addition, the attitude of white policemen toward the civil rights movement has
been generally hostile.

The use of "preventative patrolling" has tended to aggrevate relations between the police and racial and ethnic minorities. The failure of police officers
to enforce the law justly and equitably could reduce the ability of the state to
maintain its authority within minority communities. The increasing fear of
crime throughout the nation has tended to undermine popular confidence in
public authority and in law enforcement officials. Control and supervision of
police behavior has been largely ineffective.

• SOME UNRESOLVED ISSUES: A DIALOGUE

Holland: Various public opinion surveys have indicated that ghetto residents in many respects are very much in support of "law and
order." That is, given that the crime rate in various ghetto neighborhoods remains quite high, the residents there are interested in
adequate police protection. Yet it has also been demonstrated that
the relationship between ghetto residents and police departments
continues to deteriorate. In the past the police have had an excellent opportunity to provide a much needed service to a particular
segment of the American population. Yet in their understanding
of law enforcement they have gone a long way toward perpetuat-
ing tension between themselves and the community.

Hahn: While not denying that racist attitudes have been expressed by policemen in ghetto areas, I feel that many of the problems also have been promoted by a mentality that has been almost exclusively with the effort to "fight crime." Extensive research has demonstrated that the ability of the police to arrest or convict a criminal suspect usually depends upon the willingness of members of the community to provide information leading to that outcome. Hence, in the long run, the ability of the police to enforce the law must depend upon the willingness of the public to cooperate with the police. In fact, one study clearly demonstrated that ghetto residents who believed that there was equality of police protection against crime were more willing to cooperate with the police than those who perceived inequities or inequalities in police protection. Thus the ability of the police to enforce the law may depend upon their ability to develop effective relations with the community through other activities such as community services.

Holland: In large measure, the difficulty in building positive police community relations rests with the contemporary practice of having the policemen belong to communities other than the ones they are policing. This frequently leads to the feeling that "the police are not of the community and, therefore, do not particularly have the community's interests in mind in their behavior." Effective law enforcement requires the participation of community members in the surveilance of the property in their own neighborhoods. This responsibility of course must be balanced between people's right and need for privacy.

Hahn: Nonetheless, the police occupy a critical role in the community and in the relationship between the citizen and government. In this respect, this section on the police, which is located between the discussion of the courts and the discussion of protest and violence, has theoretical as well as symbolic significance. The police are fundamentally the principal agents of government responsible for the complementation of society's concept of justice in the streets.

7 PROTEST

In addition to the channels of communication provided by the courts, legislatures, parties, interest groups, and executive branch of government, minorities often have resorted to other methods of attempting to exert political influence. Institutions established by the Constitution have not exhausted the vehicles available to groups that seek to improve their status in society. Perhaps the most prominent alternative forms of political expression have been marches, demonstrations, and other displays of protest. Despite frequent charges that such tactics are either irrational or contrary to basic values, the skillful use of protest has been—and continues to be—a crucial means of accomplishing major political objectives.

THE CONSTITUTIONAL BASIS OF PROTEST

The First Amendment

Although many observers have regarded protests and similar manifestations of discontent as an unconventional style of politics, the constitutional basis for this action can be traced to the Bill of Rights, or the first 10 amendments, which were adopted soon after the ratification of the Constitution. The first of these amendments states:

> "Congress shall make no law respecting the establishment of religion, or prohibiting the free exercise thereof; or abridging the freedom of speech or of the press; or the right of the people peaceably to assemble and to petition the government for a redress of grievances."

In guaranteeing freedom of speech and the right of assembly, the First Amendment establishes another important principle to which minorities can appeal in their efforts to influence the decisions of policymakers.

Free Speech

While some judges and legal commentators have argued that the Bill of Rights was designed as an absolute prohibition against any law that might restrict freedom of speech, the Supreme Court generally has held that the First Amendment offers only relative protection for these rights. In *Schenck v. United States* (1919),[1] Justice Oliver Wendell Holmes announced an important test for determining whether or not a statute infringed on freedom of speech when he stated, "The question in every case is whether the words are used in such circumstances and are of such a nature as to create a clear and present danger that they will bring about the substantive evils that Congress has a right to prevent." The Court subsequently upheld state legislation designed to protect governments from acts that might have a "bad tendency" to produce undesirable results. In the 1951 case of *Dennis v. United States*,[2] however, the Court employed a modified version of the "clear and present danger" test to sustain the conviction of 11 leaders of the American Communist Party for violating the Smith Act of 1940, which made it illegal to advocate the overthrow of the government by force or violence. Although limitations on free speech have arisen most commonly in cases involving obscenity or the threat of violence, the Supreme Court has not interpreted the language of the First Amendment as granting total immunity to act or speak without regard for the rights and safety of others.

The Right of Assembly

The reluctance of the courts to provide absolute protection of free speech also has been evident in decisions concerning the manner in which people can express their political grievances. In a series of cases, the Supreme Court implicitly utilized the principle forbidding "prior restraint,"[3] which was designed to prohibit censorship of the press, and to invalidate state and local statutes that had resulted in the denial of permits to public speakers for persons soliciting members for an organization. State and municipal officials could not arbitrarily prevent the publication of a newspaper or the appearance of a speaker, but they apparently had the right of enacting ordinances and of arresting speakers to prevent public disturbances and disorders. In *Feiner v. New York*[4] (1951), for example, the Supreme Court upheld the conviction of a speaker who had been arrested for refusing to stop his denunciations of public officials and the American Legion, after unrest and threats had developed in a small crowd clustered around him. Although state statutes forbidding peaceful picketing were declared an unconstitutional abridgement of freedom of speech in an 1840 decision,[5] this doctrine was subsequently modified to permit

---

[1] *Schneck v. United States*, 249 U.S. 47 (1919).

[2] *Dennis v. United States*, 341 U.S. 494 (1951).

[3] Prior restraint means that governments cannot forbid the publication or dissemination of any material before its appearance. Any other action would involve a prejudgment.

[4] *Feiner v. New York*, 340 U.S. 313 (1951).

[5] *Thronhill v. Alabama*, 310 U.S. 88 (1940).

In 1963 the right of assembly when applied to black Americans meant little in Birmingham, Alabama. (Charles Moore/Black Star)

limitations of picketing when violence accompanied it or when it was used to achieve a unlawful objective.

The Supreme Court and Protest Demonstrations

The interpretation of the right of assembly became especially significant as minorities increasingly resorted to protest in their efforts to achieve important political goals. In several cases rising from demonstrations against discriminatory laws and practices, the Supreme Court reversed the conviction of black demonstrators for breach of the peace or disorderly conduct as an infringement upon their right of free speech, free assembly, and freedom to petition the government for a redress of grievances. Subsequently, however, it became clear that the right to protest was limited. In *Cox v. Louisiana* (1965),[6] the Court reversed the conviction of several black protestors; but it warned that "the right of peaceful protest does not mean that everyone with opinions or beliefs to express may do so at any time or at any place." Eventually, in *Adderley v.*

[6] *Cox v. Louisiana,* 379 U.S. 559 (1965).

Florida[7] (1966), the Court upheld the right of the police to disperse a crowd that had gathered in front of a jail. Even when they are subjected to judicial scrutiny, state and local law enforcement officers possess extensive power to control protest demonstrations. Although the outcome of legal cases frequently depended upon specific circumstances and events, Court Decisions have consistently failed to grant an unlimited right to engage in protest.

THE NATURE OF POLITICAL PROTEST

Despite the legal restrictions that have beem imposed, minorities frequently have used protest demonstrations as a means of publicizing their grievances. As Michael Lipsky has observed:

> "The list of protest episodes familiar to even the casual observer is long: the sit-ins; the freedom rides; the Mississippi Freedom Summer; the March on Washington; the Poor People's Campaign. There have been march-ins, read-ins, wade-ins, study-ins, and kneel-ins for desegregation. There have been boycotts of goods for jobs and boycotts of schools for a variety of educational goals. There have been rent strikes for better housing and migrant workers' strikes for better working conditions. . . . These political events shared common themes; they were engaged in by relatively powerless groups. The explanation for the popularity of protest among minority groups was clear. Unlike segments of the dominant white majority, minorities frequently have been unable to compromise their demands or to attract the support of powerful allies. Protests have been a major recourse available to groups that lack the influence to engage in other forms of political activity."[8]

Basically, groups engage in protest in an effort to develop resources[9] that are necessary for bargaining. While the targets of protest usually have sufficient resources to bargain effectively, protesting groups such as minorities must develop those resources. The initiation of protests, therefore, represents an effort to change the bargaining power of opposing groups, or their ability to engage in a mutually profitable exchange of compensations. Without the resources created by a protest, relatively powerless groups such as minorities would have little to trade for favorable treatment by influential segments of the population.

[7] *Adderly v. Florida*, 385 U.S. 39 (1966).

[8] Michael Lipsky, *Protest in City Politics*, (Chicago: Rand McNally, 1970), p. 1.

[9] In this kind of situation, resources can be both tangible and intangible. If, for example, the target of a protest felt that there were "significant" others in the population who might come forward to exert pressure on behalf of the protestors, this would constitute an intangible resource. If, on the other hand, the protestors themselves were of sufficient numbers to inflict damage directly on the target, they would, at that point, possess tangible resources.

Protest and Incentives

The successful outcome of bargaining can be obtained by supplying either positive or negative incentives. Positive incentives exist when the desired action is made absolutely more attractive and not because other possible results have been made less appealing. Rational persuasion and appeals to conscience might be considered examples of positive incentives. When influential groups agree to grant the demands of their opponents because they regard their arguments as logically compelling or morally justifiable, they may be motivated by positive inducements rather than by a fear of unfavorable consequences. By contrast, a negative incentive is provided if the desired action, "although no more attractive absolutely than before the change was made, is nevertheless more attractive relative to other possibilities that now exist."[10] People often may be prompted to bargain or to compromise with their opponents by the threat that the failure to take this action would cause them to suffer major losses or undesirable results. Resources are created by protestors as a result of their ability to jeopardize something that is valued by the targets of the protest.

Protest can be defined as "the exclusive use of negative inducements which rely for their effect on sanctions which require mass action."[11] Protest usually does not produce a direct trade in which the results demanded by the protestors are exchanged for the withdrawal of pressure. Instead, protests often comprise an indirect process that seeks to activate external groups that, in turn, will influence the targets of the protest. Protestors seldom can develop sufficient resources of their own to produce a bargaining situation. Minorities often launch protests not only to attract attention to their plight, but also to enlist the assistance of groups that are capable of generating more influence than they can muster.

PROTEST DEMONSTRATIONS: CASE STUDIES

The 1941 March on Washington

An example of both the advantages and the limitations of protests was provided by one of the first prominent attempts to organize a demonstration by minority groups in America. In January 1941, A. Philip Randolph, president of the Brotherhood of Sleeping-Car Porters, which was the only all-black labor union in the United States, called on 10,000 black Americans to march on

---

[10]James Q. Wilson, "The Strategy of Protest: Problems of Negro Civic Action," *Journal of Conflict Resolution*, Vol. V., (September 1961), p. 292.

[11]*Ibid.*, p. 294.

Washington, D.C., to protest discrimination in the Armed Services and in defense industries. Although the War Department reaffirmed its policy of refusing "to intermingle colored and white personnel in the same regimental organizations," President Franklin D. Roosevelt and his wife had already expressed their opposition to prejudice by making the Lincoln Memorial available for a concert by black contralto Marian Anderson after the Daughters of the American Revolution had refused to allow her to sing in Constitutional Hall.

Plans for the March on Washington, therefore, presented both the leaders of the March and the Roosevelt Administration with a difficult dilemma. Since the President had announced his intention to send military aid to Great Britain, there was a danger that the March might have been construed by the public as undermining the war effort. On the other hand, the March threatened to be a major source of embarrassment to President Roosevelt, which he could avert either by sending troops to quell the demonstration or by acceding to the demands of the protestors.

Eventually, the President chose to bargain with the protest leaders. In exchange for a promise to call off the March, Roosevelt issued Executive Order 802 on June 25, 1941, establishing the Fair Employment Practices Commission to investigate charges of discrimination in defense-related industries. Although Randolph was widely criticized for compromising with the President, the creation of the Commission did represent major progress in expanding employment opportunities for minorities. In the circumstances of 1941, the threat of embarrassment to a sympathetic administration produced sufficient resources to enable black Americans to secure a major political objective.[12]

The Montgomery Bus Boycott

Although some protests have been organized by prominent leaders as a deliberate challenge to public or private organizations, other demonstrations have emerged as a spontaneous display of frustration and discontent. Perhaps the most well-known example of an unplanned protest that produced major success for minority groups was the Montgomery bus boycott that began on December 1, 1955, when Mrs. Rosa Parks, a black seamstress who was returning home from work, refused to yield her right to a seat on a local bus to white passengers. Her action symbolized and crystallized the feelings of millions of black Americans. As a result, when Mrs. Parks was arrested and fined 14 dollars for violating a municipal code that required segregated seating on public transportation, the incident became the impetus of an eight-month boycott of

[12]For a more extensive discussion see Herbert Garfinkel, *When Negroes March,* (Glencoe, Ill., The Free Press, 1959).

Montgomery busses that catapulted several leaders including Dr. Martin Luther King, Jr., into national fame.[13]

Subsequent stages of the boycott illustrated the difficulties of conducting a sustained protest. Boycott leaders prepared a list of demands calling for more courteous treatment of black passengers; employment of black bus drivers; and the initiation of a policy requiring that passengers be seated on a first-come, first-served basis. Plans were made to create a car pool and to charge a small fee to defray costs. This proposal was held to be in conflict with a city ordinance requiring the operators of public conveyances to charge a minimum fee of 45 cents. Although it cost approximately $5000 a week to provide transportation, funds for this purpose were raised among sympathizers with the boycott outside the community. Without this financial support from external groups, it would have been difficult to continue the protests.

City officials also responded with a variety of actions that were designed to frustrate the objectives of the boycott. Initially they attempted to reduce its economic impact by raising the bus fare from 10 cents to 15 cents. Since white riders comprised only about one-fourth of the bus company's patronage, the increased fare failed to offset the losses produced by the absence of black

In December 1956 after a year-long boycott, Martin Luther King and Ralph Abernathy are among the riders on a Montgomery, Alabama bus. (Wide World)

[13]The Montgomery boycott served as an impetus for the founding of the Southern Christian Leadership Conference, which became one of the most prominent civil rights organizations in the country until the assassination of its leader, the Reverend Dr. Martin Luther King in 1968.

passengers. Second, the city sought to negotiate a compromise by agreeing to treat black passengers more courteously. Since this proposal offered no specific or tangible gains for the protestors, it was rejected. Finally, several malicious rumors about protest leaders were circulated in an effort to break the boycott. In response, Dr. King and others held a series of mass meetings to bolster morale and to prevent any dissension from arising within the black community.

When it became clear that alternative methods of ending the boycott had failed, the city launched a repressive policy of harassment. Legal action to halt the boycott was filed in court, and local police began arresting car-pool drivers for alleged traffic violations. The conflict escalated when the homes of two of the major organizers of the boycott, Dr. King and E. D. Dixon, were bombed. Despite the intimidation and violence, however, the boycotters remained determined to continue the protest to a successful conclusion.

The combination of effective protest and court litigation challenging the constitutionality of municipal codes requiring segregation produced a major victory for civil rights activists in the Montgomery boycott. Perhaps the principal factor in the success of this protest was the economic effect that it had upon the city. Estimates indicate that the boycott was 95 percent effective among the 25,000 black passengers who ordinarily rode the buses of Montgomery. Since those black passengers formed three-fourths of the patrons of the bus company, failure to grant the demands of protest leaders might have produced economic ruin for public transportation in the city.

The gains produced by the boycott demonstrated the importance of protest as a means of initiating negotiations. Prior to the boycott, black residents of Montgomery had few resources with which to bargain. After they had withdrawn their patronage of the bus company, however, the city was forced by economic considerations to confront their demands.[14] In addition, negative incentives seemed to play a major role in the resolution of the conflict. The bus company did not change its policy because this change became logically or morally attractive; the change was made because the alternative of permitting the boycott to continue was less desirable than granting the demands of the protestors. Furthermore, the leaders of the boycott were compelled to depend, to a large extent, upon external help. Both the pressure of public opinion that was focused upon the city of Montgomery and the financial assistance of outside supporters was needed to accomplish their objectives. Even in the favorable situation of the Montgomery bus boycott, the protestors were unable to develop sufficient resources of their own to produce meaningful bargaining.

[14]Even with the direct economic threat posed to the bus company by the boycott, a court suit was necessary to break the back of segregation in Montgomery. Thus, one should hesitate to conclude that SCLC was, by itself responsible for ending segregation in public transportation facilities in that Southern city.

Sit-ins and Freedom Rides

Despite the difficulties entailed in this strategy, protest demonstrations became a major means of advancing the cause of civil rights during the 1960s. A major impetus for this movement occurred on February 1, 1960, when a group of black college students in Greensboro, North Carolina, staged a sit-in at a segregated lunch counter by refusing to move until they had been served. Within six months, sit-ins had been held in many states of the South and in the North as well. This action was followed by a series of peaceful marches and "freedom rides" protesting segregated facilities in public accommodations. Combined with dramatic incidents of police mistreatment of protestors in many localities such as Birmingham and Selma, Alabama, these demonstrations aroused the conscience of America and heightened demands for an end to segregation.[15]

Freedom rides in the South were dangerous undertakings that needed military escorts. (Bruce Davidson/Magnum)

---

[15]The importance of gaining sympathy from significant others is easy to underestimate. However, while sympathy is a source of strength, it is also a major weakness. It is not a resource that can be used over an extended period of time nor does it belong directly to those who must bargain.

The 1963 March on Washington

Perhaps the culmination of this movement was reached in the famous March on Washington which occurred in August 1963. In a memo to A. Philip Randolph, Bayard Rustin summarized the mood of black Americans when he stated, "It is time to do something dramatic for civil rights." Joined by other prominent leaders including Martin Luther King, Jr., the organizers of this demonstration planned a massive display of mounting impatience with the failure of Congress and other public and private institutions to protect the civil rights of all citizens. Although Washington had been the scene of numerous

The 1963 march on Washington for jobs and civil rights. (Fred Ward/Black Star)

earlier marches demanding agricultural relief, voting rights for women, bonuses for veterans, and jobs for the unemployed, the 1963 protest was one of the most impressive demonstrations of public sentiments in American history. In the face of threats that the outbreak of violence or disorder might have an adverse effect upon public and congressional attitudes, the March remained peaceful and orderly. Furthermore, early predictions about participation in the protest proved to be conservative. Whereas the leaders of the March initially hoped to attract 100,000 protestors to the nation's capital, an estimated 200,-000 persons ultimately marched for jobs and freedom on that day.

The March on Washington seemed to mark a major turning point in the struggle for civil rights. Perhaps its most important accomplishment was reflected in the passage of the Civil Rights Act of 1964. But neither this march, nor the protests that preceded it, nor the demonstrations that followed subsequently were successful in fulfilling all of the goals that black Americans and other minorities sought to achieve. Millions of blacks, Chicanos, Puerto Ricans, Orientals, and native Americans continued to endure the degrading effects of poverty and discrimination as an endemic characteristic of their everyday lives.

LIMITATIONS OF PROTEST

Although the politics of protest has played a major role in advancing the cause of civil rights, there are several major difficulties with this tactic that may limit its effectiveness as an exclusive means of promoting social change. Protests frequently form an important means of focusing public attention on a problem and of forcing responsible officials to begin negotiations concerning a solution, but they may fail to provide a useful or an appropriate method of achieving other crucial minority goals. A comprehensive understanding of protest politics, therefore, requires a careful assessment of the limitations as well as the successes of this strategy.

The Defects of Sympathy

One of the major resources generated by protest activities often is the sympathy of the general public. This dependence on external support has prevented minorities from developing resources of their own through protest demonstrations. These resources remain the property of outside observers whose empathy has been aroused. Sympathy is not a resource that is easily exchanged or used at the discretion of the protesting group. Furthermore it may dissolve quickly. For example, when civil rights activity was focused on the South, many white Northerners were prepared to engage in massive outpourings of money and support to remedy grievances in that section of the country. After attention shifted to the North as a bastion of segregation, however, this sentiment soon evaporated and was replaced by hostile criticism of the protestors. The resources necessary for sustained action are seldom produced by the strategy of protest. Since alliances rarely can be supported "on a moral or friendly basis,"[16] protest hardly provides a firm foundation for enduring coalitions.

The Targets of Protest

To be effective, protestors usually must articulate specific grievances that can be ameliorated by a single, clearly defined decision-making unit. Protestors can easily be ensnared in the problem of incremental change. Even a major accomplishment, such as the elimination of discrimination in one institution, may have little effect on others. Demonstrators usually find it necessary to challenge each organization separately. Furthermore, attempts to attack broad social problems often flounder because the target of the protest is incapable or unwilling to provide a solution. Even if protestors are successful in gaining a limited victory, the effects for others often are minimal. As Dr. Martin Luther King, Jr., once noted, "The right to sit at a lunch counter is meaningless if I do not have a dime for a cup of coffee." Similarly, protest against general phenomena such as racism may be self-defeating because no agency of American society would be willing to claim jurisdiction for resolving this malady. Since the goals of racism and ethnic minorities tend to be collective and diffuse, the strategy of protest frequently *might be* an inadequate vehicle for the attainment of those objectives.

The Implementation of Demands

Although protest can play a crucial role in bringing issues to the attention of the public and even in securing the acceptance of policy proposals, it is frequently incapable of insuring that those policies will be implemented. Just as decision of the Supreme Court may represent a crucial success that is often unfulfilled by subsequent administrative action at the local level, protest frequently produces symbolic victories that may not result in actual changes in the programs against which the protest was directed. The March on Washington, for example, undoubtedly played a major role in the passage of the Civil Rights Act of 1964, but it was powerless to insure that many critical provisions of this law would become operative. In fact, the administration of this statute was frustrated for many months by indecision and delay. Without firm commitments to the implementation of policy changes, the strategy of protest is no

[16]Stokley Carmichael and Charles V. Hamilton, *Black Power*, (New York: Vintage, 1967).

more effective than many other methods of seeking to influence governmental decisions.

The Boundaries of Protest

Protestors also confront a difficult problem in attempting to keep confrontations with their opponents within tolerable limits. Since they are dependent upon the approval and support of outside observers, the escalation of conflict beyond thresholds that are acceptable to the general public could serve to defeat their purpose by evoking sympathy for the targets of the protest rather than for the protestors themselves.

The Moral Force of Protest

The question of morality usually is a critical issue in protest demonstrations. In any encounter, both sides attempt to demonstrate the ethical superiority of their respective positions. Since protesting groups usually are regarded as the aggressors in a confrontation, they are more likely to receive the blame for any outbreaks of violence than those whom they are challenging. Therefore, the moral force upon which protest is based can easily be undermined by public perceptions that they have employed an "immoral" use of intimidation or violence.

Incentives for Participation

Simultaneously, protest leaders face the danger that the anger of participants in a demonstration may be diffused without accomplishing any tangible result. The activity of protest can become a personal catharsis in which protestors obtain primary satisfaction from the activity itself rather than from the successful attainment of their objectives. Hence, many leaders have found that the ranks of their followers may be thinned long before the issue has been successfully resolved. This phenomena can have the effect of reducing levels of frustration without altering the conditions that produced the frustration in the first place.

Protestors also confront the threat that either success or failure may produce a dissolution of their group. The survival of many organizations is relatively secure only so long as they fail to fulfill their aims, because after they achieve their aims they have no further rationale for their existence. A prominent example of this phenomenon was the March of Dimes, a well-financed and publicly supported organization seeking a cure for polio, which was forced to undergo an extensive reorganization and reorientation after the Salk vaccine provided immunity against this disease. On the other hand, the inability to achieve the goals of protest also can threaten an organization. Michael Libsky has written that ". . . participation in protest organizations is a function of the expectation and realization of both tangible and intangible benefits. To the extent that people participate in order to achieve tangible benefits, their interest in a protest organization may depend upon the organization's relative material success."[17] When protest organizations compile a lengthy record of repeated failures, they usually have difficulty in maintaining the sustained participation of their membership. Frustration as well as catharsis can produce attrition in the ranks of the group.

Counterprotest

Under some circumstances, there is a distinct possibility that counterprotest may be organized. Although protest activity is usually discussed as though the only reference groups in the general public are potentially favorable to the goals of the demonstrators, it is possible that counterprotestors could evoke more sympathy than the protestors themselves. When the initial protest lacks popular support or employs means that are perceived as illegitimate, protestors may discover that they have lost more than they have gained.

Dependence on the Mass Media

Another difficulty confronting protestors stems from their dependence on the mass media to carry their message to others. In many circumstances the media may frustrate the aspirations of the protestors by deciding not to publicize their grievances; and even if a protest incident is covered, the participants have little control of the type of image conveyed to the general public. Since the values of the journalistic trade place a high premium on events that generate either conflict or unusual episodes, there is a high probability that major attention will be focused on violent or dramatic encounters. Thus, many protestors have criticized the press for emphasizing inflammatory or threatening statements to the neglect of substantive demands.

The Rhetoric of Protest

The leaders of protest are required to maintain a delicate balance between three major publics: the protestors, external reference groups, and the targets of the demonstration. As a result, leaders must devise a rhetoric that will accomplish three objectives simultaneously. Initially, to maintain cohesion and to prevent defections among their followers, they must resort to inflammatory language to describe the people whom they are challenging and to portray

[17]Lipsky, *op. cit.*

themselves as the uncompromising champion of the group's cause. Second, they must also avoid language or actions that would preclude them from gaining a sympathetic hearing from the mass media or with the general public. Finally, their words and actions must be calculated to induce their opponents to engage in bargaining. Thus, protest leaders are confronted with incompatible and often irreconcilable demands. Perhaps the greatest danger could result from a compromise reached with the targets of the protest that may be interpreted by rank-and-file protestors as a surrender to the enemy. While protest frequently has been a critical strategy in securing civil rights progress, it is fraught with numerous perils that make an exclusive reliance on this tactic problematic.

• POINTS TO REMEMBER

The right to protest is provided for by the First Amendment to the Constitution, which forbids Congress from passing laws abridging the freedom of speech and the right of the people to assemble and to petition the government for a redress of grievances. Although limitations of free speech have arisen most commonly in cases involving obscenity or the threat of violence, the Supreme Court has not interpreted the language of the First Amendment as granting total immunity to act or speak without regard for the rights and safety of others. Despite some legal restrictions, minorities have frequently used protest as a means of publicizing their grievances.

Groups engage in protest basically in an effort to develop resources that are necessary for bargaining. Protest is the "exclusive use of negative inducements which rely for their effort on sanctions which require mass action." A major objective of protesting groups is the activation of significant others who will bring pressure to bear on the targets of the protest.

While the Montgomery bus boycott and the March on Washington serve as examples of the effect use of protest politics, the tactic is fraught with several limitations. These include a dependence on evoking sympathy, becoming ensnarled in incremental change, an inability to oversee implementation, and the problem of keeping conflict within tolerable limits.

The difficulty minorities experienced in attempting to use conventional approaches to express grievances to the American political system erupted into the nation's most destructive riots in the 1960s. Protest by deprived groups usually has connoted an implicit faith that the public or government authorities would respond to their appeals. By contrast, violence generally has signified a growing belief that political leaders are unresponsive.

• SOME UNRESOLVED ISSUES: A DIALOGUE

Holland: As we saw in this chapter, the right to protest is guaranteed by the American Constitution. The framers went to great lengths to ensure the right to free speech as well as the right to assembly. And the Supreme Court in subsequent decisions has upheld the constitutionality of the right to protest. Yet as we have seen, protest is a tool that is used primarily by the powerless and, while it is a legitimate strategy, there is some doubt as to whether it has been a legitimized strategy. A group has the right to petition the government for a redress of grievances, but it is a strategy that has not proved to be particularly popular with the American people or with political authorities.

Hahn: I think the essential difference between protest and other methods of exerting influence rests with the reaction of public officials rather than with the actions of the people themselves. Public officials expect people to vote, to initiate suits in the courts, and to lobby in behalf of their political interests; and they have accepted those activities. But collective protests usually have encountered resistance from political authorities.

Holland: This difference in the reaction of public officials persist even in light of the reality that protests like other forms of political behavior is legitimated by the Constitution.

Hahn: I think it is interesting to note that the increasing use of protest seems to coincide with a shift in the philosophy of the civil rights movement during the 1960s. For most of American history, the objectives of minorities have focused on the effort to secure "equality of opportunity," or the removal of discriminatory barriers that would prevent one from maximizing his personal talents. The major thrust of the effort to secure civil rights, therefore, reflected a recognition that individuals should be evaluated according to their personal merit rather than their racial or genealogical background. Yet, it also became increasingly apparent that centuries of denial and neglect prevented black Americans and other minorities from competing on an equal basis for the rewards of life. Thus, the focus of the civil rights movement seemed to gradually center on the concept of "equal shares," or the representation of racial and ethnic minorities in all strata of society. The objective of securing "equal shares" necessarily implied, in many cases, the use of quotas or other institutional methods of guaranteeing equal representation for minorities. (For additional discussion of these concepts, see Section 9).

Holland: Opposition to the notion of quotas is very strong among the American people. Arguments against their use are many and varied, but in the end they all boil down to resistance to employing racial and ethnic criteria as a form of inverse or reverse discrimination. But in the few areas in which equal opportunity was realized, it was thoroughly demonstrated that the right to compete in no way insures the equal opportunity to win. In fact, it could be argued that factors other than individual merit frequently intervene in American society to determine who gets what, how, when, and where. American history is full of examples that demonstrate that European immigrants, for example, "took care of their own" without regard necessarily to merit.

Hahn: I agree. The use of quotas and other techniques based upon the concept of "equal shares" is not antithetical to American values; but it is likely to arouse controversy whether it is sought by organized protests or through other means.

There is, however, another aspect of protest that bothers me. As we have noted, the success of protest activities frequently depends upon the support of reference groups or what I might term "sympathetic others." Hence, it is a strategy that is often viewed favorably by white liberals. But, as long as their support is essential to the success of a protest, they remain in a position to control not only the nature of the protest but also the goals that are sought by minorities. This, I believe, is a highly undesirable situation.

Holland: Martin Luther King in "Letter from the Birmingham Jail," indicated that he was painfully aware of having to rely on "significant others." In that letter he alluded to the attempts on the part of white liberals within the church to call a halt to his protest efforts. The Black Panther Party likewise was confronted by the reality that outside support meant outside control, and they moved soon after they realized this to eliminate dependence on external funding.

Hahn: Protest is thus incompatible either with a separatist orientation or with political activity founded upon economic self-interest. As such, its long range utility may be questioned.

8 VIOLENCE

One of the most dramatic and significant events in the struggle of racial and ethnic minorities to achieve equality and justice was the seemingly sudden and unprecedented eruption of violence in urban ghettos during the 1960s. The message conveyed by those incidents seemed unambiguous and inescapable. Many black Americans and other minorities were no longer content with efforts to attain their objectives through peaceful or nonviolent means. Yet, the predominant reaction of white America to the outbreak of ghetto rioting was shock and disbelief. Although minority groups have been attempting to demonstrate their needs and aspirations for many years through numerous forms of political activity including voting, interest groups, litigation in the courts, protests, and appeals to legislative and executive agencies, the white majority apparently had failed to take adequate cognizance of those strivings. By engaging in acts of violence, minority citizens presented white America with their demands in a manner that could not be neglected or ignored.

Although ghetto riots had a powerful impact upon the American people at the time of their appearance, they seemed to produce few major changes in public attitudes or values. Many persons appeared willing, and even anxious, to relegate urban violence to a minor lurch in the evolution of American society. Even within a few years after the outbreak of serious rioting, those incidents often seemed to be regarded primarily as historical occurrences rather than as events that had a strong and continuing influence on social and political controversies. While the effort to deemphasize the violence may have reflected widespread guilt or shame about one of the most tragic developments in American politics, this emotion also might have had the unfortunate effect of obscuring the significance of ghetto riots. In many respects, the explosion of violence in American cities during the 1960s marked an important watershed in the development of racial conflict that was comparable, if not equivalent, to the events that precipitated the Civil War. Just as the conflict between the North and the South illustrated the deep feelings that were aroused by the issue of slavery, ghetto violence dramatized the intensity of minority demands to improve their social and economic position in society. Even though many persons were anxious to dismiss those events from their conscience or memory, a serious examination of urban riots seems essential to an understanding of the role of minorities in American politics.

History of Violence in America

Although the attempt to explain the total impact of urban riots upon American politics comprises a relatively complex undertaking, several important consequences of the upheaval became evident in the immediate aftermath of the violence. Initially, they compelled many persons to reexamine and reappraise the role of social disturbances and violent protests in attaining major political objectives. The ghetto revolts of the 1960s seemed to lead Americans to a rediscovery of their violent past. As Charles Tilly has pointed out, violence has been a common political strategy employed not only by groups seeking to acquire political power, but also by groups attempting to maintain their existent power and by groups that were losing political influence.[1] Although the study of American history has been greatly affected by what has been termed "the myth of peaceful progress,"[2] a careful reassessment of the historical record reveals that farmers, laborers, immigrant groups, and other major segments of American society frequently have resorted to violence as a means of promoting their political interests. From early attempts by farmers to resist the authority of the federal government in incidents such as Shay's Rebellion and the Whiskey Revolt, which occurred soon after the ratification of the Constitution, to the bloody struggle over the unionization of American labor, which resulted in 198 deaths and nearly 2000 injuries in the single period from 1902 to 1904,[3] violence has been a prevalent feature of political life in the United States.

Historical Violence against Minorities

Furthermore, violence in America often has revolved around racial and ethnic minorities. In the first two and a half centuries of slavery in the United States, a careful estimate has indicated that there were at least 250 major conspiracies to organize slave revolts.[4] Perhaps the most serious incident of urban violence in America, however, was the so-called New York "Draft Riots" of 1863 in which two mobs of Irish immigrants expressed their resentment against military conscription by attacking the police and by murdering at least 11 black

[1]Charles Tilly, "Collective Violence in European Perspective," *Violence in America*, Hugh D. Graham and Ted R. Gurr (eds.) (New York: Bantam, 1969), pp. 37–41.

[2]Jerome Skolnick, *The Politics of Protest* (New York: Simon and Schuster, 1969).

[3]Phillip Taft and Philip Ross, "American Labor Violence: Its Causes, Characteristics, and Outcome," in Graham and Gurr, *op. cit.*

[4]Herbert Aptheker, *American Negro Slave Revolts* (New York: International Publishers, 1952), pp. 80–82.

freedmen who were perceived as the symbolic cause of the war.[5] According to records compiled by the Tuskegee Institute, between 1882 and 1959 at least 3400 black Americans also lost their lives as a result of violence perpetrated by lynch mobs.[6] Although lynchings occurred primarily in the South, black migration to the North after World War I resulted in numerous race riots in which black workers were attacked by whites who feared the threat of job competition. The 1917 riot in East St. Louis, for example, produced the death of 39 blacks and 9 whites.[7] In 1919, race riots erupted in at least seven major American cities, including Chicago where 15 whites and 23 blacks were killed. Mounting racial tensions also provoked serious rioting in 1943 in Detroit and in Harlem, which had been the scene of another major violent incident in 1935.[8] Nor has violence been confined to conflicts over the role of black Americans. During a 21-month period between 1970 and 1971, for example, the predominantly Chicano area of East Los Angeles experienced at least eight riots, making it one of the most crisis-ridden communities in America at that time.[9]

Although many citizens have sought to erase the memory of such incidents, the urban riots seemed to promote a renewed awareness of the role of violence in American political history. Violence traditionally has accompanied the efforts of many groups, including economic interests as well as minorities, to achieve increased status and influence in society. As visible and persistent minorities that have experienced more difficulties in attracting allies and more serious obstacles in the pursuit of their political goals than other segments of the population, blacks and other minorities frequently have been the center of violence and disorder in America. From the perspective of history, therefore, the urban violence of the 1960s did not appear to be either unexpected or inexplicable.

Violence as a Last Resort

The outbreak of urban violence appeared to illuminate some basic flaws in the political process. In the context of the accelerating civil rights movement of the 1960s, violence did not occur until almost all other methods of communicating political grievances had been exhausted. The mood of minority communities seemed to reflect a prevalent belief that alternative forms of political expression had been explored and that they had been found inadequate. The willingness of many ghetto residents to resort to violence as a means of expressing

[5]James McCaque, *The Second Rebellion* (New York: Dial Press, 1968).
[6]Cited in Joe Feagin and Harlan Hahn, *Ghetto Revolts* (New York: Macmillan, 1973), p. 78.
[7]E. M. Rudwick, *Race Riot in East St. Louis* (Carbondale, Ill.: Southern Illinois University Press, 1964).
[8]Arthur I. Waskow, *From Race Riot to Sit-In* (Garden City, New York: Doubleday, 1966).
[9]Armando Rendon, *Chicano Manifesto* (New York: Macmillan, 1971).

Military forces in Washington, D.C. during the 1968 riot. (Burk Uzzle/Magnum)

their discontent seemed to provide definitive evidence that existing methods of political expression and institutions had failed to fulfill the objectives of racial and ethnic minorities.

Another major effect of the urban riots was to dramatize the pressing needs of minority groups. Many citizens considered their grievances and aspirations so urgent and so compelling that they were prepared to engage in violence in a desperate attempt to resolve those problems. Even though violence often was interpreted by the white public and their political leaders as an inappropriate strategy for improving ghetto conditions, violence could hardly have failed to impress outside observers with the critical nature of minority demands.

Protest and Violence

The dramatic character of urban riots has promoted a prevalent, but inaccurate, confusion concerning protest and violence. Protest by deprived groups usually has connoted an implicit faith that the public or government authorities will respond to their appeals. By contrast, violence generally has signified a growing belief that political leaders are unresponsive to minority needs and that efforts to disrupt the social order may comprise the only available means of securing major objectives. Although the outbreak of rioting may have played a major role in focusing increased public attention on ghetto problems, the impetus for violence commonly has encompassed many attitudes that were absent in protest demonstrations.

In addition, many persons have seemed to adopt the mistaken belief that there is a causal relationship between protest and violence. Protest usually has represented controlled and disciplined attempts to secure social and political change through peaceful methods: they have been characterized by the application of a specific and relatively limited amount of force to secure explicit objectives. Contrary to a prevalent myth, riots seldom have been started by demonstrations of protest that became uncontrollable and that exploded in violence. Although the outbreak of rioting seemed to evolve from intense and repeated efforts by minorities to secure a redress of their political grievances, protests did not have any direct or immediate impact upon the eruption of violence. The persistent struggle of minority groups for equal rights merely formed the context within which violence occurred. The ghetto riots of the 1960s may not have developed outside this context; but protest did not, in any sense, *cause* the violence.

Violence: Rational or Irrational?

Another common source of misunderstanding concerning urban violence has been reflected in the growing debate over the rationality or the irrationality of riot behavior. Violence may have represented one of few realistic alternatives remaining to minorities that failed to achieve their goals through other forms of political activity; but it also constituted an impossible, and perhaps inappropriate, method of securing an enduring solution to their problems. Although some constructive results did emerge from the riots, those accomplishments clearly were inadequate to meet the needs conveyed by the violence.

The Abnormality of Violence

In many respects, the attempt to isolate either rational or irrational components of riot behavior may be a fruitless exercise. The impetus for violence probably emerges both from our emotional origins and from an awareness of the limitations on the political alternatives available to minority groups. The controversy over the rationality or the irrationality of rioting seems to resemble a similar dispute about the "abnormality" of violence. While riots obviously represent a departure from the social conventions and laws that ordinarily control human behavior, a review of history indicates that they have not been unusual or atypical incidents in the struggle to gain political influence. Labeling riots as irrational or aberrant, therefore, may tend to divert attention from restrictions on the alternatives available to groups seeking to express political dissatisfaction. Similarly, terms such as rational or normal also seem inappropriate. Although the latter phrases contain more constructive connotations, they may not exhaust the total implications of riot behavior. Hence, it does not seem necessary or advisable to approach the analysis of urban violence by employing value-laden terms such as "rational," "irrational," or "abnormal."[10]

Violence: Expressive or Instrumental?

Perhaps more important than the question of the rationality of rioting is the issue of the expressive or the instrumental character of ghetto violence. From one perspective, riots seem to be merely expressive; that is, they constitute a dramatic and inescapable display of persistent ghetto discontent and aspirations. On the other hand, the violence also appears to denote instrumental attributes. In employing violence as a form of political expression, the rioters exceeded a simple attempt to arouse the conscience of the white public and their political leaders. Violence, fundamentally, reflects the form of political action that surpasses other methods of exerting influence.

Again, however, the two concepts may not be mutually exclusive. The ghetto riots of the 1960s seemed to contain both instrumental and expressive characteristics. Although the violence represented a massive display of hostility and

[10]For a discussion of these issues see David Perry and Herbert Hirch (eds.), *Violence as Politics: A Collection of Original Essays* (New York: Harper and Row, 1974).

resentment, it did not appear to be devoid of goals or objectives. In fact, the aims and aspirations of minorities seemed to play a critical role in the violence. By assessing ghetto riots in terms of their objectives, therefore, it is necessary to examine the behavior of both riot participants and the actions of the state that may have contributed to the violence.

Individualistic Theories of Violence

Although the demands conveyed in ghetto violence seemed inescapable, during the initial outbreak of rioting many members of the white public found themselves unable to comprehend or to explain those events. Hence, many of the initial interpretations of the riots offered by white politicians and local leaders sought to describe the violence as the product of alien, deviant, unrepresentative sectors of the community. The investigators of the upheavals commonly were depicted as hoodlums, criminals, organized conspirators, outside agitators, rootless migrants, and similar undesirables. By ascribing the causes of the riots to a small and politically powerless segment of the population, urban spokesmen may have sought to preserve the image of an otherwise peaceful and harmonious community. In addition, most of the early interpretations of ghetto riots focused on individual rather than structural characteris-

"Burn baby, burn": Detroit 1967. (Detroit Free Press/Black Star)

tics. The fault for the violence could be blamed on a few maladjusted persons rather than on basic defects in social or political institutions. As a result, public leaders were not compelled to consider the possibility that government policies and the political process itself may have been responsible for the discontent and disatisfaction that ultimately exploded in violence.

Although individualistic interpretations and the so-called "riff-raff" theory of rioting were widely circulated and believed by the public in the aftermath of violence, numerous studies of the characteristics of riot participants failed to confirm those explanations. In general, the characteristics of riot participants seemed to be representative of the ghetto populations in which the violence occurred. Although rioters tended to be young males in their twenties or thirties, they did not include a disproportionate number of excitable adolescents, persons with extensive criminal records, recent migrants to the area, or other deviant members of society.[11] In addition, several official investigations by government commissions and agencies failed to uncover any evidence that the violence had been instigated by organized conspiracies or by agitators who were imported for the specific purpose of inciting violence.[12] Empirical evidence compiled by careful research on ghetto violence discredited conclusively many popular theories concerning the causes of riots.

Collective Behavior Theories

Another attempt to develop a comprehensive explanation for ghetto violence emerged from sociological theories of collective behavior.[13] Basic to this theory was the concept of social tension or strain. According to this view, participation in collective behavior, including ghetto riots, resulted from exposure to intense social stress or tension. Although several critics have observed that the assumptions in these theories frequently spawn explanations of collective behavior that portray such activity as deviant, abnormal, or irrational, perhaps a more fundamental flaw arose from their failure to emphasize the role of the state in the outbreak of rioting. Collective violence usually has been produced both by the actions of disadvantaged groups and by the failure of political authorities to resolve their grievances satisfactorily. Theories of violence that neglected the interactive relationship between those antagonists have not provided an adequate explanation of the causes of ghetto riots.

[11]See, for example, Robert M. Fogelson and Robert B. Hill, "Who Riots? A Study of Participation in the 1967 Riots," in *Supplemental Studies for the National Advisory Commission on Civil Disorders* (Washington, D. C.: Government Printing Office, 1968).

[12]*Report of the National Advisory Commission on Civil Disorders* (New York: Bantam, 1968), pp. 201–202.

[13]See, for example, Neil J. Smelser, *Theories of Collective Behavior* (New York: The Free Press of Glencoe, 1963).

The Frustration-Aggression Model

Perhaps the "easiest and by far the most popular explanation of social violence"[14] emerged from psychological models of frustration-aggression, which posited that individuals whose basic desires are thwarted and who experience a sense of dissatisfaction and anger are likely to react to this condition by directing aggressive behavior at what is perceived as responsible for thwarting those desires. Although research based on the psychodynamics of frustration and aggression has made some important contributions to an understanding of violence, the stress on inner conflicts and on psychological characteristics frequently has seemed to divert attention from the broader social and political forces that may be responsible for the outbreak of rioting.

The Concept of Relative Deprivation

The concept of frustration-aggression is closely related to another theory, relative deprivation, which is widely used in the interpretation of urban violence.[15] This approach emphasizes the discrepancy between a person's present status and standards supplied by some other reference group. Many studies employing this theory, however, have failed to answer the basic question: relative to what? While some observers have emphasized social and economic differences within the black community, others have stressed the objective discrepancy between black and white socioeconomic levels,[16] and others have attributed violence to "the revolution of rising expectations" while arguing that the gains of minorities have not occurred with sufficient rapidity to satisfy rapidly rising expectations.[17] According to another group of scholars, violence often has occurred after a severe reversal following a period of sustained social and economic progress. Failure to achieve general agreement on the standards for measuring relative deprivation, therefore, has cast grave doubt on the value or the utility of this concept in the explanation of urban violence.

Demographic Correlates of Violence

Additional studies of the social, economic, and political characteristics of cities that experienced major violence also failed to provide firm support for the

[14]Leonard Berkowitz, "The Study of Urban Violence," in Lewis H. Masoth and Donald Bowen (eds.), *Riots and Rebellion* (Beverly Hills: Sage, 1968), p. 39.

[15]See, for example, Ted R. Gurr, *Why Men Rebel* (Princeton, N.J.: Princeton University Press, 1970).

[16]James C. Davies, "The J Curve of Rising and Declining Satisfactions as a Cause of Some Great Revolutions and a Contained Rebellion" in Graham and Gurr *op. cit.*, pp. 716–725.

[17]Thomas F. Pettigrew, *Racially Separate or Together?* (New York: McGraw-Hill, 1971), pp. 148–152.

relative deprivation hypothesis. In an early study of racial violence between 1913 and 1963, Silverman and Lieberson concluded that, "Riots are more likely to occur when social institutions function inadequately, or when grievances are not resolved, or cannot be resolved under the existing institutional arrangements[18] While another investigation found that rioting was most likely to occur in cities with a high level of absolute deprivation between black and white residents,[19] subsequent analysis revealed that neither social, economic, nor political characteristics were closely related to the occurrence or the level of urban violence; rioting was most closely associated with the region of the country in which a city was located and the size of the black population in that community.[20] Apparently, in almost every major city in the United States, the intensity of minority grievances had exceeded the threshold that was necessary to spark a serious riot.

Perhaps a major difficulty in the interpretation of urban violence has arisen from a common characterization of riots as reflecting random or irresponsible behavior. In general, most major incidents of ghetto violence have been described as chaotic, disorganized, sporadic, and confused. Those accounts have seemed to neglect some significant regularities or patterns of social conduct that emerged at various stages in the escalation of violence. Perhaps more important, the description of riots as reflecting random and spontaneous conduct seemed to contribute to a general image of riot behavior as apolitical and purposeless. Although the portrayal of rioters as a milling throng promoted the view that the violence lacked major objectives or aims, those descriptions often appear to ignore some of the most salient facets of riot behavior. The anger of rioters frequently was focused upon major targets that represented tangible and accessible manifestations of political authority, and the general configuration of violence often reflected evidence of purposive action. As a result, some prevailing interpretations of ghetto violence may have promoted misconceptions by stressing the random or unrepresentative character of those events without devoting corresponding emphasis to the purposive or political aspects of riots.[21]

The Social and Political Sources of Violence

Perhaps the most appropriate measures of both the origins and the objectives of urban violence are provided by an examination of the development of

[18]Stanley Lieberson and A. R. Silverman, "The Precipitating and Underlying Conditions of Race Riots," *American Sociological Review*, Vol. 30 (December 1965).

[19]Bryan T. Downes, "A Critical Reexamination of the Social and Political Characteristics of Riot Cities," *Social Science Quarterly*, Vol. 51 (September 1970), pp. 349–360.

[20]Seymour Spilerman, "The Causes of Racial Disturbances: A Comparison of Alternative Explanations," *American Sociological Review*, Vol. 55 (August 1970), pp. 627–649.

[21]Harlan Hahn, "Political Objectives of Ghetto Violence," in Daniel Gordon (ed.), *Social Change in Urban Politics* (Englewood Cliffs, N.J.: Prentice-Hall 1972).

ghetto riots. The outbreak of violence not only emerged against the background of the tenacious efforts of black Americans to achieve equality and justice, but it also was spawned by the failure of government leaders to adopt policies to alleviate minority problems. Governmental neglect of ghetto areas, such as those in which the rioting occurred, had produced a host of endemic conditions in housing, unemployment, crime, education, welfare, poverty, and related fields. In numerous surveys in Detroit, New York, Los Angeles, and elsewhere, those problems were cited by an overwhelming proportion of ghetto residents as the major causes of the violence. Those attitudes were summarized by the findings of a study of riot participants in New York and Detroit that concluded, "The continued exclusion of Negroes from American economic and social life is the fundamental cause of riots."[22] The circumstances and conditions that triggered the violence did not arise spontaneously; they were the products of decades of inaction and neglect.

The Precipitating Incident

In an immediate sense, however, the incidents that precipitated the riots also revealed a characteristic pattern. With the exception of the violence that erupted in 1968 after the assassination of Martin Luther King, Jr., almost every serious riot during the 1960s resulted from an encounter between law enforcement officers and ghetto residents. As the National Advisory Commission on Civil Disorders condluded, "Almost invariably the incident that ignites violence arises from police action."[23] Since policemen constitute the symbolic agents of political authority in ghetto areas, there seemed to be a close and theoretically significant relationship between the events that precipitated violence and the goals or purposes reflected in the riots.

Perhaps one of the major difficulties in many theories of urban violence has arisen from their failure to relate the causes of the riots to the immediate events that precipitated them. Attempts to interpret ghetto riots from the perspective of sociological theories of collective behavior, which place a major emphasis on social tension or strain, for example, seldom have suggested either the sources of the strain or why it has become evident in the relationship between ghetto residents and policemen. Similarly, investigations using the concept of relative deprivation frequently have failed to indicate how a sense of deprivation might be sparked by contacts with law enforcement officers. Furthermore, examinations of riot behavior based upon the model of "frustration-aggression" often have failed to specify either the type of frustration that may yield violence or the reasons why violence rather than some other form of aggres-

---

[22]Nathan S. Caplan and Jeffrey M. Paige, "A Study of Ghetto Revolts," Vol. 219, *Scientific American* (August 1968), p. 21.
[23]National Advisory Commission on Civil Disorders, *op. cit.*

sion may emanate from that frustration. Conventional social science theories, therefore, have been unable to define the association between persistent discontent, precipitative events, and the objectives of ghetto violence.

The Politics of Violence

Fundamentally, rioting has appeared to reflect a deliberate repudiation of the rules that usually govern social conduct and a continuing defiance of governmental efforts to reimpose the authority of those regulations. The violence that erupted in urban ghettos during the 1960s did not represent a permanent plan to overturn or to withdraw from the auspices of existing government institutions and leaders; but—for a brief period of time, at least until the awesome force of the state was summoned to end violence—riot participants seemed to constitute the ruling force within some ghetto communities. In many respects, therefore, the riots may have resembled a primitive form of rebellion or insurrection. In fact, the actions of public officials, in assigning massive numbers of troops and armed force to riot areas, seemed to underscore the plausibility of this interpretation. Yet, urban violence did not constitute a revolution, or a serious threat to political sovereignty. Basically, the ghetto riots of the 1960s seemed to reflect a strategy that might be termed "the politics of violence," or a desperate effort to attain crucial objectives that had not been achieved by other forms of political activity and protest.[24]

The Targets of Violence

One method of assessing the objectives of ghetto riots entails an examination of the persons and institutions that become the major objects of hostility during violence. Perhaps the two principal targets of rioters in a serious incident of violence are police officers and local merchants. Assaults upon the police might reflect an attack upon law enforcement officers as the extended arm of government authority that is required to exercise power in an effort to uphold and sustain the existing structure of public and private influence. Furthermore, the looting and theft that usually accompany major violence could be construed as an extralegal effort to expropriate consumer goods.[25] During a serious riot, property rights are ignored; and material goods are acquired primarily on the basis of their accessibility or availability rather than according to the purchasing power of the person who obtains them. Hence, assaults upon the police and upon retail stores, might be interpreted as a basic attack upon the personal and property rights that form the basis of the social order.

[24]Feagin and Hahn, *op. cit.*
[25]E. L. Quarentelli and Russel Dynes, "Looting and Civil Disorders: An Index of Social Change," In Masotti and Bowen, *op. cit.*, p. 131.

The Selectivity of Violence

Many of the assaults upon private property that occur during a riot, however, tend to be selective. Commercial enterprises may be assaulted or ignored not only on the basis of the goods they contain, but also according to prevailing attitudes toward their proprietors. The selectivity displayed by riot participants seemed to raise some serious questions about the characterization of rioting as tumultuous behavior. If riot activities were random, all businesses might be equally vulnerable. Actually, however, careful observations of riot areas indicate that some stores may be looted or destroyed, while others remain untouched. The bases for the decisions made by rioters also reflect some important components of riot behavior. Frequently, stores are looted or destroyed simply in an effort to secure revenge. Unpopular merchants are more likely to suffer damage during a riot than those who have retained the favor of the community. Attacks upon local stores may denote a general feeling that the principle of vengeance should be substituted for the values that ordinarily ensure the protection of private property. Although most citizens might disapprove of the use of this principle in the enactment of laws, during major riots it may emerge as a more salient consideration than traditional social constraints.

The Values of Riot Participants

During a major riot, the crowds on the streets participating in the violence frequently frame their own rules of conduct. The decision to break into a store, to attack law enforcement officers, and to engage in other activities often may be the product of a consensus formed by riot participants. In this process, leaders frequently emerge to mold the attitudes and behavior of other members of the crowd. Although those activities may never be formally organized, they appear to resemble, in several important respects, the basic features of a decision-making assembly. In the absence of customs and laws that ordinarily regulate social behavior, new values and new regulations are substituted. Those rules are not enforced by persons formally in power to perform this task, but they may be applied to personal conduct by a variety of informal gestures that connote social approval or disapproval.

Most of the norms that emerge during a riot, of course, are contrary—or antithetical—to the conventions and rules that would otherwise govern social conduct. The prevailing normative structure among crowds of rioters may support actions such as looting, the destruction of businesses based upon the principle of revenge rather than upon the values that normally support private property, and attacks upon police officers or other agents or representatives of external authority. Among some rioters, homocide may even be justified as a means of securing retribution. In fact, the almost total reversal of laws and values that occurs during a riot seems to underscore the significance of violence as an attack upon existing political authority. A complete rejection of traditional rules and customs might even be a necessary precondition to the willingness to resort to violence. Presumably, if individuals were prepared to accept the most fundamental rules of society, they would not be willing to participate in riots. Violence is perhaps the most extreme form of expression available, and an almost total repudiation of commonly accepted social values may be required before people are prepared to adopt this strategy.

In addition to the acts of rioters that reflect a complete rejection of basic legal standards, however, many of the rules of conduct that emanate from crowds on the street during a riot seem to connote more constructive attitutdes. Frequently, for example, the "soul brother" signs that adorn businesses allegedly owned by black merchants are respected by riot participants. In addition, members of the crowds on the streets during a riot often intervene to protect innocent bystanders or persons who hold the respect of the community. Cases of mistaken identity sometimes are resolved by the crowds in a process that appears to resemble the adjudication of legal disputes. The norms

Standoff during the 1967 Detroit riots. (Ira Rosenberg/Black Star)

and values developed by rioters, therefore, are not designed solely to permit or to facilitate acts of destruction and violence; they also may attempt to keep the violence within acceptable limits.

Street Governance

In many respects, the rules of conduct formulated by rioters in defiance of armed attempts to reimpose external authority upon the community seem to constitute a form of what might be termed "street governance." Rules are formulated, decisions are made, and leadership is exercised in a process that scarcely resembles the institutionalized procedures of established government. Yet, the behavior exhibited by rioters seems to contain many of the essential components of political decision making. For many years, ghetto residents had been separated in their efforts to communicate their sentiments *up* to government leaders; in a fundamental sense, violence represents a means of bringing political authority *down* to the people. During a major riot, many people who had been ineffective in politics previously were granted a direct and immediate opportunity to participate in the formulation of rules and in other quasi-political functions. In the process, penalties were imposed and rewards were dispensed, albeit in a manner contrary to the usual policymaking process. By forming a decision-making body in the streets, many persons exercised a form of political participation that would not have been available to them in more distant or remote governmental institutions.

Basically, the behavior of ghetto residents in various riots did not reflect an effort to destroy established political institutions; but it may have implied a desire to rearrange the existing structure of influence. In effect, the riots seemed to turn the distribution of political power upside-down. Laws and customs that ordinarily sustain the social order were repudiated; and new rules of conduct were substituted in their place. Persons who had never previously been able to exert political influence suddenly found themselves exercising almost unlimited power within ghetto neighborhoods;and government authorities who were accustomed to wielding influence rapidly began to feel impotent or powerless to halt the violence. Riot participants seemed to display an implicit—and perhaps vain—hope that they would be granted increased opportunities to participate in the process by which public policies are formulated. The riots, therefore, appeared to signify not only a call for major changes in governmental policies, but they also seemed to reflect a growing demand for the reorganization or restructuring of political institutions.

The Actions of Political Authorities

Although many studies of ghetto violence have devoted relatively little attention to the implicit desire for participation reflected in riot behavior, the actions of government authorities in seeking to curtail the violence seem to provide some support for this interpretation. Despite public proclamations to the contrary, political leaders appeared to respond to the violence less as a riot than as a revolt or an insurrection. During many serious outbreaks of violence, law enforcement agents and troops were mobilized in a massive attempt to suppress the violence; and many of those units were dispatched to guard key public utilities and installations that would be a major target in an overt rebellion. Hence, the number of deaths and injuries resulting from gunfire directed by the agents of the state against civilians greatly exceeded the harm inflicted by ghetto residents upon troops and law enforcement officers. The "official violence" employed by the state to end ghetto riots surpassed the violence produced by the rioters themselves. Massive force assigned by government leaders to control the riots undoubtedly was a major factor that prevented their reoccurrence. While the impressions implanted by attempts to suppress the violence remain in the memories of many people for an extended period of time, the tragic effect of those actions upon ghetto communities seldom was emphasized by public officials.

The Aftermath of Violence

Despite the crushing impact of the force that had been exerted upon them to stop the violence, however, the attitudes of many ghetto residents in the aftermath of major riots seemed to reflect a high degree of political optimism. Many persons whose lives have been affected by the violence were genuinely convinced that the riots would produce expanded government efforts to ameliorate ghetto conditions and increased opportunities for minority groups to participate in the policymaking process. A survey conducted in the Twelfth Street area of Detroit, which had been the scene of one of the nation's most destructive riots, for example, disclosed that most residents of the area felt that government officials would devote increased attention to this ghetto community and that the neighborhood would possess increased political power after the riots.[26] Although participants in the riots were unable to maintain the political power that they wielded at the height of the violence, many inhabitants of the area apparently were convinced that some of the major objectives of the violence had been accomplished.

Official Reactions to Violence

Subsequent events, however, seemed to demonstrate that this optimism was excessive. Despite the flurry of interest and attention that was focused upon

[26]Harlan Hahn, "The Aftermath of a Riot," in *Discourse: A Review of the Liberal Arts*, Vol. 12 (Autumn 1969), pp. 549–553.

those areas immediately after the cessation of violence, relatively few enduring changes have been accomplished throughout the country either in riot-torn neighborhoods or in ghettos. In large measure, those circumstances seem to have been perpetuated by the response of the white public and their political leaders to the violence. After an initial period of shock and disbelief, the white majority displayed increasing resistance to the massive expenditures that would have been required to effect a permanent improvement in urban ghettos. Recommendations of the National Advisory Commission on Civil Disorders, which called for massive increases in federal appropriations to improve ghetto conditions, for example, seem to have been consigned to the realm of political neglect. One commentator noted, that most serious outbreaks of violence in American history have resulted in two major proposals. One plan has generally emphasized increasing the capabilities of law enforcement agencies to suppress future disorders; and the other program has stressed the need for basic social and economic reforms. In general, the former recommendations usually have been implemented, while the latter suggestion has been generally ignored. Perhaps the principal effect of ghetto violence upon the black community has been to devote an increased share of public resources to expenditures for law enforcement agencies. Since those plans have been concerned solely with methods of controlling the violence rather than with attempts to remove its causes, they have not appeared to produce any major changes in the position of minority groups in American society.

The Growth of Black Pride

Within the black community, however, the mounting demand for equality and justice appeared to provide an impetus for major changes in public orientations and values. Perhaps one of the principal movements that developed during the 1960s, for example, was the growth of black identity and pride. This trend obviously contributed to a growing sense of self-esteem, and it may have promoted the advancement of black citizens by investing them with a growing recognition of their own potential effectiveness. However, the development of similar attitudes among other minority groups including Chicanos, native Americans, Orientals, and Puerto Ricans has had a profound effect upon American society.

The Demand for Community Control

Another important trend that developed among minority groups after the violence of the 1960s was reflected in the growing demand for decentralization or "community control" of neighborhood affairs.[27] In many respects, this

[27]Alan Altshuler, *Community Control* (New York.: Pegasus, 1970).

movement appeared to be consistent with, or to resemble, the impetus for "street governance" that developed during riots. Basically, the proposal for "community control" involves bringing political authority to the grass-roots or the neighborhood level. In this manner, ghetto residents hope to be granted an increased opportunity to participate in the formulation of policies that would have a direct impact upon their lives. The movement for "community control," therefore, seemed to reflect an effort to organize and institutionalize opportunities for effective political participation by ghetto residents under the auspices of established political authorities.

Assessments of Decentralization

In many respects, the proposal for decentralization or "community control" seemed to offer numerous advantages for minority groups. The prevalence of residential segregation had forced minorities to live in separate enclaves where they were frequently denied the services and facilities enjoyed by other segments of the community. As a result, the redefinition of political boundaries to create governmental jurisdictions that would consist primarily of minority groups seemed to be of great assistance in their efforts to improve their neighborhoods. On the other hand, "community control" also seemed to raise some serious problems. The granting of this right to racial or ethnic minorities, for example, might necessarily entail the extension of the same privilege to segments of the white community. As a result, racial tensions might be institutionalized or rigidified, and white neighborhoods could enact policies designed to exclude or discriminate against minorities. The extension of "community control" to white as well as black neighborhoods, therefore, could tend to exacerbate rather than reduce the growing trend toward polarization that has enveloped American society.

Participation and Mobilization

The problems that might result from the implementation of decentralization also illustrate another basic difficulty in the political process. Although the adoption of "community control" might facilitate extensive public participation in political decision making, it may not guarantee that the neighborhoods will be successful in gaining major political results. The American system of federalism has created numerous jurisdictions that impede the prompt attainment of major political goals. Neighborhoods, for example, might find it necessary to compete with municipal, state, and federal governments in attempting to attain the resources necessary to accomplish their objectives. Furthermore, the decentralization of political authority usually has entailed the dispersal of influence, and it has commonly inhibited the mobilization for prompt and effective political action. Since many of the problems confronting minority communities are urgent and compelling, this obstacle could impose serious limitations upon their abilities to fulfill their aims. Ironically, public policies to satisfy the demands of minorities might be more likely to emerge from centralized than from decentralized political institutions.[28]

Proposals for Metropolitan Government

The plan for "community control," however, seems to contain greater opportunities for minorities than the movement toward metropolitan government. As black residents gradually acquire increasing power in central cities resulting from the movement of whites to the suburbs, there may be a renewed interest in metropolitan government—encompassing suburbs as well as central cities —to ensure white control of those areas. Despite the technical advantages of metropolitan government to improve efficiency and to avoid duplication and overlap of governmental jurisdictions, the adoption of such a scheme would tend to dilute the strength of racial and ethnic minorities. While decentralization may tend to enhance the participation of minorities in the decision-making process, it might tend to limit the effectiveness or scope of government projects that emerge from that process. On the other hand, the adoption of metropolitan government would enable local areas to centralize their resources to achieve broader goals, but might tend to inhibit the political influence or participation of minority groups. Although neither decentralization nor metropolitan government might enable minorities to attain the goals that they seek, significant changes in political structures and institutions may be necessary to accomplish those objectives. The frustrations encountered by minority groups in their attempts to achieve equal rights through conventional means of political activity underscore the need for extensive changes in the decision-making process. As the violence of the 1960s indicated, many black Americans and other racial and ethnic minorities are beginning to demand major alterations in the methods by which policies are enacted and in the means by which authority is exercised in the American polity.

• POINTS TO REMEMBER

The initial interpretations of the riots by many members of the white public sought to describe the violence as the product of unrepresentative sectors of the community. This became known as the "riff-raff" theory of rioting, which has been discredited by subsequent research. The circumstances and conditions that triggered the violence did not arise so spontaneously; they were the

[28]Harlan Hahn, "Civil Responses to Riots," in *Public Opinion Quarterly* Vol. 34 (Spring 1970).

products of decades of inaction and neglect, and almost all of the riots erupted from an encounter between law enforcement officers and ghetto residents.

The urban violence of the 1960s, rather than constituting a revolution or a serious threat to the body politic, can perhaps best be classified as the "politics of violence." It is the most extreme form of expression available, and an almost total repudiation of commonly accepted social values may be required before people are prepared to adopt this strategy. Basically, the behavior of ghetto residents in various riots did not reflect an effort to destroy established political institutions; but it may have implied a desire to rearrange the existing structure of influence. In effect, the riots seemed to turn the distribution of political power upside-down.

The inversion effect that rioting had on the distribution of political power was relatively short-lived and the urban centers returned to "normal" in a short period of time. However, the seeds of destruction are still present and precipitating incidents such as political assassinations of minority leaders, encounters with the police, and other such events that have historically aroused the anger of central city residents could well have the effect of shattering the illusion that violence is a thing of the past.

• SOME UNRESOLVED ISSUES: A DIALOGUE

Holland: While there is considerable doubt as to the effect, if any, that the violence in the urban centers had on public policy, an important threshhold was broken. Until the riots, whites had a virtual monopoly on the use of violence. The outbreak of the riots demonstrated that the monopoly had been broken and that black Americans would no longer sit passively while their homes and churches were bombed and their lives placed in jeopardy by law breaking Klu Klux Klan members or their sympathizers.

Hahn: While I agree that the outbreak of ghetto revolts ended the white monopoly on private acts of racial violence, the force exerted by national, state, and local governments in stopping ghetto revolts also demonstrated that public institutions controlled by whites maintained a monopoly on public violence. In large measure, the awesome power exerted by governmental sources of violence may have been responsible for the end of the revolts of the sixties. But it is difficult, if not impossible, to determine whether or not the violent epoch of American history had really ended. While there was a cessation of dramatic or massive incidences of violence, fragmentary evidence suggest that violence as a form of political activity has remained on the American scene.

Holland: The politics of violence can be characterized as the politics of last resort. The solution to the nation's problems in the urban centers does not rest with repression but rather rests, in the long run, with structuring opportunities for upward mobility for the dispossessed minorities. The future of our central cities can either be determined by adding additional police while being on constant alert for the possibility of massive riots; or it can be handled at its roots, satisfying the frustrations and denials caused by decades of discrimination and neglect.

Hahn: There is another aspect of violence that I believe is worth of comment. In many respects, the use of violence represents an attempt to secure the redistribution of possessions or resources. In the looting that occurred during major acts of violence, for example, much of the behavior of the rioters reflected an effort to expropriate commodities that could not be purchased with economic resources. The participants in violence, in effect, took matters into their own hands and redistributed resources contrary to the law. In many respects, the outbreak of violence, therefore, may have reflected a frustration with unwillingness of public officials to redistribute resources through official or legal means. As the operation of the American political process had demonstrated, public resources are allocated incrementally and usually only to those who possess resources already. Seldom are racial and ethnic minorities granted benefits from the government, which necessarily entail the surrender of advantages' by the dominant segments of the population and, therefore, could have a major effect upon the political system. "The politics of redistribution" would be radically different from the "politics of distribution". If political leaders should ever summon the courage to allocate benefits to deprived and disadvantaged minorities and to whites at the bottom of the socioeconomic spectrum, they would certainly encounter strong resistance from the rich and the influential. If this type of politics should ever occur in America, one might expect to see radical changes in the nature of political alliances. (For an additional discussion of these concepts, see the following section.)

9 PUBLIC BELIEFS AND THE FUTURE OF AMERICAN POLITICS: A DIALOGUE

Hahn: Having reviewed the operation of American government in its entirety, I believe the most important conclusion that emerges from all of this material is that minority groups have not been able to achieve their political goals by working within existing institutions. Minorities have not been able to gain major objectives through any of the structures of government including political parties, legislatures, the executive branch, or the courts. Nor has the resort to unconventional tactics such as protest and violence been totally successful. Although political scientists and other commentators have urged minorities to adopt numerous strategies ranging from increased organization within their own communities and the effective use of the ballot to incessant disruption and resistance, I am reluctant to prescribe any of those palliatives. I believe that time has come to discuss—and to search for—new solutions to the dilemma posed by the existence of a persistent minority in a political system based upon majority rule.

Holland: In large measure I agree. The institutions that comprise the framework of American government have been unable to accommodate the demands of minorities. The question of whether or not the founding fathers were racists in many respects has had little to do with the inability of minorities to secure their political objectives. The difficulty can be attributed to the fact that the Constitution established a political system founded upon incrementalism, the division of authority, and compromise.

Hahn: But I'm wondering if the obstacles confronting minorities are a product of the institutional arrangement of American politics or if they reflect the failure of political leadership and of the general population to support the demands of minorities. In other words, I think we have left unresolved one of the critical issues of American politics; namely, the question of whether the fault of the political system can be attributed to institutions or to people. Perhaps the general conclusion of most students on American politics is that the principal blame can be attributed to people. But, at the same time, I am extremely concerned that persons who have devoted their lives to the study of the American political system might become overly enamored with the institutional features of that system. As a result, they may be less inclined to recognize defects in the system than to recognize flaws in the people. I believe at this point it would be appropriate to give serious consideration to the question of whether or not the people have maximized their potential to resolve racial conflict within the constraints imposed upon them by political institutions.

Holland: I certainly agree that there has been a propensity for political scientists to venerate the institutions of American politics. However, an emphasis on the potential of the people to settle fundamental racial issues might be premature. It seems to me that institutions have posed major obstructions to the demands of minority groups in America. However, I hasten to add that institutions, in some measure and on occasion, have prevented the populace from committing serious acts of racism and oppression against minorities.

Hahn: I think that's a good point. We've devoted most of this book to a description of existing political institutions. I now believe that we must examine public attitudes both to determine whether or not the public supports those institutions and to assess the perceptions of the dominant white majority concerning the needs and demands of minorities. I believe an appropriate point at which to begin this examination is simply to note that there has been a major change in public attitudes toward racial issues in recent years. At the beginning of the twentieth century, for example, most white Americans subscribed to the belief that blacks and other minorities were biologically inferior. Hence, they could ascribe the inability of minorities to achieve social and political goals to that belief. But today even few of the most extreme exponents of segregation would be willing to make that argument. There has been a secular change in racial attitudes, and I tend to believe that this change may have outpaced the extent to which established institutions have satisfied the needs and demands of minorities.

Holland: The changes in the attitudes of white America have indeed been profound. For example, in 1909 a group of whites sympathetic to the cause held a conference in New York in which they sought to discuss the issue of whether or not blacks were human beings. As a demonstration, they displayed the brains of a white, an ape, and a black. These whites—perhaps among the most liberal of their time—concluded that blacks, although human, were nonetheless inferior. Clearly, such a conclusion at a conference in contemporary America would be remarkable.

Hahn: An examination of public opinion data on white attitudes concerning the rights of minorities in housing, education, and other areas indicates a substantial decline in attitudes reflecting racial intolerance and a decrease in support for segregated institutions between 1955 and 1972. According to a survey of white attitudes in 1966, 61 percent of white Americans felt that blacks were the victims of discrimination.[1] So the evidence reflects not only a major trend indicating increased public sympathy or support for the rights of minorities, but it also suggests a growing recognition of the problems and obstacles confronted by those groups in their quest for equality and justice. Perhaps most significant, this change in white attitudes apparently has not had a profound impact upon the political system. The efforts of minorities and others to implement the growing support for their demands in the dominant white public has been met by hesitancy and intransigence at almost all levels of government. In many respects, therefore, it appears that the institutional obstacles to the attainment of minority demands have been a greater obstacle to progress than the resistance of public opinion.

Holland: I agree; but equally important are the attitudes of black Americans toward various political institutions and leaders in the United States. On the one hand, numerous surveys have indicated that blacks have displayed growing alienation from political institutions at both the local and the national level.[2] On the other hand, however, political participation and party identification remain high. Surveys conducted in 1963, 1966, and 1969 asked blacks, "Regardless of how you may vote, what do you usually consider yourself—a Republican, a Democrat, or what?" Seventy-four, 70, and 67 percent of the black respondents in those respective years indicated support for the Democratic Party.[3] This high degree of loyalty has meant that Democrats have had to make major political concessions to black Americans; and Republicans simply have refused to compete for the black vote. But as we indicated in Chapter 2, there is considerable doubt that parties act as an effective means

[1]William Brink and Louis Harris *Black And White* (New York: Simon and Schuster, 1966) p. 125.
[2]See, for example, Joe R. Feagin and Harlan Hahn, *Ghetto Revolts* (New York: Macmillan, 1973); Louis H. Masotti and Don R. Bowen (eds.) *Riots and Rebellion* (Beverly Hills, Cal., Sage Publications, 1968).
[3]Brink and Harris *op. cit.*, p. 92.

of interests aggregation. Thus, it is unclear whether the nation's dispossessed minorities should pursue a course of greater flexibility in their electoral choices.

Hahn: Black Americans and other minorities also have shown a considerable amount of ambivalence toward other major political institutions. The proportion of blacks who regarded Congress as helpful to the cause of civil rights has fluctuated from 54 percent in 1963 to 60 percent in 1966, and to 52 percent in 1969. Although relatively small proportions identified Congress as harmful to civil rights, approximately one-third of all black citizens indicated uncertainty about their assessment of legislative representation. On the other hand, the proportion of black citizens regarding the United States Supreme Court as helpful to the cause of civil rights has declined from 80 percent in 1963 to 65 percent in 1966 and to 64 percent in 1969. Again, less than 10 percent of all blacks portrayed the Court as harmful to their basic interests, but substantial proportions indicated ambivalence about this issue.[4]

In many respects, the attitudes of blacks and other minorities toward political institutions have reflected predominant tendency to personalize those institutions. The proportion of blacks who indicated that they were basically sympathetic to the federal government changed from 83 percent in 1963 during the administration of John F. Kennedy to 74 percent in 1966 in the administration of Lyndon B. Johnson to only 25 percent during the "benign neglect" incumbency of Richard Nixon. By 1969, 30 percent of black Americans felt that the federal government was basically harmful to the cause of civil rights.[5] Although blacks have been reluctant to criticize venerated American institutions, their attitudes reflect something less than overwhelming trust and confidence in those political processes.

Holland: This tendency to personalize political institutions and issues is based on the American myth that, if something goes wrong with government, the people have an opportunity to change matters by "throwing the rascals out" of office. Attention is diverted from the possibility of restructing the American system of government; and little serious effort is devoted to examining the weaknesses of existing institutions. As has been noted earlier, executives who were favorably disposed toward civil rights still encountered numerous roadblocks in their efforts to aid minority groups. In fact,

[4] *Ibid.*, p. 240.
[5] *Ibid.*, p. 238.

only in times of national crises has a President been able to act decisively on behalf of racial and ethnic minorities.

Hahn: The unresponsiveness of the American political system has led many blacks to conclude that they must resort to "unconventional" tactics in pursuing their political objectives. For example, when asked if they felt that protests had "helped Negroes or hurt them in their efforts to win civil rights" blacks overwhelmingly responded in 1969 that such efforts had in fact helped. Only 13 percent felt that protest had harmed their interests. In addition, increasing numbers of black Americans have expressed the belief that violence is a necessary means of securing fundamental freedoms.[6] According to a survey conducted in 1963, 63 percent of black Americans felt that they could achieve their objectives without violence. By 1966 this proportion had dropped to 59 percent.[7] Perhaps even more significant, additional data indicate that blacks who were militant in their beliefs about racial equality and the need for justice also were most likely to participate in conventional forms of political activity such as voting.[8] Another survey conducted in Detroit revealed that in comparison with whites, blacks were more likely to support conventional methods of expressing their political sentiments, such as voting, writing to elected representatives, and participating in political campaigns; they were also more apt to become involved in unconventional forms of political expression such as protest and violence.[9] The ominous implication of these findings is that if the increasing efforts of blacks to achieve their political objectives through available strategies are unsuccessful, we may eventually reach a point at which the system can no longer contain or accommodate the demands of minorities for their rightful role in society. At that point, we may be faced with the crisis of institutional collapse that could imperil the entire political system.

Holland: If the political institutions are unresponsive and if the attitude is one of increasing alienation, the question has to be posed at this point: Where are we now and where are we going in the future? It seems to me that the country must develop political institutions to guarantee that minorities not only have the right to express their grievances but also that their demands will elicit a sympathetic response from important decision makers. In a sense, this

[6]Feagin and Hahn, *op. cit.*, p. 275–282.
[7]Brink and Harris, *op. cit.*, p. 260.
[8]See, for example, Gary T. Marx, *Protest and Prejudice* (New York: Harper and Row, 1969), p. 71.
[9]Joel Auerbach and Jack Walker, *Race In The City* (Boston: Little Brown, 1973).

is a call for a different form of political institutions rather than a change in attitude on the part of the American people.

The unresponsiveness of the American political institutions has led numerous black Americans to assume a separatist posture. These movements can be evaluated in two ways. While they have served as alternatives to mainstream politics, they have also drained a great deal of energy from efforts to resolve the nation's most persistent domestic issue.

Hahn: The institutional obstacles that have confronted minorities in the pursuit of their political goals seem to have made any other course of action improbable. It strikes me that separatist movements and aspirations are a natural product of the existing political system. Hence, I would be reluctant to chastise the people who seek political goals independently.

Holland: Separatist groups remaining in the United States still are confronted and confined by political and economic institutions that, in large measure, determine their fate. But we must also mention that the movements to return to Africa, which have been prominent among black Americans, have been fraught with difficulties. There is considerable doubt that the majority of black Americans want to go back to Africa, and there is some doubt that they have any place in Africa to go. Africa is a diverse continent made up of many nations and many peoples. For black Americans to assume that it is their homeland is, at best, presumptuous. The battle must be fought in America, and it must be resolved here.

Hahn: Given the need to remain in this society and to cope with the issues that are endemic to our culture, it seems to me that we are then confronted with the essential problem, the role of a minority in a majoritarian system. Obviously the strength of any single minority, consisting of blacks, Chicanos, Asians, Puerto Ricans, or native Americans, is insufficient to capture the support of more than half of the citizenry. The issue of whether or not the *collective* strength of all minorities that have suffered from prejudice and discrimination in America actually comprises a majority is, I think, an empirical question that might be explored through increased cooperation between existing minority groups as well as other segments of the population that regard their political interests as essentially similar to those groups.

In the event that such a combination of minorities should fail to command the support of a majority of the population, my own feeling is that the institutional obstacles that have been erected to frustrate minority ambitions make the likelihood of a coalition between minorities and influential members of the dominant white majority improbable. Improbable in the sense that any such coalition, within existing structures, would reflect a relationship of superiority and inferiority that would be detrimental to minorities. As Carmichael and Hamilton have pointed out, the only basis for concerted political action involving blacks and whites is genuine equality.[10] I personally doubt that most whites, accustomed to the status and the prerequisites afforded by their skin color, would be willing to surrender this advantage by pursuing political goals in the interest of racial and ethnic minorities.

If, however, one is pressed to concede that the inability of minorities even to attain the status of a majority creates a need for such a coalition, the essential question then becomes: what segment of society would be most willing to align themselves with racial and ethnic minorities on a basis of equality to pursue common goals? My own reading of the evidence is that the most probable means by which the objectives of minorities can be pursued is through a coalition of blacks and other minorities with low-income whites. Although they do not form a racial or ethnic minority, many low-income whites have felt the effects of discrimination and deprivation. Extensive data from public opinion surveys indicate that low-income whites share a sense of social and political alienation with blacks. According to a survey conducted in 1963, 49 percent of black Americans believe that the rich get richer and the poor get poorer, and 68 percent of the low-income whites supported this attitude. Similarly, 60 percent of the poor whites, 40 percent of the blacks, and only 39 percent of the total population believe that what you think doesn't count much.[11] Perhaps even more important than their mutual disaffection from the political system is the fact that they have many political interests in common. The effort to improve education, housing, employment opportunities, welfare, and to eradicate the blight of poverty is a goal that is as important to many poor whites as it is to blacks and other minorities.

Holland: This has been a major strand in black protest thought throughout the twentieth century. It was a proposal advanced by W. E. B. Dubois as well as by A. Philip Randolph, the founder of the Brotherhood of Sleeping Car Porters. Randolph believed that the labor union movement could succeed most effectively if labor understood its common interest with black Americans. Contemporary

[10]Stokley Carmichael and Charles V. Hamilton, Black Power (New York: Vintage, 1967).
[11]Brink and Harris, op. cit., p. 135.

black America, however, appears to be somewhat reluctant to take this position because, as "conventional folk wisdom" has it, lower-class whites have traditionally been hostile to any consideration of the rights of non-Europeans.

Hahn: A careful analysis of questions focusing exclusively on the political objectives of minorities, however, reveals that lower-class whites are no more opposed to the rights and the aspirations of minorities outside the South than upper-income whites.[12] Similarly, a study of the attitudes of social classes toward issues of racial prejudice revealed that when the effects of education were examined independently, lower-class whites with high educations were actually more tolerant and less prejudiced than upper-class whites with relatively limited educations.[13]

Holland: Another attempt to develop a coalition between whites and blacks at the bottom of the socioeconomic spectrum was represented by Martin Luther King's efforts to solidify and direct the garbage workers' strike in Memphis, Tennessee, immediately before his assassination. However, most attempts to organize common political efforts between whites and blacks in American politics have failed, either by accident or design. It would be a positive development if such a coalition could materialize. To bank one's fortunes on experiments that have been previously unsuccessful may lack political wisdom.

Hahn: While granting that the historical record on the possibilities of common political action by minorities and low-income whites has not been encouraging, let me briefly mention several points. One is that institutional arrangements have been largely responsible for the failure to develop such a coalition. Lacking usable mechanisms for promoting widespread participation and for developing strong linkages between the public and their elected representatives, it has been difficult for dispossessed and disenfranchised segments of the population to unite and to find an effective vehicle for the promotion of their political interests.

Second, many attempts to weld an effective coalition between lower-class whites and blacks and other minorities have been frustrated by the intervention of whites who occupy higher positions on the socioeconomic ladder. The populist efforts to form such alliances in the South in the late nineteenth century, for example,

[12]Richard F. Hamilton, *Class and Politics in the United States* (New York: John Wiley, 1972).
[13]Charles H. Stember, *Education and Attitude Change* (New York: Institute of Human Relations Press, 1961).

were frustrated by the efforts of wealthy Bourbons, or upper-class segments of the white population, who fanned racial fears and hatred to thwart this movement.[14] Whenever the potential has arisen for such a coalition, institutional barriers and upper-class energies have been energetically employed to disrupt unified political activity between minorities and low-income whites, whose combined strength would constitute a majority.

Finally, and perhaps even more important, I believe that there are a number of forces at work in American society that may change the nature of American politics and that may simultaneously make such a coalition more likely. While the essential thrust of the civil rights movement in the 1960s represented an effort to gain "equality of opportunity," we are now facing an era in which genuine equality can be attained only by more direct methods. The emphasis has shifted from "equality of opportunity" to the pursuit of "equal shares," which implies quotas, the allocation of resources to minorities based upon their proportion of the population, and similar formulas that have not previously been applied to public policy. To cite only one example of the impact of this change, it should lessen the effects of job competition, which has been a persistent source of racial prejudice among low-status whites. Since minorities are demanding representation in high-paying as well as low-paying jobs and professions, the consequences of job competition will no longer be confined to low-income segments of the white population.

The demands of racial and ethnic minorities have reached a point at which their aspirations cannot be satisfied simply by allocating slight increments in resources to the deprived and the disadvantaged. The fulfillment of minority objectives may necessarily entail the surrender of resources by the people who have traditionally enjoyed them. The extent and intensity of minority demands seem to require some withdrawal of resources from other segments of the population. Essentially, we are leaving an era that might be characterized as the "politics of distribution" to enter an historical epoch of what might be termed "the politics of redistribution." Little can be gained by minorities without taking away some of the benefits traditionally enjoyed by high-status segments of the dominant white majority. Many dispossessed elements of the white population will share in the improvement of education, housing, employment, and welfare policies that comprise the core of minority demands, and high-income segments will naturally be

[14]C. Vann Woodward, *The Strange Career of Jim Crow* (New York: Oxford University Press, 1966).

reluctant to surrender their advantages. Hence, America might develop an increasingly "class-based" politics, in which the interests of high-status whites will be opposed by a combination of minorities and low-income whites.

Holland: Your points are well taken. However, I believe that political action in behalf of minorities could be supplemented by the establishment of a principle prohibiting racism in American politics. More succinctly, I am asking to close certain questions in an open society. A commitment to this position does not guarantee that people will not violate the principle; but the laws and the principles can be established nonetheless. An example of what I am talking about goes something like this: A racist should not have the right to run for elective office, and there ought to be some mechanism by which he can be prevented from doing so.

Hahn: I seriously wonder if it would be possible to fulfill all of the legitimate objectives of minorities in a system that is predicated upon the protection of their rights through the establishment of principles. Such principles may be of considerable value in assuring the opportunity of minorities to participate in the political process, but they may be less than effective in attaining the material, or social and economic, goals which many minorities seek.

I am also bothered by your example. Even if it were possible to formulate a definition of racism that would satisfy everyone, the refusal to allow a "racist" candidate to run for public office would comprise a denial of fundamental civil liberties upon which this country is founded.

With that exception, I am sympathetic with your point. Many have argued that the most effective means of protecting minorities is through the establishment of principles to which leaders can refer when they make political decisions. But there are two additional considerations that must be examined. First, any form of government that depends on the good will of those in power ultimately might degenerate into a form of paternalism. Although the rights of minorities may be protected by the altruistic concern of leaders, such a system perpetuates a posture of inferiority and superiority in the relationship between minorities and the people who control political institutions. Second, I am concerned about the question of who should be in control, who should run the institutions, who should have political power in this society. Ultimately, I think we are forced to choose between some type of elite group that maintains control of government and some form of popular sovereignty in which basic authority rests with rank-and-file citizens.

Holland: Frankly, I am not greatly concerned about who is in control, the people or some kind of elite. (It's my feeling that elites will emerge anyway.) I am more concerned with what those in control will do and how can they be limited in what they do.

I think that existing political institutions in the United States have facilitated the emergence of elites. But I must admit I am somewhat less than anxious to allow the people of the United States, the dominant white majority, to determine the fate of black America. Political institutions as presently constructed have inhibited the progress of racial and ethnic minorities; but they have also, at times, limited the power of those who are hostile to the rights of minorities.

One certainly has to have sympathy for the various racial and ethnic minorities including blacks, Asians, native Americans, Puerto Ricans, and Chicanos. Their ascendency has been excruciatingly slow. However, it may be too early to determine the extent to which the American political system can be responsive to minorities. We must recall that it was only 1967 in which blacks were finally granted full enfranchisement. I believe there is evidence of significant progress in the relationship between minorities and the white majority since that time. It may be of little consolation, for example, that whites find it more difficult to commit violence against blacks; but it is a consolation, nonetheless.

Hahn: It may be consolation but, given the pressing needs of minorities, I think what is needed is a victory rather than a consolation prize. To the person who is hungry or seeking shelter, the opportunity to vote and to write his Congressperson may be of limited value. It seems to me that we need a political system that is capable of providing basic and minimal levels of life for all members of society, and I doubt that those rights could be provided by a system in which elites control major political institutions.

I doubt that minorities will ever gain significant representation within elites, unless they are recruited through the use of quotas or a similar device. The control of political institutions by a small group, regardless of the method by which it is selected, tends to accentuate a priority among men that is contrary to egalitarian values. What we are striving for, it seems to me, is a society in which all men and women will be respected as human beings because of their unique potential and abilities. In the pursuit of that objective, I hope that we may ultimately be able to exclude extraneous considerations such as skin color and genealogy from our evaluation of individual capabilities. But I am concerned about a society dominated by individuals in positions of preeminence and power, which enables them to exercise control over others and thereby to differentiate themselves from the rest of society by stressing their alleged superiority.

In the final analysis, ultimate authority in a democracy rests with the people. I am reluctant to believe that the interest of minorities can best be served by elite leadership that enforces principles designed to prohibit racism and subjugation. My own view is that the political objectives of minorities are most likely to be achieved through the organization of a coalition involving minorities and disadvantaged whites, operating within a system in which decision makers are highly responsive to the will of the people. I realized that others with similar values may disagree about the best means of reaching common goals. But the right to disagree, and the opportunity to study the issues that we have been discussing, is perhaps the major strength of this society.

Holland: A victory is, indeed, in order. But your suggestion that it will come by way of a coalition with disadvantaged whites simply flies in the face of too much of American history; and your discussion of elites ignores their links with the masses. Politicans do, in large measure, what they think their constituencies will allow. The failure to pass the views of the citizens through the medium of representation, I am afraid, would grant a victory only to those who would have denied minorities the most basic right of all—the right to life.

**Hahn
and
Holland:** Hopefully the reader, after reviewing this work will come to a fuller appreciation of the potential role that he or she can play in American social and political life. The issues before us concerning racial and ethnic minorities are of enormous magnitude. The survival of American society depends upon a thorough appreciation of political institutions including their strengths and weaknesses. By attempting to pursue those objectives, we hope that we have aided the reader in understanding the future that lies ahead.

Throughout this volume, we have suggested possible alterations in the structure of the American political system including multiple member districts, public financing of political campaigns, initiative, referendum, and recall, and numerous others. Recall that in 1787 some of the best minds in the country met in Philadelphia to ponder serious alteration of the Articles of Confederation. Their work was marked both with outstanding success and failure. But the problems they were unable to resolve have dominated American politics from then to now. We do not pretend to be capable of rewriting the entire Constitution in a way that would bring about the desired changes. However, perhaps it is time to call for another Philadelphia meeting to come to grips with the problems and issues outlined throughout this book. A major difference between the Convention of 1787 and the one we are proposing, of course, would be the representation of persons of non-European descent. Starting anew with the experience of two centuries of intense and bitter race and ethnic conflict should provide us with the wisdom to avoid what the original Framers sought but failed to compromise out of existence.

INDEX

- 294

DATE DUE

GAYLORD   PRINTED IN U.S.A.